Praise for *Priestess of the Morrigan*

"Those seeking to deepen their practice with the Morrigan will find insight and inspiration to take those next steps."

—Morgan Daimler, author of *Morrigan: Meeting the Great Queens* and *Raven Goddess*

"I have a number of people that are dear to me that have been called, touched, and changed by the Morrigan. I have often wished for a book just like *Priestess of the Morrigan* that I could recommend to them. With the rising challenges and increasing complexities in the world, it is no surprise that a multifaceted and many-layered goddess is stepping forward to call forth the people that are needed for the tasks at hand. This book does a superb job of describing the Morrigan, the process of transformation that comes from her touch, and a wealth of modern rituals that are effective and authentic. May this book be nine times eternal!"

—Ivo Dominguez Jr., author of *Keys to Perception*

CW00553209

PRIESTESS
of the
MORRIGAN

About the Author

Stephanie Woodfield (Orlando, FL) has been a practicing Pagan for over twenty years. A devotional polytheist, teacher, and priestess of the Morrigan, she is one of the founding members of Morrigu's Daughters and is an organizer for several Pagan gatherings. Stephanie teaches classes on devotional work and magical practice in the United States and internationally. A longtime New Englander, she now resides in the Orlando area with her husband, a very pampered cat, and various reptiles. She is called to helping others forge meaningful experiences with the Morrigan, as well as the gods and land of Ireland.

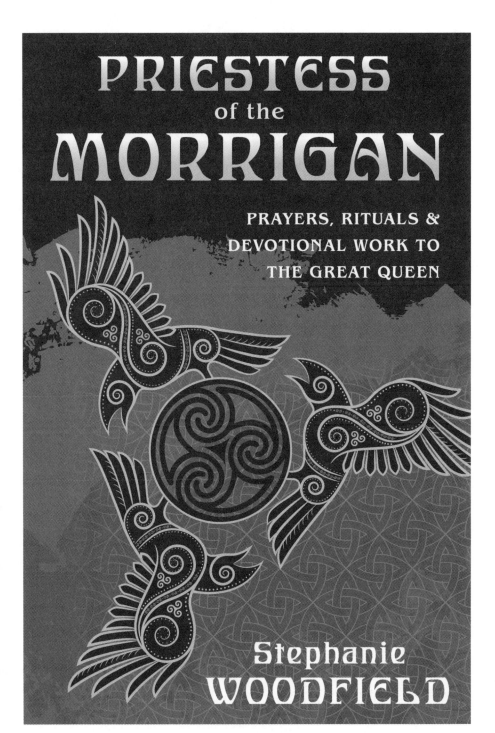

PRIESTESS
of the
MORRIGAN

**PRAYERS, RITUALS &
DEVOTIONAL WORK TO
THE GREAT QUEEN**

Stephanie
WOODFIELD

Llewellyn Publications
Woodbury, Minnesota

FIRST EDITION
First Printing, 2021

Cover design by Kevin R. Brown
Interior illustrations by Eugene Smith
Interior illustration on page 192 by Llewellyn Art Department

Llewellyn Publications is a registered trademark of Llewellyn Worldwide Ltd.

Library of Congress Cataloging-in-Publication Data

Names: Woodfield, Stephanie, author.
Title: Priestess of the Morrigan : prayers, rituals & devotional work to
    the great queen / Stephanie Woodfield.
Description: First edition. | Woodbury, Minnesota : Llewellyn Publications,
    2021. | Includes bibliographical references and index. | Summary:
    "Stephanie Woodfield, a devotee to the Morrigan for over twenty years,
    offers stories, prayers, and rituals for groups or solitaries engaged in
    devotional practice to the Irish goddess"– Provided by publisher.
Identifiers: LCCN 2020041390 (print) | LCCN 2020041391 (ebook) | ISBN
    9780738766652 | ISBN 9780738766812 (ebook)
Subjects: LCSH: Morrigan (Celtic deity) | Goddesses, Celtic—Ireland.
Classification: LCC BL915.M67 W66 2021 (print) | LCC BL915.M67 (ebook) |
    DDC 299–dc23
LC record available at https://lccn.loc.gov/2020041390
LC ebook record available at https://lccn.loc.gov/2020041391

Llewellyn Publications
A Division of Llewellyn Worldwide Ltd.
2143 Wooddale Drive
Woodbury, MN 55125-2989
www.llewellyn.com

Printed in the United States of America

Also by Stephanie Woodfield

Celtic Lore & Spellcraft of the Dark Goddess

Dark Goddess Craft

Drawing Down the Sun

Forthcoming Books by Stephanie Woodfield

Dedicant, Devotee, Priest

Dedication

For the Morrigan. I am grateful for your gifts and victories.

For Catrina, Sonja, and Terry, for being my comrades in our many adventures. Even when I accidently forget I have volunteered us for rituals. Or when I accidently lock us all out of hotel rooms, cars, and other various places.

For all those who have helped me make the Morrigan's Call a reality these many years. It has been an honor weaving magic together with you.

Contents

Part 4: Sorcery and Ritual Craft

Introduction
Priestess of the Morrigan

Priestess is a word that means many different things to many different people. Across different cultures we can see some threads of similarity, but the expression of this kind of devotion varies wildly. I suspect it is in part because in each case we find a different god, or set of gods, being worshipped. I cannot tell you what being a priest of Baal is like, because I do not belong to Baal. I belong to the Morrigan. And that devotion, that connection between the Great Queen and myself, colors everything else I do as a priestess.

My understanding of the Morrigan has been a winding road. It wasn't what I thought it would be when I first started out on this path. It has led me to Ireland, to crawl through the Cave of Cruachan, the Morrigan's cave, on the eve of Samhain and emerge feeling like a different person—a death, a rebirth, a new kind of initiation that altered my being on a deep level. To sing to Badb in a graveyard on Boa Island and feel phantom wings embrace me. To walk Emain Macha in the footsteps of the warrior queen Macha Mong Ruad. The road has led me through the heart of myself and to find hidden parts of my soul I never dreamed existed or had once upon a time ignored. It has led me to find true friends and allies. It has led me through enemy territory and skirmishes. It has led me to move a thousand miles away, to write a book about all the things I wish I had known about the Morrigan when I first encountered her. It has made me look at illusions and shadows. It has led me to grow as a priestess and to serve a growing community of Morrigan devotees.

I thought I knew the Morrigan when I began my journey; looking back now, I know I was only scratching the surface, and she would soon plunge me into the deep end. Even now when I can confidently say I know the Morrigan well, I am sure as I round another twist in the path, she will find some new way to surprise me yet again. I suppose what is surprising about the path the Great Queen has led me on is that there is still much more to say about the Morrigan.

This isn't a book about the past, about what ancient peoples did or the stories they told, or about what I wish I had known when I first met the Morrigan. I've already written that book. This book is about the future. It's about what comes next, about how we can integrate all the lessons of the past into developing a living tradition. It is a guide for devotees and priests of the Morrigan for our world today. The community of people worshiping the Morrigan is growing. It's happened on its own, not because I wrote a book or because others have; it's happening because she wants it to. Because she is walking in this world, calling to us.

In this book I will offer a further look at not only what it means to worship the Morrigan, but also what it means to be her priestess through insights from my own journey and experiences. Sometimes our own stories, our missteps and triumphs, can be the best guideposts for others on the same path. I am not who I was ten years ago, twenty years ago, or even two years ago. My path as a priestess has evolved, and there is value in looking back at that evolution, as well as speaking to where I am today.

First, we will explore the true nature of the Morrigan. Now that she is a figure people clamor to call upon instead of fear, there is a host of new misconceptions about this ancient goddess to address. Popularity comes with its own set of problems. In part 2, Vision and Prophecy, we will look at what it means to channel the voice of the Morrigan, how to handle UPG, and my own experiences with her as a goddess of prophecy. In part 3, Devotions and Oaths, we will look at how to navigate oaths in the context of Irish lore, how to build a devotional relationship with the Morrigan, and prayer. In part 4, Sorcery and Ritual Craft, we will explore her role in curse work and magic, as well as how to craft group rituals centering around the Morrigan. Each of these parts touches on an essential aspect of being a priestess of the Morrigan and is designed to deepen your understanding of the Great Queen. This is not a step-by-step guide to becoming a priestess. Instead, it's a window into what that work looks like and entails, as well as a guide to navigating your own path with the Morrigan.

Although I use the word *priestess*, all the practices you will find in this book can be of value to people of any gender. *Priestess* is the term I use, although I could just as easily refer to myself as a priest or use a more traditional Irish term. Because so much of this book is based on my own personal work, I use the terminology that I identify with when describing my own experiences, but the practices and lessons of priesthood remain the same regardless of gender identity.

I hope this book will be a continuation of my first, a deeper look at who the Morrigan is today and was in the past, and a continued guide to navigating your own relationship with this powerful goddess in modern times, helping you build and grow your own work in service to the Morrigan.

Part 1
The Nature
of the Morrigan

We are lucky enough to have pieces of the Morrigan's story left to us. We see her through the lens of the ancient peoples who told her stories and, to some degree, the filter of the monks who would in later times write down the stories of their forefathers. She is there in tales of cattle raids, in stories concerning the lore of place names of the Irish landscape, in the tales surrounding the taking of Ireland by the Irish gods. Not all gods are so lucky. Many have myths that are forgotten or names that are lost. But the Morrigan remains steadfast through time. I see the gods as living beings, and I think as humanity has changed, so too has the Morrigan and the rest of the gods with her. Modern concerns aren't that different from those of the people of the past, but they are perhaps more high-tech and complicated. And I'm sure some of that influence is not lost on the Great Queen. I am not an Iron Age Celt, and, thus, how I choose to serve an ancient goddess in a modern world will not be the same as priests of the past. Yet at the heart of what we do, I am sure we are probably the same. Priests seek a deeper connection with the divine. We serve the community as bridges between the gods we serve and those seeking a connection with them. We seek to remain in right relation with the gods we serve, honoring them and doing whatever work we feel they have for us in the world. In essence, one of the chief functions of a priest or priestess is to have a deep understanding of their gods.

Understanding the nature of the Morrigan, or any god, is not something that happens overnight. Yet I think understanding the nature of the deity one is devoted to is one of the most important functions of a priest. It is like any relationship, in which our understanding deepens over time. While we will discuss the deeper and more complex work of what it has meant to be a priestess of the Morrigan in my own experience, I think it is appropriate to start out with this chief function of priesthood. You can't understand the Morrigan if you don't have a good sense of who she is and how she operates in the world. And I don't think you can serve her well as a priest or devotee if you aren't dedicated to understanding the power you serve. This is not the same as understanding mythology, although that is certainly a needed side of it. It is instead the understanding of someone who experiences the divine in a real and tangible way.

I think the most important thing to keep in mind when trying to understand the nature of the Morrigan is to accept that your understanding of her will change. The gods are vast beings: we aren't meant to understand them all at once and probably will never fully understand them while on this plane of existence. I think the parts of them we experience have more to do with where we are on our spiritual path than they do about the nature of the deity. Let that understanding evolve as you evolve.

The lore is important, vital even, to understanding the Morrigan. Much of the Irish lore referenced here you may already be familiar with, but if not or if you need a refresher, the appendix on page 237 will be a useful tool, giving an overview of each story. But the lore is only a first step. When people come to me seeking guidance in connecting with the Morrigan, 90 percent of the time they aren't asking about the lore. They want to know what her personality is like. What does she look like? What things does she like? What pisses her off? And most of all they want to know what my own relationship with her and experiences as a priestess in her service have taught me. These are not things we can find in the lore—not all of them, anyway. While I will reference the lore as needed, much of this will be rooted in my own experiences and how the Morrigan has revealed herself to me over the years.

Chapter 1
The Morrigan: Who She Is and Who She Isn't

The Morrigan is complex; she has filled many roles for both those who worshipped her in the past and those who hear her call today. She is an Irish goddess connected to war, sovereignty, shape-shifting, magic, and much more. I remember a time not so long ago when the Morrigan was deemed too dangerous to work with by modern practitioners. Yet now she is everywhere, regaining followers and appearing frequently in modern literature, comic books, and even in TV series. The Morrigan is popular now in modern Paganism too, something I never imagined would happen. But still I fear the Morrigan is misunderstood.

Who is she really? I hope you will find the answer to that question in these pages. My own understanding of the Morrigan and her nature has evolved over time. It has come from multiple sources: first in encountering her in a dream, then through many years of reading her mythology and learning about the culture she came from in order to understand whom I had met in that dream. The lore and mythology remain my anchor in my understanding of her, but my understanding is also tempered with my own personal experiences with her over the last twenty years. For a being so vast, with so many aspects and so many competing notions of who exactly makes up this multifaced goddess, it is often difficult to sort out who or what she actually is. I've often run in philosophical and historical circles in my head trying to understand the being, the power, I am devoted to. Trying to understand the nature of a god is like trying to envision the depth and breadth of the universe, the sheer vastness of it. It is contemplating dark matter and what the life of atoms might be like. My understanding of her has certainly evolved since our first encounter, and I'm sure it will continue to evolve. Sometimes that is the point of a mystery, that it unfolds slowly and only has meaning in the context of the journey itself.

Before we take a closer look at some of the more complicated aspects of the Morrigan's nature, let us look at some of the basics about her personality as well as address some of the most common questions I encounter about her.

The Morrigan Q and A

Does the the *matter? Is it the Morrigan or just Morrigan?*

As you may have noticed, the Morrigan's (*MOR-ree-guhn*) name appears with a definite article. The *the* really does matter. It's how her name appears in Irish mythology, and we find that many Irish gods have definite articles as part of their names, the Dagda being an example. *The Morrigan* does not necessarily indicate a plural, so it is used to indicate a singular character as well as the plural grouping of the three sisters born to Ernmas. The plural of *Morrigan* would be *Morrignae* or *Morrigna*. I have seen people refer to her as Goddess Morrigan or just Morrigan, but it's just not how she was referred to in the culture she originates from. The *the* matters because it's still part of her name and how she has been referenced historically. It should also remind us that most of the time we aren't dealing with a single being but a grouping of goddesses.

Is the Morrigan one goddess, three goddesses, or a multitude?

Like many Irish deity names, *the Morrigan* can also indicate a title of a grouping of goddesses. Let's go back to the source material to see who is part of that grouping. The *Lebor Gabála Érenn*, also known as *The Book of Invasions*, contains several genealogies of the Irish gods as well at detailed migrations or "invasions" of several divine races to the island. Most modern readers would think that this work is a single book, but there are actually several versions, or what are called recensions. In it we find a very specific trio named in multiple parts of the text as the sisters who form the Morrigan. Also we find her mother consistently named as the goddess Ernmas: "Ernmas had other three daughters, Badb and Macha and Morrigu, whose name was Anand."[1] That makes Macha, Badb, and Anu the definitive trio that forms the Morrigan. Next to nothing is left to us about their mother other than her name, but the consistency in

---

1.   R. A. Stewart MacAlister, trans., *Lebor Gabála Érenn: The Book of the Taking of Ireland, Part IV*, Irish Texts Society, vol. 41 (Dublin: Irish Texts Society, 1956), 131.

which she is named with them would suggest that it was understood that this lineage and grouping of sisters was the widely accepted one.

But as most devotees of the Morrigan are aware, there is a whole host of other goddesses who are connected to or are lumped into this collective that forms the Great Queen. Because nothing can be simple with the Morrigan, this can make it rather difficult to figure out what deities are considered part of this collective. Who is the Morrigan? Is she a single being? Or many? And who fits into this collective of war goddesses?

We can say with certainty that she appears as both one and many. For example, in the *Táin Bó Regamna* she is a red-haired woman whom Cuchulain challenges.[2] Here she is identified as *the Morrigan*, even though she is a singular character. In the story of Odras and in at least one version of her yearly meeting with the Dagda at a river ford, she is an individual being identified as *the Morrigan*. In other cases, such as in *The First Battle of Moytura,* we are told the three Morrigans—Anu, Macha, and Badb—attack the Fir Bolg and rain down blood and sorcery upon them. In this instance they are three individuals yet are still acknowledged as the Morrigan. The simplest answer, and the one that seems to hold true to my own experiences, is that she is all these things. A whole and a collective simultaneously.

How I thought of and approached the Morrigan changed very much from the first time I offered her my service to my current practices. When I first encountered her, I was aware that she was made up of three individual goddesses, but I saw her very much as a single being. Even today I can say I see the collective whole that is the Morrigan as an individual being that has a separate personality and energetic feel to her. Whether this unified collective is the combined hive mind of Anu, Macha, and Badb I cannot say, only that when I speak to the totality of the Morrigan, she has a particular feel. That said, that "totality" cannot be confused for the energy and personality of Badb or Macha when I encounter them or any of her other faces as individuals. It took me a long time to learn who these beings were both individually and as a whole. Today I tend to look at it as a kind of godly multiple personality disorder or a hive mind akin to something you would see in science fiction. Anu, Macha, and Badb exist separately from one another and can act separately from one another. They are whole and complete

---

2.   A. H. Leahy, trans. and ed., *Heroic Romances of Ireland,* vol. 2 (London: David Nutt, 1906), 132.

gods themselves, yet together they form something different and unique that has its own identity and agency. At least, this is how my human mind tries to conceptualize what I am experiencing.

That all being said, when I set out to dedicate myself to the Morrigan as her priestess, I didn't realize that the process would encompass several initiatory experiences. Initiation can happen several ways. There are the experiences that we seek out, as my first initiation as a priestess was. I felt called to do this work. I spent time doing divination and journey work confirming I was going down the right path. Then I simply went out into the woods and did a simple ritual offering my vows to the Morrigan, made libations, and that was it. Or so I thought. Just because I was a priestess of the Morrigan didn't mean I was instantly a priestess of Macha, Badb, or Anu. That would come later.

What does it mean when the Morrigan is silent?

I do not think this is unique to the Morrigan, but the Morrigan's silences seem to be taken more harshly than the silence of other gods by her followers. Because of her reputation as a goddess of war, no one wants to make her angry. In general, the Morrigan isn't very shy about making her presence known, so when that presence goes away, it can seem sudden and like a harsh reprimand. When a deity's presence and voice seem to disappear from us when we are used to feeling a close connection to them or receiving messages often, it is usually perceived as anger on the deity's part. This can very well be the case. If the Morrigan is quiet or if her presence feels far away, it could be due to a misstep on the part of the devotee.

For me, her silence often means I'm not listening to what she is trying to tell me. If she has been trying to tell you something ten different times, she just doesn't think that eleventh time she sends an omen or message your way is going to make any difference. Retreating, making their presence lessened, seems to be the way the gods force our hand to make the next move. Your concern that the Morrigan might be pissed at you might make you take the time to do daily devotions, to make time to pour her an offering and spend time connecting to her. Just experiencing the gods occasionally in ritual or on a sabbat isn't enough if you want to have a deep connection to them. You have to put in the work of connecting with them in your daily life. Silences can signal that one has been neglecting those daily practices or, for me, that she has already given me the answers I seek.

Other times silences can mean that another deity wants your attention or simply that the Morrigan is going to show up only at certain times in your life. Not every deity will be one you have a lifelong, complicated relationship with. The depth of the relationship will vary from deity to deity. She may appear in your life very strongly, then step back into the background, always there but not center stage, because maybe another devotion needs to be center stage for you.

What is Anu like?

Anu (pronounced *AH-nu*) can be difficult for many to connect to because we don't have any of her stories. Because the Paps of Anu (two breast-like hills in Ireland) are named for her, I first started my connection to Anu through connecting and taking care of the land I lived on. To me Anu is the sovereignty of the land that flowed to the king. She feels strong and eternal like a mountain to me. She is every inch the queen. But she is not the queen defending her claim like Macha; she is the strong ruler who knows the weight of her crown and how to rule well. She is comfortable with power and uses it. Anu is the one I go to for the kind of strength that grows things and lets them thrive rather than tears them down. Her sisters are about tearing things apart to make them stronger and burning out the rot, while Anu is about making them whole and sustainable again.

I also view Anu as the true name of the Morrigan. Since *the Morrigan* is a title, it makes sense that she would have a name in addition to the title. As earlier noted, in the *Lebor Gabála Érenn*, which lists many of the genealogies of the gods, we are told, "Ernmas had other three daughters, Badb and Macha and Morrigu, whose name was Anand." [3] This would suggest that the Morrigan's true name is Anu (here given with the nonstandard spelling).

What is Macha like?

Macha (pronounced *MA-ka*), like Badb, is multifaceted. There is more than one Macha, or at least she has several incarnations within her stories, often dying only to pop up again alive and well. Macha is complicated; there are five different

---

3. MacAlister, *Lebor Gabála Érenn, Part IV,* 131.

faces of Macha in Irish lore, and she can easily be worshiped as a multifaced goddess on her own.

Macha embodies the kind of strength that endures against all odds. She does not make rash decisions; she is full of strategy. Even as the fierce warrior queen, Macha exudes a kind of control over her power and fury. She has mastered herself. Like Anu, I find her more concerned with building things up. She certainly can destroy and burn things down, but she also values strong foundations. She makes me think of an old general who has seen many battles and knows from experience what is worth putting her energy into and what isn't.

What is Badb like?

Like Macha, there is more than one face to Badb (pronounced *BYE-vh*). There is the side of her that is Cath Badb (meaning "battle crow"), who dances on spearpoints and is all battle frenzy and battle madness. She is not about controlled force as Macha is; instead, she is the wild, destructive energy of a storm.

Then there is Badb as the Washer at the Ford. When Badb is the Washer Woman, she is calmer, focused on the cleansing that is needed for the aftermath of battle. She can be just as dangerous and harsh as Cath Badb, but for the most part I have found her to be a source of comfort when approached with respect. Someone to mourn beside you, who guides you toward releasing grief and trauma. When I see her as the Washer Woman, she has long black hair that covers her face like a veil, her fingers long, almost like bird talons. The river that she washes in has significance in my own personal unverified personal gnosis (UPG). For me, it is the river of life, death, and rebirth; it is where we all journey to when we leave this world to be cleansed and wash away our burdens.

And finally, there is Badb the prophetess. Of all the Morrigan's faces, Badb is the most connected to prophecy. She is specifically named as the one who speaks the Morrigan's famous prophecy at the end of *The Second Battle of Moytura*, after the Tuatha Dé Danann have defeated their enemies the Fomorians, and she also appears to Maeve in a dream to warn her of her son's death. Although I see this part of her as separate from the Washer Woman, it is important to note that the entire function of the Washer at the Ford in the mythology is as a death omen. Where Badb is, there is some element of prophecy and seeing into the future. In this guise she appears to me as a tall pale woman with black hair, a regal, unbending air about her. She is calm and collected, watching the swirling factors and possible threads of future events, seeing which threads to pull. I have also encountered her as a pale, wraithlike woman, completely bone white from head to toe, as if all the color and pigments were drawn out of her skin, hair, eyes, and clothes.

Of the three, Badb is the harshest of the sisters. That isn't necessarily a bad thing. She is direct and cutting at times, but I feel her directness is mostly because she sees to the heart of things. No truth can be hidden from her. We concern ourselves with the lies and illusions we spin around ourselves, but Badb sees past those and demands that we rip out those lies from our hearts.

Isn't Nemain one of the three Morrigans?

Nemain (pronounced *neh-VAN* and alternatively spelled Neman) is given a different genealogy than Anu, Macha, and Badb in the *Lebor Gabála Érenn*. The trio we know as the Morrigan are the daughters of Ernmas, while Neman is named as a daughter of Elcmar. They clearly have different parentage, so why are they so often equated?

In his work "The Ancient Irish Goddess of War," W. M. Hennessy mentions Nemain several times, although never names her specifically as one of the Morrigan.[4] Hennessy wrote in the 1800s, and there is no doubt that his work influences modern Neopagan authors looking for information about the Morrigan or Irish war deities.

Nemain and Badb are named as the two wives of the war god Neit in the *Lebor Gabála Érenn*: "Neit son of Indu and his two wives, / Badb and Neman."[5] Although in other places, Nemain and Fea are named as Neit's two wives.[6] Badb and Nemain appear alongside each other, working together to confuse a part of the enemy host when Cuchulain lets out a mighty shout in *The Cattle Raid of Cooley,* a story that details how Queen Maeve tries to steal a bull from Ulster and how the hero Cuchulain single-handedly fights her army. Since Badb is both a proper name of a goddess and also a term used to describe a war fury, it is unclear if Nemain is simply being described as a *badb,* "fury," in the text or if the word *badb* is being used as a proper name, indicating that both the

---

4.   W. M. Hennessy, "The Ancient Irish Goddess of War," *Revue Celtique* 1 (1870–72): 32–55.

5.   MacAlister, *Lebor Gabála Érenn, Part IV,* 237.

6.   MacAlister, *Lebor Gabála Érenn, Part IV,* 123 and 131.

goddess Badb and the goddess Nemain were present.[7] If that is the case, then they have no true connection other than that they are both spirits connected to battle, and Nemain can be described as a *badb,* or war fury.

For a very long time I was convinced this was the case, and that they were separate, unrelated deities. While out of the three Morrigans Badb has always felt the most wild and fierce to me, Nemain felt even more so. Whenever I encountered her, she appeared naked, covered in blood. But over time I noticed that when Badb appeared Nemain was not far away. I would call to Badb and Nemain would show up with her in tow, so eventually I included her in my worship of Badb. I still do not see her as one of the Morrigans, but I do see her as a sister to Badb, and they can be worshipped as a divine pair.

What I think is the most likely explanation for Nemain being equated with Badb is that at one point in time they formed a sacred dyad. That is a dual-faced set of deities or a set of sisters, just as the Morrigan is a set of three sisters. Over time for whatever reason Badb became absorbed into the trinity that is now the Morrigan, and Nemain's worship became separate from Badb's. This would explain why while they have different genealogies, they still were both named as the wives of Neit, perhaps indicating they are one and the same or were seen as such at one point. They also have the same epithets, being described as red mouthed, a further indication of their connection at one point in time.

The simple answer is that Nemain is not one of the three Morrigans, but she is connected to Badb, who is. Confusing, right? Welcome to Irish mythology.

What does the Morrigan look like?
I think the reason I encounter this question so frequently is that we all seek confirmation that our encounters with deity, whether they be in dreams or journey work, are valid. If we are all seeing the same hallucination, then logically it's not really a hallucination. We want to know what we are experiencing is real. Most people who encounter the Morrigan describe her as a pale woman with dark hair. Others see her as a redhead. Is there a correct answer?

If you are a student of Irish mythology, you will notice fairly quickly that Irish lore is filled with intricately detailed descriptions about weapons and what a person is wearing. Great detail might be put into describing a person's clothes,

---

7.   Thomas Kinsella, trans., *The Táin: Translated from the Irish Epic Táin Bó Cuailnge* (New York: Oxford University Press, 1969), 167.

but rarely are details given about the people themselves. We may be told all about a character's size, his strength, and the pattern of the tunic he wears, but we don't know what his hair or eye color is, for example. He or she might simply be described as fair, and we are left to fill in our own version of that for ourselves. The Morrigan is no different.

The *Táin Bó Regamna* is the only instance where anything about her physical appearance is mentioned. Yet even this is suspect because she is a shape-shifter, so we don't really know if the description is her true form. We are told she has red hair and red eyebrows: "A red woman was in the chariot, and a red mantle was about her, she had two red eye-brows, and the mantle fell between the two *ferta* of her chariot."[8] When the hero Cuchulain challenges her in this guise, he does not recognize her until she turns into a crow. In most of their interactions the hero only seems to recognize the Morrigan in animal form, which may mean that the red woman she appears as may still not be her true form. I would argue that as a shape-shifter, she may not really have a true form, other than what she appears as in the moment at hand.

In *The Cattle Raid of Cooley* when the hero encounters her again in human form, she is an old woman. Here we are given no more description other than her age. Alternatively, in a dream Queen Maeve encounters her as a pale young woman, which I think just drives home the point that the Morrigan will appear however she wants to appear, given the situation. Similarly, in another appearance the Morrigan is described as dancing from spearpoint to spearpoint in the form of a naked hag. When she appears as an old woman, the words used to describe her are *senntaine* and *cailleach*.[9] *Cailleach*, while also the name of a goddess, means "old woman" or a "hag." This description may be why some modern worshipers conflate the two deities, even though they have no true connection in mythology. Young or old, animal or human. As far as the lore is concerned, the one time we do have a description of her, she is a red-headed woman of indeterminate age.

I don't really think there is one single answer to what the Morrigan looks like. I have experienced her as a pale woman with black hair when she is Badb

---

8.   Leahy, *Heroic Romances of Ireland,* vol. 2, 132.

9.   Morgan Daimler, "The Morrigan, Questions and Answers," Irish-American Witchcraft, *Patheos Pagan* (blog), November 17, 2017, https://www.patheos.com/blogs/agora /2017/11/irish-american-witchcraft-morrigan-questions-answers/.

and Anu, while Macha for me appears as a tall red-haired woman. She is very fluid in my mind, as I think a shape-shifter should be. I have also had those close to me experience the Morrigan appearing to them in dreams wearing my face to impart a message to them. They recognized me, but on some level, they were aware that it wasn't really me. This has happened to several different people and often enough that when I asked the Queen why she was appearing this way, the answer she gave me was simple: I wore her face when I did oracular work, so it was only fair that she could at times wear my face. I think this boils down to the fact that the Morrigan can appear any damn way she pleases.

Does being a follower of the Morrigan mean you must be a spiritual warrior?

There are several problems with this concept, not the least being that those who take up the title of *spiritual warrior* tend to have very different mindsets than military personnel and those in law enforcement who, from a modern perspective, are literal warriors for a living. A spiritual warrior is not above someone who puts their life on the line and participates in the physical side of warriorship. The simple answer to this question is no. If the Morrigan has called to you, then there is something about you that she is interested in. She may make you face things about yourself and instigate change, but no one should feel the need to take on a title or work that they are not comfortable with. Ultimately, feeling that one needs to be a warrior to honor the Morrigan is essentially turning a blind eye to her other aspects. She is just as much a goddess of war as she is a goddess of prophecy, yet I see few modern devotees concerned that worshiping the Morrigan will also require them to learn oracular work.

Warrior is a term that means many things to different people and may not be appropriate for you. That's perfectly okay. The Morrigan gives us each different marching orders, if you will. Being a devotee of the Morrigan means you are cultivating a deep connection with this particular Irish goddess; it doesn't mean you've been spiritually recruited into the Morrigan's army.

Is the Morrigan cruel? Does the Morrigan break her devotees?

I encounter this question often. Perhaps because many devotees in the Morrigan community speak openly about times when they have ignored what she was trying to tell them or weren't upholding their end of a promise and it went badly. I have a friend who tells the story of how the Morrigan hit her with a bus just to get her to start listening. No metaphor there, either—quite literally a real bus. She tends to know exactly what will get through to her followers, how exactly to break you when you aren't quite getting a lesson you need to learn. The Morrigan has never hit me with a bus, but she has broken my heart in painful ways, ways that were the only way for me to learn certain things, ways that transformed me into what I needed to be. I don't ignore the Morrigan when she is trying to tell me something anymore. Even if I don't understand at first, I listen. I seek omens and consult divination. Not listening seems to be what brings on her harsher side. But I must emphasize that this is part of having oaths to a deity or being in a deity's service. I chose to be her priestess. I chose this kind of connection to her. Those oaths have consequences. For someone who may just be a devotee of the Morrigan, who worships her and feels a strong connection to her but has offered no oath of service, priesthood, or otherwise, I do not feel the consequences for not listening to something she is trying to tell you would be the same. Breaking an oath or not doing something you promised a deity, any deity, is never a good idea. Think before you speak or make grand oaths.

As for her being cruel, there is a difference between cruelty and harshness. The Morrigan is harsh at times, yes. But not all the time. She is willing to be harsh because she expects us to become better than we are. That requires tough love, and I do believe she cares about those who call to her. This idea that the Morrigan is constantly angry is an unhealthy one. Devotional work has consequences because we are dealing with forces that are more powerful than ourselves. There is risk there, but also reward. That doesn't make her an angry, hateful goddess.

Can you worship other gods alongside the Morrigan?

Since my house is basically one giant collection of altars and temple spaces dedicated to a multitude of gods, I can safely say yes. The Morrigan's altar space is certainly the largest, since she is the primary focus of my spiritual work, but she is not the only deity I worship. I have close devotional relationships with many deities. The very nature of being Pagan or a polytheist implies one may have several gods that they worship or have dedications to. I have seen others insinuate that if the Morrigan is not held on a higher pedestal than other deities, there will be dire consequences, but this just isn't true. What I can see being a problem with any deity is if you worship a god and give them regular offerings, discover another deity's presence in your life, and then just up and stop making offerings or paying any attention to the first deity. Ignoring a deity you have made oaths to or who is used to receiving regular offerings can cause issues regardless of who that deity is. If you are going to honor multiple gods then you have to make room in your life for all of them. As long as you are holding up your obligations to the Morrigan there is no reason the Morrigan would be upset if you honored other deities. There are certain deities within pantheons that do not get along based on their mythology, but that is a different scenario entirely.

In many cases I find that the Morrigan may work with other gods to convey a message or lessons. For me, the Morrigan has often worked in tandem with Brigid as well as the Dagda. For whatever reason, I have noticed that those who have a devotion to Odin and Hekate seem to also find that the Morrigan is courting or calling to them as well.

Is Morgan le Fay the same as the Morrigan?

Although her name sounds similar to the Irish Morrigan, Morgan le Fay is purely of Welsh origin. Her name is likely derived from Old Welsh *Mori-genā*, meaning "Sea Born," *mor* meaning "sea." [10] Her epithet *le Fay*, from the French *la fée*, or "the fairy," was added in the fifteenth century by Thomas Malory. However, Morrigan is derived from Irish *rigan*, meaning "queen," and *mor*, meaning "great."

But *mor* looks and sounds similar in Irish and Old Welsh—why does it have two separate meanings within two cultures fairly geographically close to one another, you ask? Well, Celtic languages fall into two branches: P-Celtic and Q-Celtic. P-Celtic, from which Morgan le Fay's name stems, includes Gaulish, Cornish, and Welsh. Q-Celtic consists of Irish, Scottish, and Manx Gaelic. [11] Similar languages, but they evolved differently.

Besides her name having a completely different etymology than the Morrigan, it is also very clear that Morgan le Fay evolved from the stories of the Welsh goddess Modron, eventually being diminished into a mortal character, a fate shared by many of the Welsh gods. Modron, notably, does have some

10.   Rosalind Clark, *The Great Queens: Irish Goddesses from the Morrígan to Cathleen ní Houlihan* (Gerrards Cross, UK: Colin Smythe, 1991), 22.

11.   Martin J. Ball and James Fife, eds., *The Celtic Languages* (London: Routledge, 1993), 67.

similarities to the Morrigan, which adds to the confusion. But no, Morgan le Fay is not the Morrigan.

From my point of view, Morgan le Fay's energy feels very different from the Morrigan's, and I do not view them as the same deity. Similarly, many people equate Badb and Nemain, but they both have very distinct and individual energies and personalities in my opinion. They aren't the same to me. Just as Kali and the Morrigan may have similarities, that doesn't automatically mean they are the same deity. Yet many people do connect to the Morrigan through Morgan le Fay and have meaningful experiences. What does that mean? Are they really connecting to the Welsh Modron? Are their experiences just fanciful and not valid encounters with deity? This is the thing with UPG— it's never simple. And this is the reason I wrote about Morgan le Fay in my first book. Just because I didn't see the Morrigan and Morgan le Fay as the same goddess didn't mean that the people who had experienced the Morrigan in this way had anything less valid than my own encounters with her. Sometimes the gods speak to us however they wish. For those I have met who do connect to the Morrigan in this guise, working with her often revolves around reclaiming their own sexuality or healing sexual trauma. Something in Morgan le Fay's story might embody that better than the Morrigan's. Perhaps that is why she chooses this face to speak to them through. I do not know.

I think the lesson here is that the gods will speak to us through whatever medium they choose. Also, we need to be able to accept that when there isn't a connection in the lore and mythology to something we are experiencing, it's because it has more to do with us and the personal lessons we need to learn, rather than the experience being a statement about the nature of the deity.

Is the Morrigan a triple goddess?

In the sense that the Morrigan comprises three sisters, yes. In the sense of Maiden, Mother, Crone, no. Most triads of goddesses don't fit that model. It is, in the end, an interpretation by Robert Graves of how he viewed the Goddess, not something that can be applied to every triple set of female deities. The Morrigan does appear both young and old. She does have children, but she isn't a mother goddess. She happens to have children, like many women. It's not the defining aspect of herself or her function as a deity. When she appears as a young woman, she isn't very innocent, and it is usually a disguise so the hero or person she is encountering won't recognize her. She wears most of her forms as very interchangeable skins, and they have more to do with her purpose at the time than reflecting a stage in a woman's life. Ultimately, connecting the Morrigan to the Maiden, Mother, Crone concept has more to do with modern Neopagan ideology than it does with how the Morrigan was viewed by the Irish.

Do you have to be a Reconstructionist to honor the Morrigan?

The simple answer is no. I find this question cropping up a lot as there is now a stronger push to look back at authentic Irish practices. Learning more about the culture the Morrigan comes from should be very important to anyone who worships her. I think it's a good thing that people want to understand what authentic Irish folk belief is and what comes from modern concepts. Yet I also have seen many people who are Wiccan and worship the Morrigan shamed for not being "hard-core" enough because they don't worship her in the way a Celtic Reconstructionist would. I started my own path in Wicca and then moved on to a more devotional path, but it was only because that was what worked for me. I try to use what works tempered with what we know about the past and mix that with my own gnosis, which makes me an odd kind of hybrid. That may not work for you, and that's fine. It matters that you approach your devotion and worship in a meaningful way. It doesn't matter if you are Wiccan, Reconstructionist, or something else. I know devotees of the Morrigan who have deep, meaningful relationships with her and practice in vastly different ways, ways that would probably cause both parties to point to the other and say, "You are doing it all wrong!" The point is I don't think the Morrigan cares. All our modern practices probably look nothing like how she was worshiped in the past. Is it valuable to know about Irish culture? Yes, absolutely, just like it is important to understand the origins of modern occult practices and techniques. In the end, all that matters is that she is being worshiped. The manner in which that is done doesn't matter so much in my opinion. I think her devotees have stronger feelings about the subject than the Morrigan herself does.

Is the Morrigan Brigid's mother? Who are her children?

We are told that Brigid's father is the Dagda, but we are never told who her mother is. At least when we are talking about Brigid, the goddess of the Tuatha

Dé Danann. Brigid the Christian saint has her own storyline for her parentage. Since the Morrigan and the Dagda are said to be husband and wife, it is not out of the realm of possibility, but we really don't know, which is to say Brigid's mother could be any of the Irish goddesses. What is absolutely out of the realm of possibility is that Brigid is conceived during the union the Morrigan and the Dagda have at Samhain in *The Second Battle of Moytura*. Why? Because at this point in the stories of the Irish gods, Brigid was already an adult, married to Bres, the king who was overthrown and caused the battle in this story in the first place. She even already has sons who are grown at this point who fight in the battle. Could she be a child of the Morrigan and Dagda from an earlier union? It's possible, but we just don't know. The Dagda does have children with other goddesses as well, so really this is something you have to make your own judgments on. There is no real evidence for it or against it.

The Morrigan does have other children. In the *Dindshenchas*, a collection of lore concerning Irish place names, we are told Meiche (pronounced *MEH-kah* with the *k* sound as in *loch*) is a son of the Morrigan, although we are never told who his father is. Meiche comes to an unfortunate end when serpents begin growing in his three hearts. Yes, when you are a god, why have one heart when you can have three? In one recension of the *Lebor Gabála Érenn* the Morrigan is said to be the mother of Brian, Lucharba, and Luchair by her own father, Delbaeth. In other versions this trio is said to be the children of Brigid, perhaps further confusing their connection and blood ties.

Another child of the Morrigan, Adair, is mentioned in an index of *The Second Battle of Moytura*. We are told almost nothing about her other than she was a daughter of the Morrigan by the Dagda and that she later married a man named Eber.

Why are there so many versions of the Morrigan's stories?

Trying to sort out Irish mythology can be pretty overwhelming. Perhaps the most frustrating aspect of delving into Irish mythology is that there are multiple versions of a single story, known as recensions. This means the same story appears in different manuscripts, and they are not exact copies of each other. Since we have many versions of the same stories in various manuscripts, in some versions a character might do one thing, then in another version of the same story a different character is attributed to that plot point or named as the parent of someone, contradicting the other version of the story. For example, in the story of Cuchulain's wasting sickness the name of his wife keeps changing for no apparent reason. This may be due to regional variations for certain stories prior to them being collected and written down. *The Second Battle of Moytura* is the rare exception, since we have only one manuscript surviving with this story. However, although we only have one manuscript for this text, you will still find various differing English translations. Some translators may have chosen to not translate several passages if they contained difficult to translate language. In *The Second Battle of Moytura* translator Elizabeth A. Gray skips over a whole paragraph of Lugh speaking to Balor. The English text skips ahead with Balor commenting on how talkative Lugh is, which makes no sense to the English reader because Lugh seemingly hasn't said anything. You might not understand that we just skipped ahead a whole paragraph if you don't have the version that gives you both the Old Irish text and the English translation side by side. Not all translations are perfect, and some of the older translations tend to have wording that fits the translator's perspective or morals from that time rather than being true to the text. We can see this in translations that edit out the Morrigan washing her genitals at the river ford prior to her meeting with the Dagda.

To further confuse the English reader, sometimes a story will be referenced using its Irish name, and other times it may be referenced by its English name, causing more confusion if you don't realize they are the same thing.

For stories pertaining to the Morrigan, it is good to start with both of the battles of Moytura and the Ulster Cycle, which includes *The Cattle Raid of Cooley*. You will find a short description of all the stories referenced in this book in the appendix, starting on page 237, as well as links to read the materials for yourself.

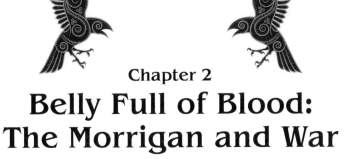

Chapter 2
Belly Full of Blood:
The Morrigan and War

*T*he woman in front of me shuffles the cards. I meant this to be a quick reading, but I feel Badb stirring in the background of my mind. She is ready. She has things to say. I draw the cards and I speak what Badb shows me. Badb seems pleased that her message has been relayed to the woman, and after the reading, we sit and talk about the Morrigan's nature and how she is viewed by modern Pagans.

Tomorrow I will be part of a devotional ritual to Badb for the conference I am attending. We plan to call on her not just as a goddess of prophecy but also as the Washer at the Ford to cleanse us, to strip away poison and grief. The woman is surprised, as are many others we have talked to about the ritual. Most have assumed a ritual to the Morrigan would include calling for war or portraying her angry and ready for blood, sword raised ready to take on a challenge. There also seems to be a general feeling that the Morrigan is angry all the time, always in battle fury mode. Always ready for blood. That this imagery must be the totality of her personality. I have been a priestess of the Morrigan for over twenty years now, and it still surprises me how often I come across these ideas, how superficially we view the gods. Still, after all this time, all we see is war in her, and even then, all we see is the romanticized ideal of war. Not the truth of it. Not the truth of her. Badb is all about cutting things away to see the truth. I feel her stirring, whispering, "I am more ... I am so much more ... Show them."

When the reading is done, I still feel Badb's shadow upon me. Offerings are made at our makeshift hotel room altar next to the coffee maker, and I ask her why her children cannot see past this one face, this one aspect of her. Badb speaks again:

"If you want war, I will give it to you. If you wish to fight endlessly, I will give you what you want, because you have asked me. I will fill your belly so full of blood that

23

you will beg to see my other faces. The lesson will be as easy or as difficult as you wish it. Some will destroy themselves and never see me fully. It speaks to what you are, not to what I am."

With the words I feel a desire to be seen. To be known fully. To move past the surface. I hope the ritual the next day will provide some of that, and I think it does. Her words leave me thinking of a time I could only see her as the goddess of war and how that has shifted. How I am more inclined to call her a goddess of prophecy and sovereignty nowadays, if I am forced to put a label on her in relation to my current practice. The Morrigan is many things. Yes, she is a goddess of war, but as I pour another offering in gratitude, I am pretty sure our modern perspective of war is all wrong too.

———

It is easy to see only the goddess of war, the screaming battle fury. It is an image that exudes power, especially to women. We are taught to be timid, to smile, to not be aggressive. This image of a raging woman, frenzied, battle cry echoing loud from her lips, breaking down all the stereotypes our culture imposes, is powerful. She is not quiet; she is bold. She does as she wills. She is dangerous and uncontrollable. The power in that image of the Morrigan, as a war fury, to a modern woman cannot be overstated. It is an image I find empowering. For a long time, this was the only face the Morrigan showed me. Because it was the only image I wanted to see. Everything revolved around battles I needed to fight, demons to overcome. And I needed it. I truly did. But I couldn't see anything else. I clung to the image of the goddess of battle, the war fury, and blinded myself to the rest of what the Morrigan was. Because that was the image I saw power in.

It was a long time before I understood that she was more than a goddess of war. Like all the Irish gods, she is not one dimensional, and we have to look at the whole picture to find a well-balanced understanding of the nature of these gods. War is brutal and dangerous, and so too can the Morrigan be. We should not declaw that side of her, yet at the same time we can't overindulge in that side of her either.

If we only want to call down war and face our personal battles, she'll keep throwing things at us until we tire. In many ways that is what she did with me. If I only wanted to see her side connected to war, fine. She wasn't going to run out of demons I needed to face or challenges I could throw myself at. There was an endless supply. In many ways she was like a seasoned drill sergeant, standing back, watching me exhaust myself, and waiting for me to figure out that I couldn't do this forever. She would let me exhaust myself and wait till my head was in the dirt, ready for a change. I had to choose to see her as something more. I had to wait until my belly was filled with blood and I was sick of fighting before I was ready to see something more in her, to stop idealizing battle. Personal battles and literal battles are the things we survive. We fight to get to an end point so we can move on, but that's a hard lesson to someone who finds the aesthetic of warrior culture appealing and powerful.

Eventually, I realized the power that I saw in her warrior face was in all of her faces and aspects. She wasn't powerful because she was a goddess of battle; she was just powerful. Powerful in all that she did and represented. It is easy to romanticize war, to see the power in the image of bold warriors, and to forget the realities and horrors of war. The combination of romanticizing war and the empowering image of a female war fury is in part why I think it is difficult for us to see the Morrigan as anything else. We choose only to see the images that make us feel empowered and forget to see the rest of the image and what it represents. In the recent past, many feared this aspect of her, but now we can't see anything else. In some ways, I think we can't see the forest for the trees. Do we really understand the goddess of war?

Ancient Goddess of War

I think the first question we have to ask is, what role did she play in ancient war? Why does she have this bad reputation? Why are modern people inspired to depict her as this angry goddess walking among corpses and carnage with a look that says she gets turned on by fresh entrails?

I think it is important to note that she isn't an Irish version of Eris. She doesn't cause conflict; the gods and mortals do that just fine by themselves. Instead she shows up when there is conflict to aid in the battle in various ways. When she helps the Irish gods in their battles, she participates in physical battle and uses magic to defeat the enemy. There is certainly a strong element of magical warfare connected to her. She uses her magic to conjure blood, fire, and fog to hinder the Fir Bolg when the Irish gods fight them for dominance over Ireland. Translator R. A. Stewart MacAlister writes in his introduction to section 6 of the *Lebor Gabála Érenn* that she is a war fury: "He [Delbaeth] has three daughters, the famous war-furies Badb, Macha, and Mór-rígu."[12] The same text also mentions the trio as a source of "bitter fighting": "Badb and Macha, greatness of wealth, / Morrigu, springs of craftiness, / sources of bitter fighting."[13] Translator Whitley Stokes writes in the preface to *Three Irish Glossaries* that the contents of Macha's acorn crop, "Mesrad Machae," are the severed heads of battle.[14]

When the Morrigan meets the Dagda at the ford in *The Second Battle of Moytura,* after their union, she tells the Dagda to gather the hosts to the river ford to meet her and that she would take on one of the enemy kings and "take from him the blood of his heart and the kidneys of his valour."[15] Later she gave two handfuls of that blood to the hosts that were waiting at the Ford of Unshin.

Before the Irish gods prepare to battle the Fomorians, they indulge in a round of boasting about what skills and power they will bring to the fight:

> *"And you, Morrigan,"* said Lug, *"what power?"*
> *"Not hard to say,"* she said. *"I have stood fast; I shall pursue what was watched; I will be able to kill; I will be able to destroy those who might be subdued."*[16]

This indicates she isn't shy about participating in battle as well as influencing the outcome of battles.

The Morrigan was also said to take part in a historic battle, the battle of Mag Rath in 637 CE fought between the high king of Ireland and his foster son. She is said to have appeared as a thin, gray-haired hag who flew through

---

12.   MacAlister, *Lebor Gabála Érenn, Part IV,* 103.

13.   MacAlister, *Lebor Gabála Érenn, Part IV,* 217.

14.   Whitley Stokes, trans., *Three Irish Glossaries: Cormac's Glossary Codex A, O'Davoren's Glossary, and a Glossary to the Calendar of Oingus the Culdee* (London: Williams & Norgate, 1862), xxxv.

15.   Elizabeth A. Gray, ed. and trans., *Cath Maige Tuired: The Second Battle of Mag Tuired,* Irish Texts Society, vol. 52 (Dublin: Irish Texts Society, 1982), section 85.

16.   Gray, *Cath Maige Tuired,* sections 106–7.

the air, dancing from spearpoint to shield rim of the warriors who were destined to be victorious in the battle.[17]

Overall, I don't think this paints the picture of a bloodthirsty goddess. When her people need her, she is there, ready and willing to fight. The Dagda and many other Irish gods who participate in these same battles are not viewed as vicious. It is clear her favor is pivotal to winning a battle. She can fight in both a physical sense and with magic. She has some sway over the outcome, as we see with her touching the weapons of those who will be victorious in the Battle of Mag Rath and her association as a war fury. I think what we forget is she is less the warrior woman on the battlefield, and rather the force behind it all. She pulls the strings and moves the chess pieces on the board to her liking. She participates in and understands war, but she isn't out seeking it. Even her acorn crop is not the heads she takes in battle; it's the ones on the battlefield taken by the armies she watches and oversees. As long as there is war and conflict in the world, she will be there. Not because she craves the gore and bloodshed, but because she understands the nature of why we put ourselves into those situations, in which the only way through the problem is fighting your way across a battlefield.

Goddess of Modern War

When I lived in New England I worked for a bank for many years. When you work in a small town in banking, you get to know everyone. You see them when they come in to cash their paychecks, when children come in with their parents to deposit their birthday money, when they want to apply for a mortgage or need a loan to pay for a wedding. Across the street from us was a retirement home, and sometimes we just had little old ladies come in for the free coffee and wanting nothing else except to chat with us and promise one day to open an account. Maybe over tomorrow's free coffee, but probably not. I remember one young man coming in often to make sure his paycheck cleared faster than it would at the ATM. He would tell us about his plans in life and how he wanted to join the military. Eventually, he did just that. He came into the bank in his new military uniform and told us he was about to go to boot camp, politely asking that his last paycheck for the job he was leaving not be held. He was hopeful and excited about the future. That was the last time I saw him.

---

17. Daragh Smyth, *A Guide to Irish Mythology* (Dublin: Irish Academic Press, 1988), 127.

We didn't hear from him for a year or two, although his mother came in and told us about where he was stationed and how proud she was of him. Then we got the news that he had been killed when his unit was attacked. When they brought his casket home, they closed the main road, which the bank was on, and we even closed the bank for an hour as they escorted his body with a motorcade of police and local military vets who wanted to honor him. I remember standing along the side of the road with my coworkers, paying our respects as he passed. I offered a silent prayer to the Morrigan that he might be at peace. A crow watching from a phone pole called out, and I took it as a sign my prayer had been heard. For a long while after, I would light a candle for this fallen solider. It was my way of remembering that while most of the battles the Morrigan has helped me overcome were metaphorical ones, she still ruled over actual war. Wars didn't stop in the Iron Age. I needed to remember that war was a real, literal thing. Even now in modern times. She didn't just rule over long-forgotten battles or battles fought with archaic weapons. She still ruled over war as it existed today.

I think understanding war is essential to understanding the nature of the Morrigan. War is both why many fear the Morrigan and why so many fail to see her complexities. One of the beauties of the Irish point of view is that they embraced the complexities of life. Nothing is black and white or simple. Like the knotwork in their art, ideas and concepts double back, circle around each other, and become entangled and complicated. Everything is connected to something else. There are no clear-cut answers to most things. The Morrigan isn't the goddess of war, because the gods weren't the gods of a single facet of reality but many. She is just the Morrigan, by that way of thinking. War is just one strand, one thread, among many that form the tapestry of her being. Everything is interwoven; nothing is a straight, easy-to-define line.

But it is hard to understand a goddess of war when you have never gone to war, in the literal sense, yourself. Perhaps this is why we make so many attempts to tame our war gods, to make them harmless, toothless lions. The qualities they embody are powerful and vital to us, yet we feel the need to make their images more palatable to our modern sensibilities. It's a dangerous game to play. War is horrifying and scary, and many times it is brutally unfair and gory. The wrong people die, and sometimes the bad guys win. Sometimes the people who are supposed to be the good guys aren't. Many times, life is lost senselessly. But it doesn't change the fact that there are things worth dying for in war or that we need soldiers to protect us no matter how much we would like to deny it. Or that the same gods who rule over gore and bloodshed also rule over the spirit of perseverance and over the will to survive and fight for what is meaningful.

One of the primary reasons many in the past have discouraged modern worshipers from honoring the Morrigan was that she was connected to war. In many ways modern Neopaganism in the 1990s was dealing with the aftermath of Hollywood's negative depiction of the growing Pagan movement in movies such as *The Craft*, and there was a general air of *We need to pass. We need to not look dark and scary*. Curses weren't things Witches did, no sirree, we were all "love and light" and an all-loving Mother Goddess. If you mentioned the Morrigan in a Pagan circle, you were promptly told she was too dangerous to work with. Fast-forward twenty years and when I mention I am a priestess of the Morrigan, people's reactions are usually something like "Oh, cool, she's that badass war goddess, isn't she?" Our war gods have become less taboo in Paganism, and that is certainly an improvement. But that shift to war being cool and edgy is problematic. Instead of seeing the many other sides of the Morrigan, we fixate on this single angle. We aren't scared to talk about dark and dangerous gods anymore. Witches admittedly doing public cursing has even made the evening news a few times recently. But just because the dark and scary things are coming out to play in the light doesn't mean we should romanticize them or tame them. It also doesn't mean that we really understand them any better, either.

There is a story in the *Dindshenchas* in which the druid Tulchaine prays to the Morrigan to help him win the love of a faery woman. The faery woman won't leave her favorite cow in the Otherworlds, so he basically asks the Morrigan to open the doorways between worlds so that the cow can graze on the pasture he owns in the mortal worlds and his love can be with him. Basically, he is asking her to steal the cow from the Otherworlds, but it wouldn't be the first time the Morrigan had stolen someone's cow, so it all works out in the end.[18] The point is he isn't praying to her for war; to Tulchaine the Morrigan has many layers. No one sane prays for war.

---

18. Whitley Stokes, trans., "The Prose Tales in the Rennes Dindšenchas," *Revue Celtique* 15 (1894): 470–71.

War is utter destruction. It is seeing everyone you love harmed or dead. It is the destruction of the land and infrastructure around us. War is brutal and ugly. To glorify that is dangerous. It certainly doesn't make the Morrigan an evil figure. No, she is the force that helps us survive that kind of horror. She is alpha and omega, the one who goads us on to fight the battle and the one who says the time of fighting is at its end. She is not an angry goddess who only wants us to be tied up in an endless cycle of destruction, and I think that is a very important point to make. Because if we idealize the war and the gore, if we focus on making ourselves emulate that badass warrior image, then we will never want to leave the battlefield. The Morrigan embodies power, and I think in many ways it is easiest to see that power in her warrior side, but power can be found in all aspects of her nature, not just war. Power is something that she is—it is not lost when she is weaving spells, stealing cattle, or predicting the future, rather than fighting on the battlefield.

In the end I think we must separate our concept of power from war. Being strong and surviving struggles are what makes the Morrigan appealing to many people. The power she embodies is something woven throughout the thread of her being. It's time to stop looking at just the single thread and see the greater whole of what and who the Morrigan is. The Morrigan is simply what she is. No more, no less, not evil, not good, just herself.

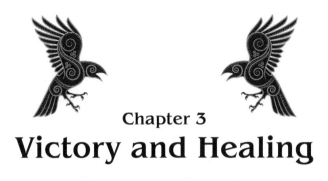

Chapter 3
Victory and Healing

*T*he guardian at the temple door leads someone through the temple entrance and ushers them to come toward me. Me, but not me. I don't quite feel like I'm floating. It's more like I'm dreaming. I'm dreaming and I'm trying to hold a vast, almost uncontainable force within me. The Morrigan is that vast sea of energy. It is not uncomfortable being filled—possessed, in all honesty—with that divine presence. The priests have been training this whole past year for just this purpose: some will become vessels for the Morrigan in her temple, some will guard her vessels, and others hold space at the entrances to her temple where petitioners gather to speak with and be within the presence of the Great Queen.

I am dimly aware of holding people's hands, of speaking. I think I touch someone's cheek. I put my hands on someone's chest and speak words filled with purpose. But the part of me that is me doesn't pay much attention to that. My mouth moves but I don't know what is being said. The part that is me is consumed with a feeling. I want to weep, I want to weep, I want to weep. There is so much pain, so much sorrow. I feel it all. Because she feels it.

Afterward, my friends and some strangers whom I am not even aware of meeting or seeing in the temple will come up to me and tell me some of what I have said. What the Morrigan has said. It's odd to have a conversation about something you have said to someone else yet have no memory of. Because in the end it isn't me. It's the Morrigan, and her conversations with her children are not my business. I'm the vessel. Something else is speaking through me. I don't know what my body is saying or doing because in the process of holding the presence of the Morrigan, I am feeling all that she is feeling, and that is all consuming. I see the thoughts that are behind whatever words she is *speaking through me. It is not unlike how an empath experiences the feelings of others, only this is the vast energy and feelings of a goddess.*

What strikes me the most is how much her children think they are unworthy of her. That if they trudge onward, without rest, without sleep, without care for themselves, that will somehow prove they are good soldiers. Prove they are worthy. They think she wants them to destroy themselves on the battlefield. "Do they not see I am trying to save them from that fate?" she says to me. "I will see them off the battlefield. I will see them to victory. I would have my ravens thrive. What good are they to me broken and dead upon the battlefield?" And I want to weep for the sorrow of it, for the sorrow I feel in the Morrigan. There is strength there too, but still there is that overwhelming feeling that what her followers think she wants the most isn't what she wants at all. There will be battles, there will be blood, and she will be harsh at times, but she will also offer them victory. Will they take it? Will they know when she wants them to sit and be still, to heal their wounds, just as much as she may want them to stand tall and enter the fray of battle? Battles end: the goddess of war knows this. But do her followers understand it? Would they guess their goddess weeps for them?

———

War isn't just the battle itself. There is the part that comes after, when the warriors have to heal and put themselves back together. There is the part when we come home, changed, and have to deal with the aftermath. We *visit* the battlefield; we can't *live* on it, not unless we want our lives to be destructive messes. Part of what the Morrigan teaches us is understanding that action and force are necessary at times. They are potent and destructive catalysts, and they are vital to change. But as in all things the dose makes the medicine or the poison. Digitalis can save you from heart failure, but too much will kill you. Forgetting how to leave the battlefield, how to accept the victory the Morrigan offers us, neglecting to heal ourselves—that's a poison too.

We can't define war solely by conflict. There are reasons we go to battle, and usually those reasons are to create a desired end result. We go to battle to seek victory, to gain something for the blood and tears we shed. If we went to war to stay in a state of constant struggle, what would be the point? But it is often very easy for followers of the Morrigan to get locked into a cycle of endless struggle. Many of her followers are survivors of abuse and trauma. Being in survival mode sometimes becomes our default state of mind. We understand it. We are used to being constantly in a stressful environment. We are used to always being on guard. Even when we move past trauma, it is very easy to stay in that mindset. Peace, being at rest, being happy? That's scary. We might lose those things. It's just easier to remain in fight-or-flight mode instead. It also stops us from looking at our wounds or looking within and healing our scars. Because the next battle takes priority, we don't have time to sit still and fix ourselves. Instead we take the noble path of bleeding out while battling onward.

The Morrigan isn't the goddess of constant conflict. She is a goddess of war, yes, and most importantly victory. Victory means the battle has to stop at some point. At some juncture we have to put our swords down. For that to happen we have to acknowledge that any conflict has a beginning, middle, and end. As children of a goddess of war that means we have to understand the whole process, not just pick the parts of the cycle we like the best.

Putting Down the Sword, or Why Soldiers Crave Battle

There is an odd phenomenon among soldiers. After coming home from war, many soldiers miss war, often even those who suffer from PTSD. Sebastian Junger speaks to this in his book *Tribe: On Homecoming and Belonging*. War is horrific. It can scar a soldier for life, physically and mentally, but still many veterans miss it and find it difficult to reintegrate. How is it that someone can experience something so horrible and miss it? When you are in a highly stressful situation such as war, everything matters. If you forgot to put something in your bag or pocket this morning before you head out to work, it is not the end of the world. If you are in war and forget to pack the right equipment, it could kill you or the person next to you. There is also a deep sense of comradery. Junger describes this as a "brotherhood" in which you are willing to put the good of the group before your own safety. He defines it as something different from friendship.[19] A friend is someone you choose to like. The bonds formed between soldiers don't necessarily have anything to do with liking the other person, but instead knowing they have your back and you have theirs. When soldiers return from war, they lose that sense of purpose that all their actions

---

19. Sebastian Junger, *Tribe: On Homecoming and Belonging* (New York: Twelve, 2016), ix–x.

are meaningful and that sense of comradery and knowing someone has your back. They are just everyday people again. They don't know who they can trust, and their actions can feel meaningless. They crave the experience again—not the killing or the fear or the bloodshed, but the other components of war.

If you are a member of the military, you may be familiar with these feelings. If you are not, as I'm sure most reading this will not be, I find there is value in understanding these sentiments. I have never served in the military, but I can tell you that happiness for a long time was a difficult thing for me to endure. The trauma of my past made me feel more at home in stressful situations. It made me take on more than I probably should have in many cases. I felt as if I shouldn't get used to being happy, because one day I'd probably lose it. I felt the need to prepare and tensely await the next battle that surely was just over the horizon. That was something I understood how to deal with. Happiness wasn't. There was a kind of guilt attached to it as well. I was a priestess of the Morrigan; I needed to be able to take on things. What battle was I facing if I were happy? If I rested, if I were content, would the Morrigan turn her back on me? I think that is the real fear. When I have no more battles left, why would the Morrigan want to talk to me anymore? Again, this fear is born out of her not being viewed as anything but a goddess of battle. If we have a healthy understanding of the Morrigan and that she has many faces, I think perhaps we will be less afraid to put down our swords and explore those other sides of her. We would not be so hesitant to accept victory.

Not surprisingly, this tends to be a common sentiment among devotees of the Morrigan. We feel guilty if we aren't being a badass and taking on some kind of struggle. We see the need for others to take the time to heal themselves, but we often neglect that same need in ourselves. We crave the metaphoric battlefield, in part because we are more comfortable there. Learning to accept victory and healing can be a difficult thing.

The Hag and the Cow

After the Morrigan and the hero Cuchulain battle in *The Cattle Raid of Cooley*, both hero and goddess are wounded. She keeps her word, attacking the hero in the form of an eel, a wolf, and a hornless heifer. Cuchulain, being a demigod, has certain powers, one being that a wound dealt by him would not heal unless he gave his blessing. In their angry exchange before the battle he tells her he will never give her that blessing. Of course, the Morrigan being the Morrigan tricks him into doing so:

> *When Cuchulainn was in this great weariness, the Morrigan met him*
> *in the form of an old hag, and she blind and lame, milking a cow with*
> *three teats, and he asked her for a drink. She gave him milk from a teat.*
>
> *"He will be whole who has brought it," said Cuchulainn; "the bless-*
> *ings of gods and non-gods on you," said he ...*
>
> *Then her head was healed so that it was whole. She gave the milk of*
> *the second teat, and her eye was whole; and gave the milk of the third*
> *teat, and her leg was whole. So that this was what he said about each*
> *thing of them, "A doom of blessing on you," said he.*
>
> *"You told me," said the Morrigan, "I should not have healing from*
> *you for ever."*
>
> *"If I had known it was you," said Cuchulainn, "I would not have*
> *healed you ever."* [20]

For many, this story is an example of the Morrigan's use of shape-shifting and trickery. But I see another layer to it, especially since the Morrigan has often had to trick me into seeking healing. The Morrigan and the hero have a strained relationship. At times they are at odds with each other and other times the goddess aids him. Cuchulain is kind of thick headed. He chooses to take up arms on a day it was foretold that anyone who took up arms would die young but would have his name remembered forever. This seems inauspicious to us, but it is exactly what he wants. As long as his name is remembered and he has glory in the end, he brushes off the price of an early death. He takes on an army single-handedly. Even when the odds are against him, he marches onward stubbornly. Sometimes that stubbornness helps him achieve his tasks and sometimes not. Usually he just makes things more difficult for himself. I have been guilty of the same, and just as the Morrigan has to trick Cuchulain into healing, so too has she had to "trick" me into seeing the value in my own healing. We tend to focus on the idea that the Morrigan is seeking to heal her own wounds dealt by the hero. No doubt she is, but the hero is also healed by her in turn. They bless each other, with her offering the milk from her cow

---

20.   L. Winifred Faraday, *The Cattle-Raid of Cualnge* (London: David Nutt, 1904), 81–82.

and him offering the words that will heal her. It is not one sided. They heal each other. Afterward, the goddess aids him in battle. Things are, for a time, set right and put into balance. To me, this story will always be about stubbornness and a reminder to seek healing. When I seek a gentler side of the Great Queen, my offerings are usually milk in remembrance of this story.

Ironically, when the Morrigan made me sit down and heal, it was perhaps the most difficult battle I faced from her. She put roadblocks in my way when I tried to take on too much. The more I received the message to heal and rest, the more I fought against it. I felt like I was failing her until I realized the whole point was she wanted me to make healing a priority. What use was I going to be to her if I was running myself ragged? That perhaps was her hardest lesson. To heal, to accept happiness. To recognize I didn't have to constantly be doing and struggling to be her priestess. I was allowed to have good things, to be rewarded for my service.

During that time I went to a friend who has oracular training for some answers, mostly because I was being too thickheaded to understand what she was telling me. I felt like the Queen was going to tell me I wasn't trying hard enough and that was why I was meeting with such resistance. But when the Morrigan spoke through my friend's voice, she called me a "stubborn mare" and told me that things would go easier for me if I did not fight her, if I went where she led me, and that I was making assumptions about what she must want of me, instead of listening to what she *actually* had been telling me she wanted all along.

The answer took me aback. When I stopped fighting against her, things did get better. The roadblocks went away, and I learned to trust the Morrigan in a way I hadn't before. I recognized that I had been telling myself she must want XYZ from me because she is a goddess of war. I had made assumptions.

American culture in general puts a high value on productivity. Productivity is good and means you have value. The more productive you are, the more valuable you are. Resting and not being productive with your time is considered lazy and lessens your value as a person. It's a hard idea to escape. Try doing nothing for a minute and see how it makes you feel. Put down this book for a full sixty seconds and do nothing. If you are like me, you might start a mental list of all the things you absolutely have to get done today. Don't. Just sit, relax, and exist. No mental lists, no productive use of time in any way other than relaxing. How did that feel? Did you feel guilty for not being productive with your time?

Ultimately, I had put no value in my own healing. In fact, I viewed it as a waste of time, a burden even. The things I had been struggling to achieve, the things I had asked the Morrigan for victory in—once I accomplished them, I didn't cherish them. I didn't pause to enjoy what I had fought for before moving on to the next struggle. Why would she keep giving me victory if I didn't value it? Well, the answer, I thought, was that she probably wouldn't. So, I sat still. I took time to tend to my own wounds and heal as best I could.

Washing the Blood Away and the Price of Victory

We imagine victory as the hero with their sword raised high. All the enemies are beaten, and the day is clearly won. Victory isn't so simple. For me, victory has never been accomplished in such a cheerful or simple way. Victory has always come first with a visit from the Washer at the Ford. Perhaps because victory and death go hand in hand. To overcome an obstacle or an enemy, usually something must die, whether that be your foe or a part of yourself or your perspectives. Something needs to crumble and give way for forward motion to be accomplished. Even if in your battles you start out on the side of the angels, the fight itself will change you no matter what. No one comes back from war the same. Not the winner or the loser or anyone in-between. That sort of change is something the Washer at the Ford rules over.

None of the imagery of the Washer at the Ford is given to us by accident. The Washer Woman purifies the treasures she's gained. She washes armor, chariots, and spoils of war in her stories. When it is not gore, the items, though bloody, are valuables and treasures in many cases. The blood is the cost of the purification. She washes away the pain and sorrow so we can enjoy these things without the stain of how it was gained. When she washes us, we gain possession of ourselves. When she washes us clean, we can look back at what we have endured and be grateful for what we went through, all our trials, to become what we are now. The blood that she washes, which stains her river red, is the sadness and regret, the pain that covers the treasures she washes.

It is a kind of baptism, a recognition of the cost of transformation. You didn't have to die in those battles, but you bled for the knowledge gained. If you didn't release that sorrow attached to that transformation, and the hard lessons that came out of it, you wouldn't be able to enjoy the treasure you gained from it. I use the word *baptism*, but this is not a cleansing of sin. Instead, it is a restoration, the restoration of peace and balance. After all, what is the end of war but a restoration of things? We trick ourselves into thinking that war is the hard part. It isn't. War is easy; it is not complicated. It is hardship and full of discomfort, certainly. And sometimes at the end of it all you don't even feel like you have won since you are still covered in blood, covered in the sorrow and pain of it all. Restoring right relations, healing, is harder. The Washer at the Ford's role stands here, at the end of war and on the precipice of victory. Because one day you too will be there down at the river washing your armor because you don't need it anymore. One day you will find you are going to put your sword down and stop being at war. You'll never stop being a warrior, but your war will end, and it will be time to go back to your real life. Because you can't live on the battlefield. If you don't wash away the gore, all you will know is the smell and feel of blood. You will just seek to pour more of it upon yourself because you have become so accustomed to it. And nothing grows on a bloody field.

This, I think, is the price of the victory the Morrigan offers. You'll gain her blessings on the edge of a blade. You'll bleed for it, but when the blood has stopped running, when you have cleansed yourself in the waters of the Washer Woman, the victory will be all the more precious. It is hard won. Part of the cost of that victory is putting your sword down for a time. Really claim victory and enjoy it, and know when it is time to rest and enjoy her blessings. Perhaps the hag will have to trick you, as she did Cuchulain, or perhaps you will be brave enough to accept it willingly.

A Prayer for Blessings and Healing

To be said over milk or cream that is either poured as a libation or drunk to receive a blessing.

I seek the healing of An Morrigan
I seek the blessing of the milk given to Cuchulain
The blessing of peace after conflict
The blessing of balance being restored

I seek the blessings of the daughters of Ernmas
Fierce in battle, mighty in victory
May you heal that which is broken
Bring your strength to what is weak
Bring your blessings to (me/the one who received this milk)

A Prayer for Victory

Victory as high as the sky
Sky to earth
Earth to sky
Morrigan, you who proclaim high deeds
And grant victory
Look favorably upon us
May there be victory
May there be the restorations of wrong doings
May there be joy where there was sorrow
May our hearts be open
Strong rulers, and wise counsel
Victory as high as the skies
May it be so!

Chapter 4
Not for a Woman's Backside: Sex and the Morrigan

*T*he room is dark. Outside the wind blows cold and bitter. We begin the Yule ritual by calling upon the Morrigan, Cerridwen, and the Cailleach. A large cauldron sits on the central altar, and we each say blessings and pour libations and herbs into the cauldron, asking for blessings. We ask that new growth and light come from this time of darkness. The ritual goes well. We share food that everyone has brought to the feast. We exchange gifts and enjoy the company of good friends.

I go home expecting the ritual to be a happy memory with friends. Several months later I am surprised to find myself the topic of debate on the internet. It is not about what happened during the ritual. It is about what I was wearing. It is also about whether or not I was too sexy and revealing and whether or not my wardrobe sexualized the Morrigan. Because, you see, there is another internet debate broiling about whether or not the Morrigan is a goddess of sex. On one side of the argument is someone who attended my ritual and comments that I looked powerful and sexy embodying the Morrigan in the ritual wearing a black dress and a corset. And on the other side of the debate are people who did not attend the ritual who feel I have damaged the image of the Morrigan with my unabashed sexuality. I have a very well-endowed chest, and while I didn't feel the corset was distasteful in any way, apparently not hiding the fact that I have breasts or not choosing to wear a turtleneck to ritual has now made by boobs enemy number one in the fight to not portray the Morrigan as a sex goddess.

I really didn't know how to react. It is not every day one must defend their cleavage online, after all. I had always viewed my religion as one that included a body-positive mentality. My body was a sacred temple. I shouldn't feel ashamed of *it. But it did illustrate that something was wrong—wrong with our views about sex, sexuality, and the goddess of battle.*

———

One of the things I like about Irish mythology is that the gods, while immortal, are imperfectly human in so many ways. The gods make mistakes, occasionally die (only to reappear alive and well shortly after), fall in love, feel jealousy, and even fart. Yes, fart. One of the Dagda's epithets, *Broumide* ("Farter"), even references his abilities in this area.[21] And yes, they have sex. Just like everyone else.

The concept that the Morrigan is overtly sexual has snowballed recently to the point where I often see the Morrigan referred to as a goddess of sex. Not that she *is* sexual and *has* sex, but instead that sex is a part of her role and function as a deity. That's a very important distinction. In Irish mythology, there is a great deal of sex, people having sex with other people's spouses, and even time travel magic to cover up the fact that someone knocked up someone else's wife because "oops, we need to speed up time and hide the resulting baby." Sexuality is part of human nature, and the behavior of the Irish gods certainly reflects that. So why has the Morrigan been singled out among them as a sex goddess by modern Pagans? The answer is complicated and in many ways has to do with our own modern hang-ups about sex and power and some skewed modern iconography.

When it comes to the Morrigan, her modern worshipers have very strong opinions on what her sex life indicates in relation to her divine nature. It tends to swing to two extremes. The first camp, inspired by many modern artists who portray the Morrigan as a kind of sexy grim reaper, views her as a goddess of sex or sexuality. The embodiment of death being portrayed as a beautiful or sexy woman is not a new motif. What is interesting to note is that this sexy pinup death imagery has shifted how modern people view and worship the Morrigan. Then there is the opposite camp, which rejects this image and takes it to the other extreme, turning her into an asexual being. Neither view, in my opinion, describes the Morrigan.

---

21.   Isolde Carmody, "Names of the Dagda," *Story Archeology* (blog), December 23, 2012, https://storyarchaeology.com/names-of-the-dagda/.

To understand the nature of the Morrigan, it is imperative to get a little personal and really take a look at the Morrigan's sexual history.

The Morrigan's Sexual Encounters in Mythology

Is the Morrigan off having excessive trysts and encounters with gods and mortals? Well, there are only two references to the Morrigan's sex life in her mythology. The first we will look at is her interaction with Cuchulain. During *The Cattle Raid of Cooley*, Cuchulain faces Queen Maeve's army single-handedly. They agree that each day the hero will face her champions, whom the hero continually beats, creating a standoff for some time. During this time, a young woman appears to the hero:

> "Who are you?" he [Cuchulain] said.
>
> "I am King Buan's daughter," she said, "and I have brought you my treasure and cattle. I love you because of the great tales I have heard."
>
> "You come at a bad time."...
>
> "But I might be a help."
>
> "It wasn't for a woman's backside I took on this ordeal!"
>
> "Then I'll hinder." [22]

In this version of Cuchulain's encounter with the Morrigan, she appears disguised as a king's daughter and attempts to seduce the Irish hero while he is guarding a river ford against his enemy. He turns down her advances, telling her he has not come here for a "woman's backside" (sex). Not pleased by his rebuke, the Morrigan reveals her true identity and promises to attack the hero during his struggle with the enemy in various animal forms. An almost identical exchange between the two is made in another story, the *Táin Bó Regamna*, in which the hero encounters the Morrigan in her chariot and accuses her of stealing a cow. Their conversation similarly ends in insult being taken, the Morrigan again promising to come against the hero in animal form, and Cuchulain promising to cause harm to the goddess in turn.

It is generally believed that the version of this story found in the *Táin Bó Regamna* is closer to the original source material, while the encounter with the king's daughter more than likely is a later creation. After all, let's be realistic: in

---

22.   Kinsella, *The Táin*, 132–33.

the rest of the stories involving Cuchulain, it was pretty rare that he *didn't* fall for or impregnate someone other than his wife on his adventures. One could say the hero was a bit busy at the time he encountered the Morrigan incognito. Due to a curse that Cuchulain was immune to, he was the only able-bodied man available to defend Ulster against Queen Maeve's army. I don't think having an army at his heels is much of an excuse given his behavior in other stories. Regardless, the story of the Morrigan disguised as a king's daughter is often looked at by modern readers as evidence of her wanton and overtly sexual personality.

Oddly enough, the myth that most people point to when claiming the Morrigan is a sex fiend doesn't actually have her having any sex. Certainly, she wants to have a tryst with Cuchulain but nothing actually happens. We should take into account that the real purpose of this story is to explain a future plot point: the two promise to inflict harm on one another at a later date due to being insulted. The *Táin Bó Regamna* is almost exactly the same story. They insult each other, and then the Morrigan promises to come against him as a wolf, eel, and hornless heifer. The hero in turn promises to wound the goddess each time she attacks him in animal form. These threats are later carried out in *The Cattle Raid of Cooley*. The slights that anger the Morrigan are different in each story. In one the hero turns down her advances; in the other he verbally spars with her, accuses her of theft, and physically threatens her at spearpoint. The only part of these stories that is identical is the promise by each to wound the other in very specific ways. That would suggest that the two stories exist simply to explain why the Morrigan attacks the hero later on in the story.

The second sexual encounter can be found in the *Cath Maige Tuired*, or *Second Battle of Moytura*, where the Tuatha Dé Danann (the Irish gods) fight with other mythical races for control of Ireland. On the eve of the battle, the Dagda and the Morrigan encounter each other by a river ford:

> Now the Dagdae had to meet a woman in Glenn Etin on that day year
> about the Allhallowtide of the battle. The (river) Unius of Connaught
> roars to the south of it. He beheld the woman in Unius in Corann,
> washing (herself), with one of her two feet at Allod Echae (i. e.
> Echumech), to the south of the water, and the other at Loscuinn, to
> the north of the water. Nine loosened tresses were on her head. The

Dagdae conversed with her, and they make a union. "The Bed of the
Couple" is the name of the stead thenceforward. The woman that is
here mentioned is the Morrigan.[23]

This encounter with the Dagda is most likely a meeting between a husband and wife. After all, the Morrigan is named as the Dagda's wife in the story of Odras told in the *Dindshenchas*, a collection of lore concerning Irish place names.[24] The place where the two have their sexual encounter is named "The Bed of the Couple" in Gray's translation, but as Morgan Daimler points out in her modern translation of this material, it is more accurately translated as the bed of the "married couple."[25] I doubt either today or in the past it would be odd for a married couple to have sex.

So what do these two stories tell us? For one thing, like most of the Irish gods and people in general from the Iron Age through today, the Morrigan has sex. What do these encounters mean? Well, they can mean several things. As I've written, both stories involving Cuchulain may simply have been a way for the storytellers to explain why the Morrigan attacked Cuchulain in *The Cattle Raid of Cooley*. We can also look at both stories in relation to the ancient concept of sovereignty in which a goddess representing the sovereignty of the land sexually confers this power and her blessing to a king. In the Dagda's case, he benefits from this conferring of power and the Irish gods go on to win their battle with their enemies, while Cuchulain, who spurns such a union, meets an untimely end.

Like any myth, you can view the story on several different levels. I do think it is clear in both of these instances that the Morrigan isn't a goddess of sex. If anything, her husband the Dagda fits that role far better. His "club" is so large that he has to carry it around in a wheelbarrow, and he has far more trysts in

---

23.   Whitley Stokes, "The Second Battle of Moytura," *Revue Celtique* 12 (1891): 85. Parentheses are Stokes's.

24.   Edward Gwynn, trans., *The Metrical Dindshenchas*, vol. 4 (Dublin: Royal Irish Academy, 1924), 198–99.

25.   Morgan Daimler, "The Morrigan, The Dagda, and Unions," *Living Liminally* (blog), April 14, 2015, https://lairbhan.blogspot.com/2015/04/the-morrigan-dagda-and-unions.html.

his stories than the Morrigan.[26] Yet we label him and many of the other male gods that would fit better into the role of sex deity as "virile" or "manly" and nothing more. Why? Because we assume that having lots of sex is going to be a natural part of the male, godly or otherwise, personality. When it shows up as a quality in the female personality, even when it is not in excess, we make a bigger deal about it. This is where we move into the real crux of the problem: our own modern hang-ups about the Morrigan and sex.

From a modern perspective, sex equals power. Our culture uses it in advertising to sell things. It is used as a weapon against others and against each other. It's a primary feature in our own modern version of mythology. In film and TV the hallmark of a powerful woman, from a power-suit female CEO to Madam Satan in the *Chilling Adventures of Sabrina,* is that she is either dominantly sexual or promiscuous. Women are blasted with so many ideas from others about their bodies. We are taught that so much of our self-worth and value is tied to the way we look and how others perceive our bodies. Sex is intrinsically tied to these ideas, and reclaiming our bodies, setting our own ideals and expectations about sex, and controlling who we can have it with and how often is empowering. I know many people who have embarked on that journey of reclaiming their sexuality after trauma through their connection to the Morrigan. It is perhaps no wonder that we equate a goddess who is seen as powerful with a trait we give to almost all our modern mythological examples of powerful women.

Iconography and Modern Depictions

The next problem is iconography. Iconography is the use of religious symbols, characters, and imagery in art. We are perhaps the most familiar with this artistic expression from Christianity, in which there is a long tradition of icons and other religious art depicting Christ and the saints and other scenes from their mythology. Studying how this art has changed over the years reflects changes in religious doctrine and gives us an understanding of the religious views of a particular time. Pagans are no different: our changing views of the gods and religious and cultural norms of a given time have influenced how we portray our gods too.

26.   Morgan Daimler, *The Dagda: Meeting the Good God of Ireland*, Pagan Portals (Alresford, Hants, UK: Moon Books, 2018), 46.

Let's do a little field research! An easy way to see how iconography has changed is to do a quick Google search. Let's use Aphrodite as an example. If you Google Aphrodite and then click on "Images" you will find something very interesting. You will see examples of early art in which she is depicted in statues as a young woman considered beautiful for the time. Note that this depiction of beauty is not particularly thin or perfectly toned and in many cases includes generous hips and love handles. She also is not in a particularly alluring pose either. As you scroll down you'll find classical paintings of Aphrodite, again very similar: pretty, young, and love handles still seem to be okay for the goddess of love's look. We see a slightly demure Aphrodite, though, with artfully arranged flying silk cloths hiding certain parts. Keep scrolling and I'm sure you will find, as I did, several modern depictions. Aphrodite now has a teeny-tiny waist, is skinny with an enormous chest, and in one case was in an alluring playboy pose, pouting her lips in a pillow-filled clam shell. Was this just some kind of fan art? An artist who liked the genre of mythology? In this case I clicked on the site connected to that image and—you guessed it—it led to a page about modern Paganism. Not everyone who paints or creates art that depicts mythology is going to be a practicing Pagan. Mythology is a popular topic with modern fantasy artists. But what is disturbing is that modern Pagans are using questionable modern images of the gods that skew the way we relate to them. It is one thing to not particularly like a modern image of a god and another to have a print of that image as a focal point on your altar. That image reinforces how we perceive our gods. It becomes a focal point to how you perceive them.

When it comes to the Morrigan, the problem is that we have no ancient depictions of her. Not a single one. There is one brief description of her physical appearance in the *Táin Bó Regamna* where she is described as having red hair and red eyebrows. Not really much to go by, and as Cuchulain did not recognize her in this form, it is unclear whether or not this was her normal appearance. She is a shape-shifter, after all. We have historical examples of how ancient people portrayed gods from other pantheons, but not the Morrigan. Literally all we have to go by are modern depictions, full of modern cultural biases. So when you Google images of the Morrigan, you will find the vast majority of them depicting her as alluring or in some kind of sexually implied pose among heaps of corpses and severed heads. Because you know, ladies, we always feel sexiest when there are fresh entrails around! This isn't to say the Morrigan doesn't have bloody imagery around her in her stories. She is said to wash the bloody clothes and entrails of those doomed to die in battle, but she is also said to be keening and mourning as she washes them. She isn't pushing up her bosom and winking suggestively at passersby to deliver her death omen in a sexy purring croon.

Modern statues in many cases continue this trend of suggestive poses and scant or transparent clothes. In one particularly horrible rendition, she is holding a sword that looks larger than her body and is half lifting it up and half humping it. How the Morrigan is portrayed in modern art is troubling and certainly needs to change, although I doubt it will until our own attitudes around sex and power shift. Interestingly, some of her followers have reacted to this sexy pinup goddess of battlefield gore by doing a complete 180 and removing any hint of sexuality from the Morrigan at all. In some circles it created a bit of a backlash at any depictions that portrayed the Morrigan nude. In her stories the Morrigan does appear naked at least once, although not in a sexualized way: as a hag hopping from spearpoint to spearpoint. In my journey work and visionary experiences with the Morrigan, she almost always appeared nude to me. My favorite statue of the Morrigan, one created by Dryad Designs, also depicts her nude. But the key difference in this depiction is that she is not posed in a sexualized way. She is in a position of power, with a sword and shield, and she just happens to be nude. Similarly, in my own personal experiences, the fact that she doesn't always seem to be wearing clothing is more of a statement in my mind that she is not hiding anything and that she is in complete control of her power—she wears her skin without shame. That is completely different from the sexualization of an image, whether she is portrayed nude or scantily clad.

Modern iconography matters. Our modern depictions of the gods in many cases, not just the Morrigan's, may be the only images we have of that deity. We can't control what modern artists create, but clearly our attitudes about the Morrigan and how we view powerful women have colored these depictions. So much so that the idea that the Morrigan is overtly sexual on some level has become widespread.

Sex and the Morrigan tends to be a touchy subject. More than just the two extreme choices of sex goddess or asexual goddess are needed. Extremes are never good, so I suggest a middle ground, the ground I think the Morrigan has always resided on anyway. She asks us, what does it mean to be sovereign over oneself? Does it include one's sexuality? Does the Morrigan not reside in this reclaiming? I think she does. She is there to help us reclaim the parts of us that have been damaged, the parts of us that have been shamed. Ultimately, we have to remember that we are the ones with the hang-ups, not the gods. The Morrigan likes broken things. She likes to help us put the broken bits back together, to poke and prod at the things we would rather ignore. If our view on sex and reclaiming our own sexuality is one of those things, I have no doubt she will help us reclaim that power. It still doesn't make the Morrigan a sex kitten, nor does it make her a goddess whose primary function is sex. It makes her, as always, a goddess of sovereignty and a goddess who makes us face dark truths and move past them.

Chapter 5
The Price of a Crown: Goddess of Sovereignty

March several years ago ...

It is a few months before our group's yearly gathering in honor of the Morrigan. I have been having odd dreams, snippets of feelings and emotion, but nothing I can remember. Often shortly before we are about to gather, the Morrigan visits many of us in dreams. Sometimes there are messages, other times warnings. It is like she is pacing somewhere in the Otherworlds, impatient for us to begin the work. The magic we weave together in her name isn't just for the few days we gather. Many of us feel the effects of those days throughout the year, the lessons learned playing a role in the year between us gathering. Even the theme is one chosen through divination, reflecting the lessons we feel the Great Queen wishes us to understand that year. This time our gathering's theme will be sovereignty. I think I have underestimated how complex and difficult this concept can be.

On this day I wake up to find a message from a friend and fellow priestess. The echoes of my own mostly unremembered dreams still cling to me. She tells me about a dream she just woke from, one in which we were at the camp we use for our gatherings. "It was a musical," she sends. I quickly make some coffee and contact her.

"Morrigan the musical?" I ask, a little bemused.

"It was the oddest dream. I kid you not, it was a musical. People singing everywhere. Macha herself was wandering around, just in a bigger scale than everyone else. She was a giant, walking forcefully around, singing about knowing your worth. No idea what this is all about. You were singing too." I have a feeling I know. It has something to do with this feeling of foreboding that is settling in my gut.

"I was singing?" I sound like a dying toad when I attempt to sing. Singing is not what I do.

"Yes, you were singing. I told you, it's all sorts of strangeness. Macha was singing too. I wrote it down. You were singing about blackbirds—

> *They will help you if you let them*
> *A flock of blackbirds flying*
> *A cloak of feathers on you*
> *Bringing strength when times are trying*

"It was a pretty tune. Then there were drumbeats from her giant stomping steps, and this is what Macha was singing:

> *We all have value to the world*
> *And we all have value that is hidden*
> *Know the worth that others see*
> *And know the worth that rests within*
> *Because the world will never stop*
> *Judging you by their measure*
> *But you can't let yourself forget*
> *That your inner worth is a treasure"*

We both ponder over the meaning for a while. This is not the first time the Morrigan has sent me messages through the dreams of others. We joke that maybe it's because I don't always remember my dreams and she is getting a bad "connection." She can't log on to my dream wifi, so she has to route the messages through the dreams of others. Now, looking back, I think it is because at this point on my path I would have doubted the message if I had dreamt it. Coming from someone else, it is harder to ignore. It also helps to send your messages through someone with a photographic memory when sending song lyrics as your message. We ponder over that too. The singing and the poetry. It is very much in line with how the Morrigan works, and the poems that are left to us in her stories. Inspired poetry was both a type of prophetic practice and a kind of battle magic, reflected in her use of rosc poetry. What does it all mean? I don't know yet. But I will.

———

June several years ago …

I am about to be betrayed. By someone I trust, in a very public and intentionally hurtful way. I just don't know it yet. We don't see eye to eye on some topics. To me that doesn't matter so much. I'm not afraid to have conversations or friendships with people that have different opinions than my own. I just ask that my opinions be respected, as I respect theirs. But that isn't good enough for this person, even though they have been happy to make money and bolster their reputation through events I run. What they want is conformity; if I'm not exactly like them, then I'm an enemy.

It's the first night of our gathering and we are doing a small private ritual before the rest of the group arrives. Two priestesses have taken up the role of oracles. They hold space for the Morrigan and let her speak through them. We have burned offerings and asked for blessings and advice. It is my turn to approach next. One of the priestesses belongs to Badb, the other to Macha. Thinking of the strange dream my friend conveyed to me and feeling drawn to the energy of Macha I feel flowing through my friend, I make my choice. She takes my hands, then Macha speaks:

"There will be battles you win and battles you will lose. But know this. I watch over those who are mine. And you will win the war."

These words have more weight and meaning when events unfold the next day. This will be a painful lesson, but one that I need. My name means "crowned one." On one side of my family, my grandmother left Ireland and eventually married an American soldier, perhaps even more scandalously one with an English last name, and came to the States. On the other side, my great-grandmother emigrated from Greece. Stephanie comes from the Greek word for crown and is reflected in the word still used for marriage crowns, stefana, in Greek ceremonies. I have been thinking about the meaning of my name leading up to this gathering that will center around sovereignty. Because names have power. Because a crown—leadership—has a price. And this is my price.

When the betrayal comes, I don't even see it. It's other people who bring to my attention the hateful things being said about me. I have only ever wanted everyone to get along. I have always believed that that was possible. I have been too kind to people I should not have been kind to. I believed stupidly that because someone is popular in our community that they are a good person. I have tried to get people with different views to come to the table and find common ground in the deity they all worship. That should be how it works. But it isn't. Not always. Sometimes, people will take advantage of your willingness to see their points of view, even if you don't agree with them, and use it as a weapon against you. And that is what has happened.

This betrayal will change me. It will make me question my own worth. Suddenly, I understand Macha's song in my friend's dream. I will learn that not everyone can get along no matter how much I want them to. That others do not determine your value. Sometimes you have to cut cords and make strong boundaries. Sometimes you have to go to war when all you want is peace. But as I walk to the temple to speak with the oracle on the last night of our gathering, I feel none of those things. I am ready to throw in the towel. I'm ready to stop doing anything public and stop doing anything for anyone ever again. I do not even ask the oracle a question. Tears run down my face and she takes my hands and speaks. Her face is veiled, yet I feel the Morrigan's gaze upon me all the same.

"You will not avoid leadership." It comes out as a demand. A reflection of my inner thoughts that I have not voiced to anyone. There is no room for argument in those words. "Do not struggle against me, my stubborn mare. Go where I lead you, and it will be easier for you. You are my priestess. Go with my blessings, with the blessings of the Morrigan." There is a warmth flowing from her hands to mine. I feel lighter and warm within, a little less raw.

The price of my bloody crown, the price of sovereignty, will be won through heartbreak and tears. It will be not letting others control how I practice my faith or how I think. The price will be becoming harder and less kind, but a better leader. Being a leader, knowing your worth, wearing the crown of sovereignty isn't fun. It's bloody, heart-wrenching stuff. I choose not to avoid the task the Morrigan has given me.

———

Language is tricky. If you are bilingual, you probably already know that translations aren't always exact. Some languages have words that don't exist in other languages. I distinctly remember my maternal grandmother, who spoke fluent Greek, trying to explain to me how there was a word in Greek that there was no English equivalent for and being perplexed at the concept. There are also nuances and double meanings that can be lost in translation as well. When we are talking about older forms of a language, there are layers of meaning that can be lost when trying to reference an idea in a modern context. After all, words are just ideas and descriptions of the world around us, and our ideas on some things have changed since the Iron Age.

Sovereignty is a word we use today as a placeholder for an ancient one, one that had a different meaning to the ancient Irish than it does today in a world where sovereignty is less a function of nations and the land than it is about individual autonomy. In Western culture we put a lot of emphasis on personal freedom. The rights of the individual are paramount in a way they were not in the past. When we talk about sovereignty in the context of ancient people and goddesses who bestow sovereignty to kings, it is very alien from our modern understanding of the concept. What the Morrigan and other goddesses of sovereignty are bestowing on kings and leaders is *flaitheas*. In Old Irish *flaitheas* means "rulership" or "to rule." What is bestowed is the right of rulership over the land and people, with the understanding that they will rule well. This is very different from personal rulership and self-ownership.

So where does that leave us? If the Morrigan bestows *flaitheas,* what does that mean to us today? Is she the goddess of self-sovereignty, rulership, or something else? I believe the gods evolve along with us. If you think about it, that's a rather big statement—that the gods are beholden to time, that they change and evolve too, that they are subject to the consequences of time and are not encapsulated eternal and unchanging beings. I think on some level as our needs change, as our cultures evolve, some part of the gods shift as well. Not because we forced them to change or have some power over them, but rather to fit the shape of the world as it exists today, not unlike how your parenting skills might change to fit the needs of a three-year-old versus a teenager. While I believe that the Morrigan does incite us to claim self-sovereignty (or more correctly, autonomy), I feel there still remains the older roots of rulership and leadership in her sphere of influence as well.

Conveyor of Flaitheas

If the Morrigan bestows *flaitheas*, where is it in her stories? Well, it is more about reading between the lines. Goddesses in Irish mythology don't waltz up to a would-be king and just say, "You're a fine lad. Here, have some of my *flaitheas*," and *bam*, he's king. Goddesses connected to sovereignty are generally tutelary goddesses connected to the land. They are usually connected to certain animals, such as horses, which were connected to wealth and kingship. There is usually a sacred marriage or sexual union between the king and the goddess or a female representing the goddess. With the Morrigan we can see a strong connection to horses as a sacred animal in her guise as Macha. Additionally, we find the various names of the Morrigan reflected in a large number of the place names across Ireland, such as the Paps of Anu. As far as sexual unions go, she is the wife of the Dagda, who did rule as a king of the Irish gods at one point. If we believe that Macha of the Tuatha Dé Danann was wife of Nuada, as they fought and died side by side in *The Second Battle of Moytura*, then that links her to a second king. Again, as with many goddesses of sovereignty, her connection to the concept is all about looking at the symbols associated with her rather than them being named outright as a goddess of sovereignty.

Flaitheas as Rulership

For me, this idea of rulership brings to mind the story of the trials of Niall of the Nine Hostages found in *The Adventures of the Sons of Eochaid Muigmedóin*. There is some dispute over who will inherit the kingship from Niall's father. His stepmother goes about having her children and Niall tested to deem who will be worthy of leadership. She of course wants one of her sons to inherit the kingship. In one test the boys are told to save the most important thing from a burning hut. The other boys bring out a pail of beer, a chest of weapons, and other items easier to carry. Niall drags out an anvil. Just think about how heavy an anvil is. Also it's a metal object in a burning building. I picture him struggling with the weight of dragging it, the progress slow, and, as the fire burns down the hut, his hands blistering from the metal of the anvil becoming hot to the touch. But it pays off, and the anvil is deemed the greater prize.[27] It is not an easy task, and while the other items have value, the anvil was a tool for making things needed for agriculture and making weapons. It sustained the people and provided for them. Niall didn't take the easy way out when in the service of others. That is rulership—that is *flaitheas* in the old sense. Leadership is perhaps a better modern synonym. Leadership isn't about you. It's about everyone else you are responsible for. You are carrying the anvil out of the burning building, risking yourself for the benefit of others, sometimes others who aren't even grateful.

If we can equate *flaitheas* with leadership and rulership, then how can we strive to be good leaders? To be worthy of this gift the Morrigan bestows?

---

27.   Standish Hayes O'Grady, *Silva Gadelica (I–XXXI): A Collection of Tales in Irish*, vol. 2, translation and notes (London: Williams & Norgate, 1892), 369–70.

The Morrigan often instigates circumstances in which a poor ruler loses *flaitheas*. This is perhaps a reminder that even though one was worthy of being bestowed with rulership, it is something one constantly has to live up to.

Leadership isn't easy, but good leaders are something we desperately need. I think it is fair to say that some of the best leaders are the ones who didn't want the job in the first place. Usually the ones who crave the role are fueled by ego trips and the delusion that leadership is easy or that it will put them on a pedestal above others. Taking on the mantle of priesthood in many ways requires one to develop the skills of a good leader. One can be a priest and be solitary, but more than likely the gods will call you to serve others at some point.

When I think of leadership, I think of a night after a ritual when my partner and I were left to clean up and those participating had left. We were the first to get there early in the day and the last to leave. Sweeping the floor, tossing the trash, and, yes, even plunging the toilets were all the glamorous jobs left to us after the chanting was done and the magic cast. We tiredly joked that we were plunging toilets for the Morrigan, and that this was the hidden side of priesthood no one told you about when you started out. And it's true. Leaders take on a great deal. The preparations and aftercare for spiritual gatherings may not even be things others see. The time and money to run events and host rituals and the vacation time taken to serve the community rather than resting can take a toll. We don't have a community in which we fund and support our leaders in the same way mainstream religions do. We kind of just hope they figure it all out while holding down other jobs to support themselves. I think Paganism will always work a little differently from other religions in this regard. That is okay, but it does require us to support our leaders and also for our leaders to take the time to develop good leadership skills. The most successful Pagan leaders I have encountered all have used leadership training from their everyday jobs in their spiritual jobs. There are many non-Pagan resources out there at your disposal, and finding training that fits your needs is essential to becoming a better leader.

For a long time, I only understood sovereignty in the context of personal autonomy. We see sovereignty as ownership of self rather than in its most literal sense as a nation or people's right to self-rulership. The Morrigan exudes power, and she can help us transform from a state of feeling powerlessness to empowerment. She has certainly done this for me. The concept of *flaitheas* is nuanced and will mean something different to us now in modern times, as it will probably mean something different to people five hundred years from now. But I like the idea that the Morrigan is concerned with making good leaders, that she rules over the qualities that can help bring communities together and make them stronger. So often we are concerned with her tearing things down, but in *flaitheas* I see how she can teach us to build something meaningful. Eventually, I realized that whenever I focused my personal spiritual work on the concept of sovereignty, the challenges the Morrigan faced me with were less and less about personal sovereignty and all about leadership. I certainly made blunders along the way. All leaders do. But once I focused on the meaning of *flaitheas* as rulership rather than the modern word of *sovereignty*, with all its modern connotations, I understood what she was trying to show me.

In many ways I feel the Morrigan has made me face both sides of *flaitheas*. There are times she has made me take ownership of personal autonomy, and yet all too often when sovereignty is the theme of a ritual or gathering, the challenges and lessons I am faced with revolve around how well I can act as a leader. These are two very different things, yet I find she rules over both, and I see both reflected in the idea of *flaitheas*.

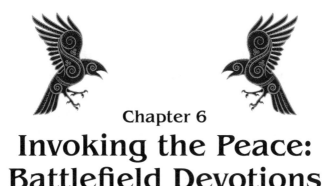

Chapter 6
Invoking the Peace: Battlefield Devotions

The Morrigan's Call Retreat, a ritual to Macha …
I stand in the center of the field we have prepared for ritual. It is dusk and every-thing is washed in the last bit of sunlight, giving it a dreamy kind of look. We have called to Macha for this ritual. My friend stands in the center of the circle, a bronze sword in hand, speaking with those who choose to come forward. Everyone else stands in a loose circle chanting softly, far enough away to give those who choose to speak with the priestess channeling Macha in the center of the circle privacy. When it is my turn to stand before the goddess, the rest of the field seems far more distant than it truly is. There is only myself and a goddess looking through my friend's eyes.

Channeling deity can be a strange experience, both for the questioners and the ves-sel. I feel Macha's presence, a steady thrum of energy through the ritual area. Every-thing seems to fade away compared to that brilliant presence. Macha has many sides to her, but I have no doubt that the part of her that is with us tonight is the warrior queen. I know it is Macha Mong Ruad I am about to stand before and face. The tip of the bronze sword is held up and my friend looks at me with eyes that are not her own.

There are things that have been weighing on me, battles I did not seek yet find myself facing anyway. I feel heavy and tired with the weight of them. I have been attacked unjustly, I have been betrayed more than once. I am always on edge now, always on the lookout for the next person to turn on me. Always trying to figure out if someone is trying to use me for their own goals.

Sometimes we have to cut away certain people, and I have. My general good-naturedness has been perceived as weakness, and weakness always welcomes attack. So, I have fought back. My heart and will have become harder, a fine-edged blade. I have learned much, but I am tired and I fear I will never be able to put down my own sword. When will the battles end? When can I just relax and not be afraid anymore?

As if reading my thoughts, Macha Mong Ruad speaks. "You are my priestess," she says, "but do you know when to raise your sword? And when to put it down?" The words are not what I expect. Is the goddess of war seriously telling me to put my sword down? How can I not be ever prepared for attack? Ever vigilant and waiting for the next betrayal to happen? I need to keep my sword ready and waiting, don't I? Macha looks at me, as if sensing my resistance. "Will you do this for me?" It is less of a question than a challenge. I will ponder her words for many years to come.

"I will," I say, meaning it. I may not yet understand what she wants from me at this moment, but I will do as she asks.

―――――

A few years later at Pulse Nightclub, Orlando, FL ...

It does not escape us that the unmarked car parked next to us is an undercover cop car. It idles in the Dunkin' Donuts parking lot next to Pulse and no one gets out. The windows are tinted and someone behind the window watches us for a moment as we get out of the car and walk across the street to the memorial. In a few days it will be the anniversary of the shooting that happened here. The energy still feels raw. Silently, I say a prayer to the dead who I still feel are present and haven't quite moved on yet.

The old nightclub is surrounded by a large barricade wall that people have hung posters on and have painted. There are all sorts of objects left in honor of and deference to the dead: flowers, painted stones and sculptures, stuffed animals. Everything is colorful. Messages of love and sorrow. There are others there with us. No one speaks. Some cry. The energy is thick in the air and the silence is that of a graveyard. Because this is a graveyard. It's a battlefield, and this is in part why we have come. Not only to honor the dead, to remember them, but to invoke the peace at this modern battlefield. My partner and I kneel down and place a crow feather in the middle of rainbow-painted stones someone has arranged in the shape of a heart. We softly speak the words of the Morrigan's peace prophecy, words we have spoken while making offerings to the dead at other, much older battlefields. The dead are more present here than on the battlefields of the Seminole wars or the Revolutionary and Civil War sites we have visited, in part because it is our town and it is our dead, not the dead of some time long ago. We finish the whispered prayer and spend a few minutes asking for the dead to find peace and for peace for those who visit this place.

I think about the words Macha spoke to me in ritual. Within the heavy feeling of grief that fills this place, I know with certainty why a goddess of battle is concerned with peace. The peace that she embodies is that after bloodshed. It is found in all the posters and pictures and love that have been poured out over this battlefield. All war has costs, and so many battlefields are the graveyards of people whose blood didn't need to be spilled nor who deserved their fates. I now see her less as the goddess who stirs up war frenzy, although I know she is that too, and more as the goddess who helps us survive the horrors of war. Who helps us survive the battlefield, so that we can build something better when the fighting ends. Who makes us look back at the bodies and spilled blood, at our own wounds, and demands: Was it worth it? Did you fight for something just? Or did you fight for your own ego? Will you choose the right battle next time? Or will you be the cause of more sorrow in the world?

———

Perhaps the most ignored aspect of the Morrigan is her role in invoking the peace after the battle. It is an aspect of her that is almost nonexistent in conversation about her in modern worship. As I've said before, we tend to concentrate on her as a war goddess and whatever war means to us in a personal context. But we never really consider what comes at the end of war, or that there even is an end. No general worth their salt will go into a war without a clear idea of what victory looks like to them. All wars have a clear end game, a clear goal. More often we approach our personal battles as endless struggles and make them so in self-fulfilling prophecies. We are so eager to call out to the Morrigan for war, for blood, or to smite those we view as having wronged us. If war is what we call to the Morrigan for, she will surely give it to us. She will keep giving us what we want until we destroy ourselves or until we spit out the poison within and call to her for peace instead.

In most cultures, gods associated with destructive forces were also seen as being able to cure, or hold back, these same forces. They held power over them, and the tide could turn in either direction as far as many of our ancestors were concerned. For example, the Egyptian goddess Sekhmet was attributed to be a bringer of plague, yet she was also the patroness of physicians. The idea was that she could be both the cause and the remedy for an affliction. Holding power over something didn't just mean she could banish it; she *was* that power, for good or ill, in excess and in its diminishment. That the Morrigan is both a force that encourages the battle and also the force that proclaims the peace when enough blood has been spilled should come as no surprise.

In *The Second Battle of Moytura* the Morrigan is a pivotal figure in instigating the war between the Irish gods and the Fomorians. She tells the god Lugh to "undertake a battle of overthrowing."[28] She encourages the gods to go to war, urges them onward during the battle itself, and takes on a portion of the host, and yet she is also the one who stands over the carnage and announces to the gods, and the land itself, that the battle is done, enough blood has been spilled. The prophecy she speaks after proclaiming that the battle is over is often the focal point for modern worshippers. But it's important not to take the prophecy out of context; as she speaks these words, she stands on the precipice of a new beginning. She stands amid the blood and death and reminds the gods that there is a future, there is something that comes after the carnage, something that hopefully makes all the losses and stacked-up bodies worth it in the end. Because there is nothing worse than shedding all that blood and realizing it was for nothing. Her prophecy, which predicts a good future followed by difficult times, emphasizes that now is a time for peace. It will be peace from the heavens down to the earth, perhaps not permanent, but a time for healing and cease to the slaughter. A time to rest and prosper before the next struggle.

You will find many slightly differing translations of this prophecy. Different translators favor different translations for certain words. The problem with many translations from the Victorian era is also that translators often will skip entire sections completely, choosing not to translate some of the more difficult-to-decipher verses. Personally, I tend to favor modern translations, which include the following by Morgan Daimler:

The Morrigan's Peace Prophecy

Sky to earth.
Earth below sky,
strength in each one,
a cup overfull,
filled with honey,

---

28. Gray, *Cath Maige Tuired*, section 83.

sufficiency of renown.
Summer in winter,
spears supported by warriors,
warriors supported by forts.
Forts fiercely strong;
banished are sad outcries
land of sheep
healthy under antler-points
destructive battle cries held back.
Crops [masts] on trees
a branch resting
resting with produce
sufficiency of sons
a son under patronage
on the neck of a bull
a bull of magical poetry
knots in trees
trees for fire.
Fire when wished for.
Wished for earth
getting a boast
proclaiming of borders
Borders declaring prosperity
green-growth after spring
autumn increase of horses
a troop for the land
land that goes in strength and abundance.
Be it a strong, beautiful wood, long-lasting a great boundary
"Have you a story?"
Peace to sky
be it so lasting to the ninth generation[29]

---

29. Morgan Daimler, "The Morrigan's Peace Prophecy," Irish-American Witchcraft, *Patheos Pagan* (blog), November 17, 2015, https://www.patheos.com/blogs/agora/2015/11/irish-american-witchcraft-the-morrigans-peace-prophecy/.

Peace is often a dirty word to many people. For some it implies giving up or bending to the will of others. We think of peace as something a pacifist who is not willing to fight might favor, instead of it being something every warrior who survives war will have to come to terms with. The peace the Morrigan offers us is not the peace of hippies in tinted glasses or a pacifist's peace akin to Gandhi. It is the peace that comes after hardship. It is the peace we must claim when we come back from our struggles with haunted eyes and shattered souls. Peace can be something that is even more hard won than the battle itself. Seeing ourselves through a battle, a struggle physical or otherwise, is about surviving the skirmish. Winning the peace is about thriving, and knowing the blood we spilt, the sacrifices we made, and the scars we bare were the price of better things to come. They are the coin we use to pay for our self-knowledge and freedom.

We are never the same after the battle. The trick is learning how to put the broken pieces back together again when we aren't faced with constant crisis. If you think the Morrigan is hard on you during times of struggle, just wait until you reach the edge of the battlefield. Will you turn around and go back the way you came? Returning to the battlefield, learning nothing? Or will you leave the struggle behind and face the more difficult task of what comes after battle? Tearing things apart is always easier than building new walls over the rubble. Yet this is the Morrigan's realm too. I have often said that I think the Morrigan is a collector of broken things. She would be that person who never throws away a chipped teacup but has a collection of ones glued back together. She breaks us more often than not, but always with the intention of putting the pieces back together to form something stronger and more beautiful. She makes us something better than we were, urging us not just to war, but to survive, to thrive when we have had our fill of sadness and destruction. When she asks us what is worth fighting for, it is not to urge us into endless battle, but to see us through to its end, till we are ready to count the bodies and our losses and decide it is time for peace. That it is time for growth and healing so we might be strong when the time comes to face new battles.

All too often modern worshipers assume the Morrigan will drive them toward struggles, and never consider why she does so. Several years ago, I had a very moving experience when facilitating a temple space for the Morrigan at an event. Each year we have priestesses trained in channeling act as oracles for those who wished to speak directly to the Great Queen. These encounters can be very emotional, and we had priestesses staffed outside the temple space to help people through those moments. After one person came out of the temple, I spent some time with them as they wept. Later the next day the person sought me out and we spoke for a while about what they had experienced with the oracle. What had profoundly moved this person was that the Great Queen through the oracle had told them she wanted them to be happy. There were things that needed to be fixed in their life, struggles to overcome. But that the goal was the goddess wanted them to be *happy* was a revelation. They assumed that all they would ever hear from a goddess of war was that there were more battles to fight or that they weren't fighting hard enough. That their goddess just wanted their happiness, that there could be a time to build and grow and have happiness, that battle wasn't eternal, gave them a completely different perspective on their goddess. They realized that the challenges they felt the Morrigan had made them face were intended to get them to a place of strength and peace. The battle had an ending point.

Weaving the Magic of Peace

The Morrigan's prophecy has always held a special fascination for me. On our first pilgrimage to Ireland, my cofacilitator read the prophecy while we stood on the Hill of Tara, the mystical seat of power for the Irish gods and kings. There is a small church at the entrance to the grounds, and we had all spent some time feeding the crows that lived there peanuts. Many of us had been gifted feathers, and I held a black and gray feather from a scald crow as I listened to the words of the Great Queen's prophecy. It sent shivers down my spine to hear the Morrigan's words spoken in such a sacred place. Her words are a prophecy, but I have often looked at them as a spell. After all, *dichetal do chennaib,* or spontaneous use of spoken poetry, was a type of prophetic magical practice that historically existed. The words of a god have power, and I have often wondered if it was not so much a vision of the future but a weaving of power to make the future she wished come to pass. *Rosc catha* poetry, a type of battle magic, uses a similar technique. For example, in *The Second Battle of Moytura* the god Lugh takes on a magical body posture and proceeds to describe what he wished to come to pass in poetic meter, saying it as if it had already happened as a way to will it into being: "Bursting forth, overthrowing, dividing. ... I am not reduced by battles at borders ... deadly brilliance, burning, greatly subduing them."[30] Eventually, this idea that speaking the words of the Morrigan as a spell, as a thing that held inherent power because it came from her, inspired a new kind of devotional work.

I have never lived far from historic battlefields. It is hard to find a New England town that hasn't had some Revolutionary War skirmish pass through it or doesn't have a public park that is said to be the site of one battle or another. I grew up down the road from a massive oak tree that had a small plaque on it naming it as the place George Washington planned a local battle underneath. When I moved to the South, it was very much the same. Florida may not have been very involved in the Civil War, but it has its own conflict-filled past. There were three Seminole Indian wars and forts built by the Spanish that endured numerous battles. Then there are the modern battlefields. Not that long ago I lived ten minutes away from Pulse, a nightclub where a man struggling with his sexual identity killed over forty people. Even now, while the club is closed, people have created a shrine to those lost lives. It remains covered in prayers and messages to the dead, in art, and colorful rainbows. All these places I have visited with the intention of calling on the Morrigan's peace, honoring the blood that has been spilt on both sides, without judgment, and the lives lost senselessly. The results have been quite astonishing in some cases.

When I first moved to Florida, I was a bit surprised there weren't many local Pagan events, since there was quite a large number of Pagans in the area I lived in. Eventually, I learned that the community had been fractured over the bad leadership of a few individuals, and the ensuing drama had caused a lot of hurt feelings on both sides. It had been several years since the incident, but many people still did not speak to one another. So I started organizing local events. While we set up for one such event, I made offerings to the Queen. I invoked peace, speaking her words. I went off into the shade of a tree and made offerings, invoking the Morrigan's peace and pouring libations. It wasn't the peace of someone sitting in lotus position trying to find nirvana. The overwhelming feeling of peace I felt from the Morrigan was different. It was the peace of dried blood or tired and weary warriors. It was the kind of peace you feel after you fought hard and recognize it is now time to rest and rebuild. It was an overwhelming sense of calm.

---

30. Morgan Daimler, *Irish Paganism: Reconstructing Irish Polytheism,* Pagan Portals (Alresford, Hants, UK: Moon Books, 2015), 60.

I didn't really expect much to happen, I just wanted everyone to be able to come together without splitting up into warring factions. I took the energy I had felt when I made my offerings in the morning as a good sign. The event did go well, and everyone had a good time. Sometime around the middle of the afternoon someone showed up who didn't realize me and my partner would be there. My partner and this person had been on opposite sides of the drama from the past, and after greeting each other, they went off and talked for a while. The end result was they buried the animosities of the past, there were realizations that others had fed them lies, and in the end a peace was formed. It was a resolution that both were happy about and left my partner feeling hopeful for the future. It wasn't quite the peace I thought I was invoking, but it came all the same. It may seem like a small thing, but these two parties resolving their differences was a huge deal for them. As I watched them embrace and smile together as friends once more, I could hear the Morrigan in my mind, saying, "The true price of invoking peace is that you bless even your enemies, that all might be whole again." Because how you end the battle is sometimes far more important than how you began it in the first place. Or how you fought it. People become emotionally invested in the prosecution of war, but not in the ending of it. The irony is that after the battle is over, all people will remember is how it ended. How you ended it, and how you invoked the peace, like the Morrigan standing on the heights after the battle of Moytura, counting the bodies, counting the sacrifices we've had to make for our victories. We have to decide if the price we paid was worth it. Peace really isn't peaceful. It's earned only when you are willing to fight for it.

Invoking the Peace

Visiting historic battlefields, and some modern ones, continues to be a meaningful devotional practice in my work with the Morrigan. In part they are also a reminder that not all wars are symbolic ones. Those dedicated to the Morrigan talk about battles a great deal. We talk about them in rituals, perhaps reenact our imaginings of the battles of myths in ritual drama, and spend time conceptualizing what warriorship means in a modern context. But 99 percent of the time it is not literal warfare. Many times we fall victim to idealizing the harsh realities of war. It is important to see the ugly side of war too. To see the ramifications the battles of the past have had on us today. To stand on the ground where battles were fought; to honor the dead, to honor their sacrifice, and at times to recognize the destruction that hate can cause, and then ask the Morrigan to bring peace to the echoes that remain there. This work has become a kind of sacred duty. It grounds me in the idea that she encompasses all kinds of battle and that I can't forget that war is a real thing, not just a metaphor for my own personal struggles. It is brutal and not something to idealize or glorify.

If you feel called to do such work, I invite you to use these or words of your own making. I promise it's worthwhile. Maybe it's a historic battlefield you visit, a place that has known violence, a war memorial, or at an event where you want to heal fractures in the community, or maybe you speak it with a hand over your own heart, calming the battlefield within. There are lots of battlefields to invoke peace upon.

There is no ritual that needs to accompany this. Offerings of some kind, libations or otherwise, should be left afterward. They can be something simple and should be appropriate to the place and battle. At sites connected to the Seminole Wars I've left tobacco, while at other sites whiskey or clean, fresh water felt most appropriate.

The following uses lines in part from the Morrigan's peace prophecy, as translated by Morgan Daimler, with a reworking of a line from Isolde Carmody's modern translations of the Morrigan's more difficult-to-decipher poetry, as well as my own wording. If you are uncomfortable with using the Irish at the beginning, you can omit it. Phonetically, these lines are pronounced *SHEE-eth co nev, nev co DO-van,* and *DO-van fo nim.*

Sith co nem
Nem co doman
Doman fo nim
Sky to earth
Earth below sky
Strength in each one
A cup overfull, filled with honey
Sufficiency of renown
Morrigan, you who see all

Who are born in the blood-zealous vigorous battle[31]
Hear us: we speak to the blood-soaked earth
We speak to the battlefield
We speak to the fallen friend and foe alike
The land remembers and we remember
The clashing of wills
The hosts giving battle
The strife of men
May the dead be honored
May there be peace
Peace as high as the skies
Summer in winter
Spears supported by warriors
Warriors supported by forts
Strong leaders
Justice when asked for
Banished are sad outcries
Peace as high as the skies
Sky to earth, strength in everyone
Both the living and the honored dead
Macha, whose harvest is upon the battlefield, may there be peace
Badb, who washes the sorrows of the dead and spurs on the battle, may there be peace
Anu, whose sacred land receives the bodies of the dead, may there be peace
Great Queen, may we remember why we sharpen our swords
That we fight for the peace that comes after strife
And may we remember that peace has a price
And may we honor that price now in this place
Great Queen, honored dead
Accept our offerings[32]

---

31. You can find the Morrigan speaking about a "blood-zealous vigorous battle" in Isolde Car-mody, "The Mórrígan Speaks—Her Three Poems," *Story Archeology* (blog), June 23, 2016, https://storyarchaeology.com/the-morrigan-speaks-her-three-poems-2.

32. Morgan Daimler, "The Morrigan's Peace Prophecy," Irish-American Witchcraft, *Patheos Pagan* (blog), November 17, 2015, https://www.patheos.com/blogs/agora/2015/11/irish-american-witchcraft-the-morrigans-peace-prophecy/.

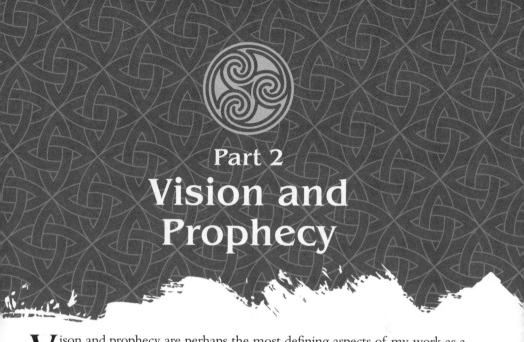

Part 2
Vision and Prophecy

Vision and prophecy are perhaps the most defining aspects of my work as a priestess of the Morrigan. Wherever the Morrigan goes there are prophecies spoken over bloody battlefields, there are visions of the future, and there are omens and warnings given in prophetic dreams. Prophecy is perhaps the most overlooked aspect of the Morrigan's nature, yet it is in almost all her stories.

When I look back at the most profound moments I have had with the Morrigan and the encounters that have changed the course of my path, prophecy has played a role in all of them. I have had visionary experiences that have changed my understanding of the Morrigan's nature, humbled me, and made me a better priestess. I have had prophetic experiences that have deepened my personal connection with her and guided me on my path. At pivotal moments I have had the Morrigan show up in the dreams of close friends who have relayed information to me when needed. Currently, as part of my work as a priestess, I practice oracular work, letting her speak through me. Thinking back to the very beginning, my very first encounter with the Morrigan was in a dream, which is a sort of vision.

We have stories of ancient sibyls, of temples ancient people traveled to on pilgrimages just to hear the words of a prophetess. Even in Irish lore we see kings and queens consult the wisdom of druids to see into the future. Queen Maeve even consults a faery prophetess before making war on Ulster. She of course refused to believe the vision of the faery woman, even though it turned out to be quite accurate.

Prophecy and the work of oracles is more than just predicting the future. It is holding the presence of the gods within ourselves. It is offering to let the gods speak through us for a time. Feeling the presence of the Morrigan is quite different from literally hearing her speak. It is perhaps the most difficult and sacred act of priesthood. Giving others the chance to speak directly to their gods is a deeply moving and profound experience. Learning to be a vessel is something that isn't really taught in many Pagan circles. Possession and channeling aren't the same as holding space for a god or simply invoking their presence into a sacred space. It is deeply personal work, work that requires absolute trust between yourself and the deity that will speak and act using your body. It is not something that every priest will be comfortable with or capable of doing and can take years of practice before one can safely take on such a role.

In this section you will find information on the practice of oracular work as it pertains to the Morrigan's modern worship. You will also find accounts of how prophecies delivered through the Morrigan, in dreams or trance, have shaped the course of my own work. In addition, we will look at personal gnosis and how it fits in with understanding the images and words we receive from visionary experiences.

No matter how long we have been priests, we stand on both sides of this exchange. Sometimes we are the prophet or the sibyl, the gods speaking through us in trance. Other times we are the petitioner coming to seek guidance. In each case, the words of the Morrigan, whether delivered through a dream or through one standing as her oracle, have made me reconsider aspects of her or how I chose to worship her. At times, they were words desperately needed during difficult times on my path. I think it is important to consider not just how we can serve as vehicles for prophecy through trance, but also what we do with the information we receive after we have left the oracle and the words are spoken. Knowing how to be a channel for the gods doesn't always mean you automatically understand how to decipher a message given in trance. So, in keeping with that idea, the chapters you will find here cover a variety of topics, all connected in some way to aspects of vision and prophecy. Some will be my own experiences when channeling, and some will be when I have had to puzzle out the messages the Morrigan has given me.

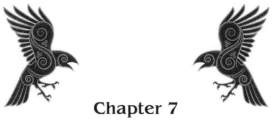

Chapter 7
Becoming the Vessel: Visionary Work and the Morrigan

A ritual in the woods ...
I kneel near the fire, pricking my finger and letting the drops of blood drip onto the soil. A routine offering, one I've made many times before. That's when I feel her, a presence standing across from me at the other end of the fire. We speak, and I am lost in that connection for several minutes. A new agreement is struck, a new deepening of the work I will do with and for her.

Then I feel Badb at my side, resting a hand on my shoulder somewhat possessively. Something in me relaxes and is no longer afraid. When we all created the ritual for this night, we left it open to each priestess whether or not they would go into trance at a certain part. If they are not comfortable going into trance or if the Morrigan doesn't want to speak, they will say a prewritten line as they give those who came to them an item that will serve as an omen. I don't expect to channel. I thought I would say the line and that would be it, but Badb has different plans. Tonight I will speak with Badb's voice. I will speak what she speaks. That is part of the bargain. When I pull the veil over my face, all I hear are the words I must say. I do not know the faces of the people who come to me. I do not know even what question I am answering or if they have even asked questions. The Badb speaks and I speak. I feel her standing beside me, that clawlike hand still on my shoulder. I have always feared doing such work. Letting go enough to give yourself over to something else, to let it speak through you and use your body, has always seemed like a difficult thing. Yet right now it is not. Even now I know it is just the beginning. Later it would be less of a comforting hand on my shoulder and instead full trance possession. But this is how it began. In the woods, in the dark, with Badb standing beside me, speaking through her priestess. It would not be the last time.

———

A year later …

The priests of the Morrigan's Call have been working the past year together to prepare for oracular work in the temple at our yearly gathering. Each night of the event we open the temple to those who wish to speak directly to the Morrigan. For a year the priests work together to refine their skills and deepen their connection and devotion to the Morrigan to be able to fulfill this service to others.

It's not the first time I have done this work. This past year, after my encounter with Badb, she has called me to make this work a more prominent aspect of my service to her. Yet some part of me hesitates. We are working on the schedule for who will stand as the oracle and who will be guardians. There is so much going on during this event, so much to organize, that I wonder if I will be able to let go. To not think about the list of a thousand things I must do to make this event happen long enough to be able to let the Morrigan in.

I think of all this early in the morning as I sit in the drive-through of a Starbucks. Do I stand as oracle or not? Will I be able to do the work when I have so much else on my shoulders? Am I being practical? Or am I making excuses to take the easy way out? I message my friend who is the temple mistress. I tell her that I'll just act as guardian this year. Too much to do. It makes sense not to take this on when I'm running the event, this year anyway. I feel like I have made a good, practical adult decision. I tell myself I know my limits; I'm not trying to take on too much. Yet I feel the Morrigan stirring somewhere at the edges of my consciousness. I tell myself and that presence that I am making a responsible choice. I am adulting. There is always next year.

I give the woman at the drive-through window my card, then she hands me my coffee. The message doesn't quite come in words. It is more feelings. "Do not avoid the work I have given you." And then the coffee explodes. I'm not squeezing the cup, nor is the woman handing it to me. There is a split second I am just grateful I ordered ice coffee and not hot coffee. It explodes in a giant wave of coffee going everywhere. For absolutely no reason. It's like a mini bomb has gone off. The woman is as confused as I am about what just happened. She apologizes and rushes to make a new coffee and hands me a giant handful of napkins. I scramble to sop up the coffee that covers myself and *most of the car with the napkins. All the while I'm having a mini spiritual meltdown inside my head.*

I text my friend that I have changed my mind ... and that I think the Morrigan just made my coffee explode.

———

Three months later ...

Before I leave my cabin for the temple, I prick my finger. A ruby red droplet is left in offering on the ground outside. The ritual has begun. It is not a ritual in the usual sense: this is the ritual and routine of trance. It is like walking down a long spiraling staircase, each step taking you down deeper and deeper. One cannot skip from the first step to the bottom landing.

The temple priests have spent much of yesterday warding the temple. When one enters the cabin, which we have filled with altars and shrines, it feels calm, safe, quiet. A little pocket of stillness. Some of the wards are etched in chalk on the walls by the doorways and others are less visible, but all are clearly felt. That is always the first step: the space for the oracle must be prepared. Our wards have made it safe and keep out the things we don't want around while someone is letting themselves be open to channeling.

It is dark except for the candlelight and electric twinkle lights. I run a finger across my palm in a spiral pattern and begin to meditate and still my mind as I walk to Badb's altar. I pour my offering of clear spring water, thinking of Badb standing by her river ford. I reach out to Badb and speak the words I use to bring on trance as I pull the shawl around my shoulders, then up to cover my head and face. "Badb's waters cleanse me." I dip a finger into the clear water and run it down my forehead, down the bridge of my nose, across my lips, to my chin. "Empty me and fill me." I am reaching those bottom steps in my spiral down into trance. With my head covered and the words spoken, I am almost gone. I feel Badb beside me and I welcome her, stepping back and out of myself and making room within myself at the same time. I feel like I am trying to hold the ocean within me. I feel Badb's readiness.

My friend who is acting as the guardian of the temple oracle has picked up that Badb is here now and she asks Badb if those waiting to speak to her may approach. She bows to me ... no, to Badb ... and then I am aware of little except what Badb is feeling and concentrate on trying to hold the force that is a goddess within myself. There is one moment where it is not just Badb anymore. Macha is there for a moment or a lifetime.

Then another time is it Nemain beside Badb. Her faces change depending on who comes before me, although Badb always remains present in some way, holding me steady. It is as if Badb stands beside her sisters as they come and go, but she is the constant.

Then I feel Badb begin to step back. What she needed to say has been said. I distantly become aware of my feet hurting a bit from standing for so long. Her presence beginning to leave me is my signal that it is time to end. I stop trying to hold her vast presence within myself, and slowly Badb is receding away from me. I say her names in my mind with gratitude: "Badb, Macha, Anu, Morrigan." She is what I was holding within, and she is what is receding. I acknowledge this. Now it is time to become myself again. I say a different set of names. My own. All of them. Some everyone knows, some only I know. When I say the last name, I am myself again. Slightly ungrounded but myself.

My guardian acknowledges this as well and hands me a bottle of water. I drink some, then go to Badb's altar and pour some more in offering, sending my thanks to Badb.

———

Prophecy is woven through the Morrigan's stories. At the end of *The Second Battle of Moytura* she speaks a prophecy predicting both good and ill times to come. She appears to Queen Maeve in a dream warning of her son's death. As the Washer at the Ford, she appears as an omen of coming death. As Macha, she sees a vision of the destruction *The Cattle Raid of Cooley* will cause years before the events occur. Wherever the Morrigan is, there is prophecy and vision.

At this point in my journey with the Morrigan, her connection to prophecy is the aspect of her that has taken the forefront. It has become an integral part of the work I do for her as a priestess and the practices of the group I work with. Yet, I can also say when I began my journey, and even when I first became acquainted with oracular work, I never thought I'd be the one acting as the vessel. But that all changed when Badb decided it was time to claim me as her priestess.

Trance possession, channeling, or oracular work is something that isn't often practiced or talked about in Irish spirituality or Neopaganism in general. Yet the lore indicates it existed. There are at least three historical types of this art that we know were practiced in Ireland because we have references to two of them being banned by St. Patrick because they invoked Pagan gods. These practices were important to Pagans of the past and have relevance to our work today. My own modern approach utilizes some of the elements found in these historic sources. Even looking to cultures beyond the Irish, we find rich traditions of going to oracles and prophets to seek advice and stand in the presence of the gods.

I have been lucky enough to work with people in my community who were adept at such work. Some found it through Heathenry and *seidhr* work, in which a person is veiled and goes into trance to answer questions. *Seidhr* in many ways bears a resemblance to some of the historical Irish practices that we know of. Others had a natural propensity to such work and stumbled their way through learning over time. I wasn't sure what I thought of oracular work until I experienced a friend channel the Morrigan in a ritual. What was very disconcerting was that she looked different. I'm almost six feet tall, and she is at least a head shorter than me. But when I stood before her receiving a message, I could have sworn she was taller than me. Even her eyes looked different, and the way she moved was oddly unfamiliar. I found the messages I received during these encounters deeply meaningful and profound. I felt I could sense some of the things the gods were trying to tell me, nudges and omens, but to hear a god speaking through a vessel—that was an entirely different experience. The Morrigan's words were less cryptic and harder to ignore when literally spoken to me, and over time I found myself seeking counsel during difficult times with those who knew this art and whom I trusted.

While I valued the advice I received, some experiences even shaping the direction of my own work, I had always felt it was for someone else. Macha and Badb had connections to visions and prophecy, but I only called upon that side of them for divination and nothing more in-depth than that. To relinquish one's control over their body to act as a vessel was a level of trust I wasn't sure I was ready to hand over, even to the Morrigan, for a long time.

There is no requirement that oracular work must be something a priest practices. Admittedly, it was well over ten years into my dedication and relationship with the Morrigan before I felt like I had the depth of connection and level of understanding of her to do such work. Part of being a priestess is holding space for the divine. Oracular work takes that to a more intense and literal level, in which you are holding that divine presence within your body and allowing it to use your body. It's not a parlor trick, and it's not something that anyone should do lightly. Some may never be ready, and that's okay. For those who wish to take that step within their devotion to the Morrigan, there are few guideposts to help you build such a practice with her. While the information outlined in this chapter does not cover the totality of such work, it should give you a good groundwork to start with. First, we will look at what oracular practices might have been used in Ireland, and then we will see how we can use these methods in a modern tradition.

Historic Irish Prophetic Practices

From the lore we know that the druids cast lots, used the behavior and appearance of birds to decipher the future, and were sought out for knowing what days were the most fortuitous for different things. This indicates a multitude of divinatory and prophetic practices. For our purposes, we will be looking at three specific practices that have been documented, two of which were banned later as Paganism transitioned to Christianity in Ireland.

Imbas Forosnai

Poets, or *fili*, were said to have oracular power as well as being able to curse. A modern person equates poetry to pretty words and love sonnets. But in Ireland, poetry and the power of words were often seen as a way to weave magic or convey prophetic truth. Poetry can be inspired by the gods and is like the words of a spell holding magical power. Our own modern spells usually feature words in some kind of poetic measure. There is even an Irish class of battle magic, *rosc*, that uses poetry to weave its magic. It perhaps is no surprise that the *fili* were the ones associated with the kind of oracular practices we will be looking at. In *Cormac's Glossaries* we can find a detailed account of the practice of *imbas forosnai*, or "knowledge that enlightens" that is attributed to the poets.

> IMBAS FOROSNAI *["knowledge that enlightens"] i.e. it discovers everything which the poet likes and which he desires to manifest. Thus is it done. The poet chews a piece of (the) flesh of a red pig, or of a dog or a cat, and puts it afterwards on the flag behind the door, and pronounces an incantation on it, and offers it to idol-gods, and afterwards calls his idols to him and then finds them not on the morrow, and pronounces*

incantations on his two palms, and calls again unto him his idol-gods
that his sleep may not be disturbed; and he lays his two palms on his
two cheeks and (in this manner) he falls asleep; and he is watched in
order that no one may interrupt [?] nor disturb him till everything
about which he is engaged is revealed to him, (which may be) a minute
or two or three, or as long as he was supposed to be at (the) offer-
ing ... Patrick abolished [banished?] this and the teinm lagda, and he
adjudged [testified?] that whoever should practise them should have
neither heaven nor earth, because it was renouncing baptism.[33]

It is important to note that the practice of *imbas forosnai* was not limited to poets. The practice was also attributed to Scathach, the warrior woman who trained Cuchulain, as well as the faery prophetess Fedelm. When Maeve visits Fedelm to learn who will triumph in the conflict between Connacht and Ulster, she asks the prophetess if she has attained the knowledge of the *imbas forosnai*. The techniques of *imbas forosnai* seem to be used in part in another prophetic practice, the *tarbh feis*. *Tarbh feis* means "bull feast," and it was used to prophetically gain information about who would be the new king. One person would eat meat from a sacrificed bull, while others chanted over them and would obtain the prophetic knowledge through a kind of vision dream while sleeping.

What can we take from this? Looking at it as a magical technique, let's break down the elements. First, offerings are made to a Pagan god, which is why it was banned by Christianity. Chants, prayers, or special words are said over the offering. Participants place their palms on their cheeks, which may seem odd, but if we think about it, when one puts their palms against either cheek, their fingers will cover their eyes. I see this as an indication of a kind of sensory deprivation. The person wishing to receive the vision says words beseeching their deities, while another person keeps watch over them. This really isn't that different from modern oracular practices. Offerings are made to a deity, and there is someone to watch and protect the body of the person acting as the vessel for deity. The oracle reaches trance; in many modern practices, such as *seidhr* in Heathen traditions, this also involved sensory deprivation by wearing a veil or

---

33.   John O'Donovan, trans., *Sanas Chormaic: Cormac's Glossary,* ed. Whitley Stokes (Calcutta: O. T. Cutter, 1868), 94–95. Parentheses and brackets are O'Donovan's.

cloak to commune with deity. Special words are spoken, which could be a trigger to induce trance. The wording may be archaic, but at its core the technique isn't that much different.

Tenm Láida

The second type of visionary art is also referenced in the same passage of *Cormac's Glossaries*, also being noted for it being banned by Patrick: *tenm láida* (also spelled *teinm lagda* or *teinm laegda*), or "illumination of song."[34] It isn't always clear what the *tenm láida* is. This practice is attributed to the hero Fionn mac Cumhaill (also known as Finn MacCool). After the druid Finnegas caught the Salmon of Knowledge, he asked young Fionn to cook the fish for him. Fionn burnt himself while doing so and sucked his thumb to cool it, accidently acquiring all the salmon's knowledge. *Tenm láida* also seems to have been associated with touching objects, in Fionn's case his thumb, to receive answers to questions while in a trance state.[35] Afterward when the hero sucked his thumb and sang, information would be revealed to him. The use of singing and poetry to gain visionary inspiration seems to be a technique used in many Irish prophetic practices. Both the *tarbh feis* and *imbas forosnai* incorporate the use of chanting or songs to be sung over the person receiving the vision or by others surrounding the person as they prepare for visionary experiences. *Tenm láida* and *imbas forosnai* are often mentioned alongside one another, indicating they were connected or related in some way, perhaps as practices that could be used separately or together depending on the situation. A further overlap is in the touching of objects. *Tenm láida* and *dichetal do chennaib* both seem to have involved touching objects with the fingers (or in Fionn's case, his finger was the focal point) to trigger prophetic speech.[36] Again, this is not terribly different from the modern use of chanting to achieve altered states of consciousness or the use of psychometry, in which touching an object triggers psychic information.

---

34. O'Donovan, *Sanas Chormaic: Cormac's Glossary,* 94–95.

35. Morgan Daimler, *Where the Hawthorn Grows: An American Druid's Reflections* (Alresford, Hants, UK: Moon Books, 2013), 166.

36. John Matthews, *Taliesin: The Last Celtic Shaman*, with Caitlin Matthews (Rochester, VT: Inner Traditions, 1991), 190.

Dichetal Do Chennaib

Dichetal do chennaib, or "extemporaneous poetry," can be seen as spontaneous inspiration. The Morrigan's prophecy in *The Second Battle of Moytura* could be a type of *dichetal do chennaib.*[37] It is seemingly spontaneous, carries a prediction of the future in it, and is spoken in poetic form. While *tenm láida* consists of singing or chanting to bring about visionary experiences, the wording of the song itself is prophetic here. Of the three, this practice was not banned since it was seen more as a poetic art and did not specifically require calling upon Pagan gods.

Modern Oracular Work

Oracular work had a place in the ancient world. In some corners of Paganism it remains, such as in the *seidhr* work of the Heathens and in African traditional religions where gods and spirits ride their priests. The chance to speak directly to one's gods through a priestly vessel is a powerful experience. It allows us to be in the presence of our gods in a tangible way. It is a service both to the community and to the gods, because I believe that gods respond to what they hear through the vessel. But it isn't easy. It's not something you can learn in a day, but rather something that will probably take years.

My oracular practice is my own modern version of *imbas forosnai.* I begin by making an offering. Usually, it is clear water, which to me represents the waters of Badb's ford. I trace a certain pattern on my palm to trigger going into a meditative state. My trigger to go into trance is dipping my fingers in the water, anointing myself in a specific way, and saying a particular phrase, one that is said every time I do this work. I then cover my head and usually most of my face with a long shawl I have specifically for this purpose. Covering my head and face in this way is my final step of the trigger for deep trance. Whether the Morrigan comes is up to the Morrigan, but usually you can get a sense of whether she wishes to speak or not long beforehand. I also do not do oracular work without someone acting as a guardian who essentially watches over me as I do that work and steps in if there are any problems, just as the person performing the *imbas forosnai* had someone watching their body.

---

37. Matthews, *Taliesin,* 164.

All of this is a deceptively simple explanation for something that is anything but simple. Let's look at some of the skills one needs to master to be able to do this work, many of the precautions needed to make it safe, and how to set up a protected space for oracular work. In many ways the majority of the work is done long before you invite the Morrigan to speak through you. It might take a year or several months of daily meditation and fine-tuning the triggers used to induce trance. Several months may be taken to create and charge a ward specifically for channeling. Then there is the rapport one needs with the person or people acting as your guardian. All these things won't come together if you haven't been working on them long before you are about to do the work. That takes time, patience, and dedication to mastery.

Know Thyself

You can't let deity fully come through your physical form if you don't know yourself. This kind of controlled possession requires that you step away from your physical form and let something else take charge for a time. If you don't have a clear understanding of what makes up your soul, mind, psyche, and very being, you won't know how to gather that part of yourself and step away from your physical form when making room for deity or how to regain that sense of self afterward. You might not step away from yourself at all, and it may be your ego or higher self speaking instead of deity. Or deity may come through and you may not be able to fully release that presence from your body because you don't have a clear sense of where your energies start and the deity's end. One technique I use when it's time to come out of trance is to say the names of the Morrigan, seeing all her energy collecting and coalescing, separate from myself, contained and defined. Then I say my own names, magical and otherwise. It's like a kind of countdown. I am separating the parts, or the beings in this case, that are inhabiting my form. In my mind I see the pieces of energy that are the Morrigan separating from me, become distinct and outside of myself. Then I name my own names, ground myself in naming them, and concentrate on those anchors to my being.

You also need to know when not to channel. If you have a lot going on and your life is a giant stressful ball of crazy, it's not the time for you to do this kind of work. That doesn't mean you don't know how to do it or aren't good at it. It just means it is not the right time for you to take it on. Just like when you have too many drinks, you shouldn't operate a car. It doesn't mean you don't know how to drive. You just aren't in the right state to do so right now. If your world is about to fall apart, you won't be in the headspace to let go of your ego. And if you can't let go of your ego, you probably will only manage to channel your ego instead of the gods. When we have lots of stressful stuff going on in the physical world, we tend to stay very grounded and focused in the physical, again making it difficult to achieve deep trance. You need to be able to be very, very honest with yourself. Know your limits. Know when to say no.

You also need to be honest about your reason for doing this kind of work. This is perhaps the most selfless and taxing work one can do as a priest. It's not about you, and it's not about being able to do a cool trick either.

The flip side to knowing yourself is that you also must know what you are welcoming to speak through you very well. You wouldn't let a stranger have the use of your form and body, right? There needs to be a relationship and trust between you and deity. You must know what their energy feels like. That requires you taking the time to do devotional work. Make offerings. Learn what their presence of voice sounds like.

Trance

Oracular work is impossible without trance. More than likely, you'll be doing this work standing and while there are things going on around you that could be distractions. Personally, I have always preferred walking or active meditations. Cultivating the skill to meditate anywhere is essential to being able to do oracular work. You basically need to become a meditation ninja. If you can meditate anywhere, and I mean anywhere, then you can do trance. This also means you must cultivate an everyday practice. It doesn't have to be for long periods of time; a few minutes a day will work. You just have to be consistent and make it a routine that is familiar and easy for you. Essentially, you are training your mind so that something that might have been difficult becomes a learned behavior. One you have done this many times, it becomes second nature.

A good starting point if you are not familiar with walking mediations is to slowly ease into the practice. Begin your daily meditation sitting, then spend the last few minutes meditating while walking slowly. It could be in a slow circle around a room, or it could be walking a particular pattern. Eventually, work yourself up to where you spend less and less time sitting and your moving meditation is longer, until finally your entire meditation is spent in motion.

Triggers

These are the good kind of triggers. If done properly, they can be an easy and effective way to enter a trance or meditative state. A trigger can be anything you want it to be: a motion like running your thumb in a circular motion on your palm three times, saying a specific word, or reciting a prayer. It could be putting on a certain set of clothes or even putting on specific makeup. It's a kind of Pavlovian response. What the trigger is doesn't matter so much as the consistency of use. If you use your trigger every time you go into trance or every time you meditate, then eventually the trigger by itself will have trained your mind to immediately put you into an altered state.

I use several triggers. I have a specific trigger for meditation to help me start the process of going into an altered state. It's kind of like starting the car. Everything is getting ready to go by the turning of the key, or in this case my trigger.

While in that meditative state, I have a specific trigger to initiate the deep trance I need for channeling. In my case that trigger is specific for the Morrigan compared to channeling work involving another deity. The more times you do it the easier it will become. Like all the things we will be discussing, it requires practice. Once you become comfortable with trance work and have set triggers in place, you need to spend time using them. At first this should not be in a public setting but a controlled, safe space where the process of going in and out of trance can be done safely and become routine.

Veiling and Sensory Deprivation

We can see the use of sensory deprivation as a technique to enter trance in the *imbas forosnai,* and it is also used in *seidhr* work in Heathen traditions, for which the oracle wears a veil. Those who are blind have always been linked with supernatural inner sight. Even in our modern folklore, this idea of sensory deprivation remains prevalent, as fans of El in *Stranger Things* know.

During my first experience standing as a vessel for Badb, I was directed by Badb to wear a long black scarf and use it as a kind of veil. My head and eyes had to be covered along with most of my face. Since then I have continued to do this, and it works well for me. Another technique I have seen used is lying down and covering oneself with a blanket, cloak, or an animal hide as a form of sensory deprivation to bring on trance. While in *imbas forosnai* the person who goes into trance would reveal the information gathered in that state after coming out of trance, most modern practitioners reveal this information while still in a trance state.

Allowing the Divine In

The actual act of drawing in the presence of the Morrigan will be different for different people. I know some priests who experience it as seeing her step into their body. They might visualize this happening while in trance to induce the trance possession. Personally, I visualize it as if I am trying to make space and hold on to a giant ocean of energy that is the Morrigan. It is like I am holding my arms out wide to try to hold on to and contain it all. You might experience her presence as something completely different. As with trance and triggers, this will take practice and will be something that should be slowly added to your meditation and trigger practice. You might take several months working on easily achieving an altered state and your triggers before making any attempt at welcoming a divine presence within you. Then work for several months on being able to contain and hold that presence well. Each skill builds on the other until you have a fluid practice.

Agreements

Just because you are channeling a deity doesn't mean the deity has free reign to do anything they want while inhabiting your body. Boundaries are important, even with gods. The agreement you make with deity is something you need to foster when you first begin this kind of work. It should be something that is already set into place long before you are channeling. This is to protect both you and those coming to speak with deity through you. With the Morrigan I think it is especially vital, as she can be very direct and cutting in her messages at times. Also you must consider that those who come to speak with someone who is acting as a vessel for a deity don't always know how the process works. This isn't something done on a regular basis in most Pagan circles, and I have had people come to me when I am channeling and ask for inappropriate things. For example, in one case even though the person was told he was only to ask a question, he instead asked Badb to perform a soul retrieval. I'm not sure what would have happened if I hadn't already had a standing agreement in place. Part of my agreement with Badb is that we only answer questions while in trance. I don't even remember the face of the person asking for the soul retrieval. But what I was aware of, while Badb inhabited my body, was the exchange between me and her. While Badb was talking to this man, she was also simultaneously talking to me in that dream state I exist in while she is using my physical body.

She was quite clear with me that she could do what this person asked but, first, that he wasn't missing part of his soul as he believed. He had placed knots and bindings around himself, perhaps intentionally or unintentionally. Sure, she could remove them. It would be painful for him and probably wouldn't be in his best interest either, but he had asked her. She could do it, but it stepped over a line in our own agreements. Did I want to cross that line? I had the feeling that in her conversation with the man using my face, she expressed it was not a good idea for him and that it was something he had to go down another path to achieve. But he kept insisting, and sometimes if we are stubborn, the gods aren't above giving us the things we think we want, even if it's a bad idea. Badb is like that sometimes. It is as if she says, "I told you it was a bad idea. Oh, you don't believe me? Okay, go ahead. Let's see how this plays out and find out who is right."

I didn't budge in our agreement, and instead of giving him what he wanted, Badb basically cut him off from continuing the conversation, since he clearly wasn't listening, and dismissed him. After I told Badb I did not want to cross the line of our agreement, I became more aware of my body. I heard myself saying the pre-agreed-upon line that I say to signal the end of someone's session with the oracle. The person acting as my guardian knew this was their cue and led him out of the temple.

Agreements can take many forms. They are about limitations on what actions a deity can perform while in your physical form. Are you willing to allow deity to eat or drink while in your form? If so, consider they might eat or drink something you would not want to eat or drink. Can they touch others in any way? Are they prohibited from taking any harmful actions against others or your own body? Can they have sex while inhabiting your form? Is there a specific amount of time they can be in your form? Be specific. Don't leave room for loopholes.

Although I was not present for this incident, I know several friends who were at a ritual where a priestess was channeling and the deity possessing her slapped one of the participants. You must have a very clear and specific idea of what is and isn't allowed to be done with your body. Just because it is a deity possessing you, that doesn't mean they won't go too far or won't do something that in their eyes is acceptable but is not okay at all in your eyes. You still own your body and have every right to say what happens with and to it. Think of these agreements as a rental contract, and add as many clauses and as much fine print as you feel is necessary. The amount of agreements may also vary depending on the deity you are preparing to channel and what your experiences and trust levels are with that deity.

In your daily work on trance and triggers, this is a good time to weave your agreements with the Morrigan. If you are to stand as her oracle, if you would be her vessel, what lines are you unwilling to cross? You can say them out loud formally as part of your process of going into trance, or it can be an ongoing conversation with deity. Regardless, it is essential to hammer out these details before you begin this work. Doing so will ensure the safety of both you and others when you do this work as well as influence how successful you will be at it.

Wards

Wards are an extra safety precaution. Like the person acting as your guardian, they are there to keep you and your environment safe while you are not fully aware of your surroundings. Wards can be something you draw on the wall in your temple space or something you embroider on your clothes and keep hidden from the sight of others.

The symbols or combination of symbols only have to have meaning to you. It can be something you created yourself or someone else created, like a pentacle from the Seal of Solomon. This should be charged and energized on a regular basis and prior to any oracle work. It may be something you keep on your person, like a piece of jewelry or a symbol drawn or sewn onto your clothes. I've even seen people magically charge tattoos for this purpose. Clothing tags, like those sewn into the back of your shirt, are an excellent place to draw a ward that will always be with you while wearing that piece of clothing. A ward drawn in chalk on the bottom of your shoe is also an easy way to have a ward on your person and not be something that is easily noticed by others. Your ward could also be incorporated into an object that is left in the room where you will be channeling. Wards don't have to be hidden from others, but I find they tend to work better when someone else isn't observing them and trying to puzzle out their meaning or adding their energy to them.

Creating the Space

I can't emphasize enough the importance of doing oracular work in the right place. Can you go into trance and channel anywhere? Probably, but that doesn't mean you will be doing it safely. Just because you can do something doesn't mean you should. Outside influences, whether they be background noise, the various energies of a place, or the presence of other people, will make it harder to get to the trance state needed for this kind of work. Furthermore, if you are working in an unprotected space, you run the risk of something other than the being you wish to channel coming through. Personal wards can serve as protection against such things but are not as effective as properly creating a space for oracular work.

A protected space for oracular work can take many forms. If you are working in a small group of people who are comfortable with each other, casting a circle and calling on protective beings and deity is sufficient. Whatever space you use should be warded in some way. This can be done with sigils or wards, by casting a circle around the space, or by walking the space that will be used and creating an energetic boundary. Creating an energetic boundary isn't necessarily the same as casting a circle. When casting a circle, in general the intention is not to cross the boundary, lest the energy being contained in it be disrupted. An energetic boundary or ward for this kind of work will have people crossing in and out of it as they enter to speak to the person channeling. Think of these energetic boundaries as more fluid, keeping out harmful energies and beings, while being inviting to the Morrigan or whichever of her faces will be called upon. The guardian who works with the oracle will help maintain and move the energies within the space, but it is still important to energetically create the boundaries of this space ahead of time.

Other practical things also have to be taken into consideration. Are there background noises? Can you eliminate any of them? For example, make sure people who are waiting to enter the space do not speak too loudly or cause any kind of distractions that can be heard where the oracle is. Lighting is also another practical concern. The sensory deprivation of being veiled is helpful but being able to turn off the lights or making it fairly dark in the space the oracle is working will also be beneficial to maintaining trance. It doesn't have to be pitch black; you don't want anyone to trip as they are coming to stand in front of the person channeling. Candlelight or twinkle lights that allow for some soft light work well.

Most of the oracular work I do is within a temple space with altars created for the Morrigan. Even when it is within a cast circle, some kind of small altar is present to represent the Morrigan in some way. Part of my own process of trance work revolves around making specific offerings before I go into trance. This doesn't necessarily mean I need an altar to make an offering, but it is helpful and I find it to be a way to welcome the Morrigan before I even begin the work. It invites her presence and is a way to mark an area as sacred for her work.

Guardians

Guardian is a term generally used for the person who stands with the oracle in sacred space. They may also be the gatekeeper who directs people approaching the oracle. This role can be a single person or a group of people. For work with the Morrigan, I prefer two to three guardians: one to stand with the oracle and tend to their needs in the temple or sacred space that the oracle is occupying, another to stand at the entrance to that space and challenge each petitioner before they speak to the oracle, and one setting the expectations of those who are gathering to speak to the oracle. Each part is important. Not many do this kind of work, and often there are no set expectations for those approaching someone who is channeling. The guardians set the tone. While people gather, the guardians can help them refine what question they might want to ask and help those seeking to speak to the oracle understand how the process will work.

Most people tend to focus on the oracle and don't realize that the work of the guardian is just as important, and probably more important, to the success of oracular work itself. While in trance, the person acting as the oracle can't always attend to the needs of the physical. You aren't usually aware of what's going on with your body. If the oracle is swaying, needs water, or needs to stop, the guardian is there to step in. Also, if someone has decided it's their time to have twenty questions with the goddess and is taking too much time, the guardian can also step in to intervene. Likewise, if the petitioner coming to speak with the oracle has a strong emotional reaction or needs help, the guardian is there to intercede.

This sounds like a no-brainer, but I can't tell you how many times at an event, private or public, someone has arrived drunk and wanted to speak to the person channeling. Or when in front of the oracle, instead of asking a question, they want something else, like spiritual healing or another inappropriate request. Having a good group of guardians can help you avoid such issues.

Going into trance and allowing oneself to step back from the physical and let something else take over what you are doing and saying is an act of trust. It can't be accomplished well if you don't feel safe. Besides setting expectations for those asking questions, the guardians are whom the oracle relies on to keep them safe. It's not something you would want to do for someone you don't know. It is essential that the oracle and their guardians are familiar with working with one another in a magical or ritual sense. They need to be able to trust one another and be familiar with each other's energies.

Guardians should also be those who are proficient in moving and shifting energy. Guardians are monitoring not only the people but also the energy of a space, sending anything disruptive or negative away.

An easy exercise for someone doing guardian work is to pick a room in your house and sit and meditate. Take some time to ground and center yourself. Become aware of your own energies. Then expand your energies outward to the rest of the room. Don't change those energies, but become aware of them. Energetically, what is going on in the room? Next, try this in a place that is not empty. This could be at a park, at work, or at a mall. Read the energy. Become aware of what is going on.

After you have practiced this for a while, try to move the energy of the place. First, try in an empty room, then somewhere where there is a lot going on. Can you move the energy so it is calmer? Can you ground or push away any negative or unwanted energy?

Aftercare

Channeling requires you to be ungrounded in many ways, so it should be no surprise that your aftercare should involve grounding yourself. This is also where a good guardian comes in. The guardian should be the one who reminds you to drink water and eat something. Something carb heavy is usually a good choice. A bit of salt on the tongue would work in a pinch. After one particularly intense and long channeling session, a friend who was acting as the oracle and is fairly mild mannered basically threatened us on pain of death to find her something to eat "that had a face and a family who misses it" in order to help her ground herself after the work. If you don't want a channeling hangover, I suggest keeping something on hand for afterward. A small plate of food and water set aside in the temple for the oracle will be immensely helpful.

Don't Force It

No matter how close your connection to the Morrigan, there will be times when she doesn't have anything to say to someone or the timing for doing oracle work is not right. You have to trust her. You should respect that she doesn't appear on demand—none of the gods do. Even if you have people who are expecting to have this kind of experience, in which they can speak to the gods through you, if the gods say no, then they say no, end of story. There are also times when I'm in trance and everything is going as it should. Then I'm sucked back into my body, and someone is talking to me, the Morrigan hanging out in the background telling me, "I've got nothing to say to this one." You do this enough and eventually this will happen. It doesn't mean there is something wrong with the person; just for whatever reason it's not the time for that person to be given a message, or maybe they need to talk to another god. It is just not for you to decide. In these cases, it's good to have a preplanned blessing to say to a person if this happens. This in many ways falls into the category of agreements you will have made with the Morrigan. It's kind of like getting the Morriganic Answering Machine. *The Morrigan can't take your call right now. Leave your message at the beep.* Or in this case, *receive a blessing and be on your way.* In many cases after someone has received the divine answering machine, her presence returns, I walk through my steps of letting go and returning to trance, and everything's fine again.

———

If I can emphasize anything about oracular work, it is that it is immensely rewarding but, like anything with the Morrigan, comes with an element of danger. One can have a natural propensity for mediumship or channeling and still put themselves in danger if they aren't diligent. All too often folks rush into this kind of work thinking they already know how to do it and don't think taking the time to cultivate the practices that we have just discussed are necessary. Taking the time to cultivate all these practices will be essential to doing this art well and to deepening your relationship to the Morrigan. It is something that should take time, care, and practice, but it will be endlessly rewarding.

Prayer to Macha the Prophetess

Raven woman
Who stands upon the plain
Seeing past what is
Knowing what can be
Lady of the liminal spaces
Let me see as you see
That I may know what path to take
What future to nurture
And which way lies destruction
Raven woman
Let me see as you see

Prayer to Badb

Prophetess
Weaver of men's fates
You who stand upon the high places
Announcing prophecies
Phantom, seeress
May your wisdom fill me
May I see with a raven's eyes
All possibilities
All paths that lie before me
May I track, with a wolf's knowing
The knowledge I seek
Seeress, prophetess, let it be so!

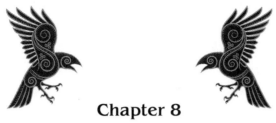

Chapter 8
The Morrigan's Wolves: A Vison Regarding Community

*M*y friends and I have just finished a long day of teaching at a local conference. *Heading back to the hotel room we are sharing, we chat about various things. We make offerings to the gods and sidhe at our makeshift altars around the room. An altar to the Morrigan with a small statue I have bought sits on the nightstand. There is also an altar to the sidhe on the hotel room desk. Sitting on the floor in my PJs, I don't really expect to be butt dialed by the Morrigan. We chat a bit about how the infighting in the community bothers us, and I notice my friend is quiet. She looks distant, tells us she feels really ungrounded. We are three floors up in a hotel full of Witches, and I reprimand myself for not remembering to bring some salt. But this isn't just being ungrounded— this reveals itself to be something different. If a deity needs or wants a message to come through, sometimes there is very little you can do to stop them. My friend is well versed in channel work, so she decides to stop fighting it and let it happen. When she looks up at me, her eyes are not her eyes. They are wild and fierce. I see Macha looking back at me, and the anger in her eyes makes me want to get up and run from the room. But I do not move. I look into Macha's eyes, I sit still, and I listen.*

"My followers are a headstrong, proud people. They are strong willed. This is good. But nothing is accomplished when all fight among themselves like dogs snarling over a bone. To achieve anything of worth, you must find common ground and seek what unity can be had in diversity. I would have a hunting pack fit to take down any prey, not feral hounds fighting over scraps."

More was said, but they were private messages for each of us. Still those words stuck with me. Slowly, my friend came back to herself. She told us that part of the imagery she had seen was devotees fighting like dogs over scraps of bones. That the Morrigan wanted wolves, the finest of hounds. She did not need them to be a pack per se but demanded that they at least ran in the same direction and not against one another. Afterward she saw those wolves running together and going off into all the directions of the globe, accomplishing their own work and purposes.

The Morrigan's words both weigh on me and give me hope. There are many times over the coming years I will wonder if we are living up to the vison of what the Morrigan wants of us. Are we the Morrigan's wolves? Or are we dogs fighting over bones picked clean of meaning and meat?

———

Visions can shape us and our work. This is one that has shaped my own work as a priestess ever since my friend spoke those channeled words. It's not just the words themselves but the feeling behind them, the emotion and energy I felt from the Morrigan as they were spoken. Anger, hope, sorrow. I didn't want to disappoint her, and I still don't.

Recently, I followed an internet battle between devotees of Hekate over some minor detail of her worship. People on each side of the argument had very strong opinions, and as with most internet battles, whether it's the comment threads on passive-aggressive blogs or reactionary blogs, the commentary got ugly and personal. By the end of it, the arguments had little to do with Hekate at all. I wasn't involved in either side, but as I watched from the sidelines, a comment someone made caught my attention. The person in question found it amusing that someone was fighting over Hekate and that for once it wasn't about the Morrigan. And I hate to say it, but the comment struck home. We really always are fighting.

If there is one downside to being a devotee of a goddess connected to war, it is that her followers have a tendency to fight a lot. Although perhaps it's not just something rampant in the community of Morrigan devotees. It's a growing thing I keep coming across a lot in Paganism in general. We've kind of forgotten how to get along with one another, unless of course the other person believes exactly what we believe. In part I think it's the product of our time. The age of meeting other Pagans at the local New Age store is long dead for the vast majority of us. We interact and connect online and in mostly anonymous ways. There is no need to be polite when one can simply block people who don't agree with them. No need for manners or civility when you don't have to use your real name on a forum. And it gets ugly out there because of it.

When I first starting writing about the Morrigan, and for that matter when I first began my dedication to her, there was no Morrigan community to speak of. There was me, some dusty old Irish books on mythology, a few pale mentions of the Morrigan in Neopagan books, and my own experiences with her. Today there are enough people who worship and honor her to create a subset within the Pagan crowd. Although most of these folks will tell you the Morrigan is more than just a mere goddess of war, we sure do tend to focus on our own warlike tendencies. We are a strong yet stubborn lot, to say the least. And with the Morrigan meaning so many different things to different people, perhaps it is not surprising that we all don't always get along. It is something that troubles me and has for quite some time. That joy of meeting someone who understands your devotion can be easily overshadowed when others feel they are the one true voice of a god or feel you must practice exactly how they do. In many ways this is a problem in most Pagan subsets and communities. There can be a holier-than-thou syndrome and the shaming of newbies, who are told they can't find their own ways to worship but must follow the approved dogma. It's a kind of contagious poison.

But for all the bad ones, there are plenty of amazing folks I've met through my devotion and work as a priestess. I've come across other devotees who relate to the Queen in completely different ways than I do. Some are new to their relationship with her, while others have had a relationship with her for just as long as I have or longer. To be quite blunt about it, some of us never will relate to her in the same way. And probably shouldn't. The marching orders she gives one person might be very different from the ones she gives to another. Any good general isn't going to send all the troops off to do exactly the same task. A tribe is only a tribe because of its differences, the myriad of talents, coming together that support the whole. And you know what? That's okay. She shouldn't want the same things from each of us because we are not all the same. We don't all need the same things in life or to learn the same lessons, nor can we as devotees all offer *her* the same things.

The gods don't always care about the mundane things we care about. The gods always have the long game in mind. They are looking at the big picture.

These forces that set the stars in motion and the planets spinning move in the world with a purpose. They have work for each of us to do, if we choose to take on the task. Sometimes that work is just simply learning to be better than we are. Problems occur when we assume the things we care deeply about must also be something the gods care deeply about. And when we encounter other devotees who don't care about the same things as we do, we take it as a trespass against the goddess we both worship. It's a dangerous path to go down. It alienates those who should be our allies. It also teaches those new to Paganism that different ideas are not welcome.

The work of oracular visions and prophecy changes you. In my case, they can change the direction of your work. Hearing the words of our gods can be a deeply powerful experience. Sometimes we can get a sense of what the gods want. We feel nudges and we see meaning in omens, but direct messages are a bit different. They are less ambiguous and harder to ignore. The words the Morrigan spoke through my friend that day changed how I approach my work. I remember the strength that came through in the Morrigan's words, the demand in them to not disappoint. To not fight over scraps of bone. I remember the look in my friend's eyes that were not her eyes anymore. If we value diversity in our community, then we have to accept that our path isn't going to be for everyone. Each devotee will have their own approach to how they honor and connect with the Morrigan. Just because we worship the same goddess doesn't mean we will have the same points of view or even the same beliefs in other areas of our lives. The things that are important and meaningful to one devotee may not have meaning to another. We aren't meant to be clones of one another. So it doesn't matter to me if you are Wiccan and worship the Morrigan or if you are a Reconstructionist or any variation in between. As a priestess of the Morrigan, to truly serve her means I have to accept and see the value in all these expressions of devotion to the goddess I serve. Because, honestly, I think the Morrigan just cares that we speak her name, that we worship her all in our own ways. Not that only certain people do it the "right" way. Because what's right to you might not be what's right for me, and there can be beauty in that diversity, rather than strife.

We really are a headstrong bunch. But even if we disagree with one another—even if we are given different marching orders in this world by the Great Queen, have different takes and viewpoints on life, or if you see the

Great Queen as simply the Irish Morrigan or the Gaulish Cathbodua while someone else instead connects to her as Morgan le Fay or Nemain—I hope that we can respect each other despite those differences. Let us not be stray dogs, but the finest of wolves.

The Morrigan's Wolves

In both *The Cattle Raid of Cooley* and the *Táin Bó Regamna* the Morrigan and the hero Cuchulain have an exchange in which she promises to fight against the hero in different animal forms, and he in turn promises to deliver his own attacks. One of the shapes she takes is that of a wolf. While most are familiar with the Morrigan's connection to crows and ravens, her connection to wolves has a particularly important connotation for me.

Wolves feature prominently in Irish mythology and folklore. They were once an integral part of the Irish landscape but are now extinct on the island. The last wild wolf in Ireland was thought to have been killed in 1786. The Irish word for wolf is *mac tíre,* meaning "son of the land." There are a multitude of stories of gods, mortals, and Otherworldly beings who could transform into wolves. The three daughters of Airitech came out of the Cave of Cruachan each Samhain and took the shape of wolves to hunt sheep. Although they are not connected directly to the Morrigan, it is interesting that other wolf-women come out of the cave that she calls home.

So what does it mean to be one of the Morrigan's wolves? More importantly, the finest of wolves, ones who do not fight over scraps. Wolves fill many roles, they are loyal, and they understand a large group can take down prey far bigger than itself to feed the pack. But they are also predators and will hunt what they see as prey. They are strong yet can be vicious. Much like the followers of the Morrigan.

Although the Morrigan fights Cuchulain in other animal forms, there is a bit of irony to fighting someone in wolf form whose name means "Hound of Cullen." Wolves and hounds aren't exactly the same, but similar enough. Dogs are for the most part domesticated wolves. Yet Cuchulain, the domesticated animal's namesake, has trouble recognizing the goddess on frequent occasions. There is something lacking in him. He is not a wolf but a diminished shadow of one.

For me, being a wolf of the Morrigan means seeing value in all members of the "pack." It's knowing when to strike and hunt, but also when to work with others. One can be strong and not give in to fighting useless battles. Wolves have better things to hunt than scraps of bone, after all.

When I think of the Morrigan's wolves, I think of what it means to be worthy. Is it possible to hear the call of the Morrigan, be a priest, a devotee, and so on, and still not be worthy of such a title? I think so. Just as there are many Christians whose actions go against their god's edicts. We can probably think of many people who hold a title and are unworthy of it, even if they themselves disagree. Wolves have been seen as noble animals as well as villains. They are perhaps capable of both sides of their nature. Being called to service is not the defining trait of having worth. It's something we have to earn and strive toward each day. I think being the finest of wolves means having mastery over oneself rather than trying to force dogma on others or being the overseer of how others worship. It's living well and being humble. It's recognizing that we all hear the Morrigan's voice in different ways, respecting each other even when we can't agree, and recognizing that fighting among ourselves isn't the way forward. I am a priestess of the Morrigan. That means I serve all the Morrigan's children, not just the ones I agree with and not just the ones I like.

A Prayer to the She-Wolf of Cruachan

She-Wolf of Cruachan
Morrigan, shape-shifting bane of Cuchulain
Noble, cunning huntress
Who knows well the battlefield
Who knows when to emerge
And when to be cloaked in shadow
Let me be like the finest of your wolves
Straying not from my goals
Not being distracted on my path
Let my aim be true
Let my goal be attained
Morrigan, She-Wolf
Guide me

Chapter 9

Poisonous Hearts:
A Vision of Serpents

It's a day like any other. I've just gotten home from work, my partner is making din-
ner, and I'm taking a few minutes to do my daily devotions. I pour an offering and I
sit quietly meditating. Smells of curry are wafting into the room from the kitchen, and
I'm about to end the meditation ... and then I am suddenly not in my body anymore.

I am suddenly in the darkness of the Cave of Cruachan. The home of the Mor-
rigan, an entrance to the Otherworlds, a dwelling place of the sidhe and entrance to
their halls as well. There is the thick mud that covers the bottom of the cave and the
ever-present darkness. I probably should be scared, but it is warm, comforting. This
place always is. This is where the Queen lives. In the deep, in the dark. I climb to the
deepest part of the cave through the unpierced darkness. The cave floor rises up, the
stone and mud creating a shelf where a cave-in happened long ago, blocking whatever
else once lay deeper in the dark. The shelf curves a bit, and I have always envisioned
it as a sort of throne, the higher parts on either side enormous armrests not unlike the
large stone on the top of Loughcrew called the Hag's Chair. A similar throne for another
goddess. This is usually where I see the Queen these days, sitting enthroned in her cave,
deep in the womb of the earth, one foot in this world, the other in the Otherworlds. I
feel her there now, keening, mourning, holding court. I have the vague impression that
she is moving chess pieces into play on an unseen board. There are other shadows in
the cave. People that are there but not there, the chess pieces she is moving around or
watching.

"The storm is coming," she says. I almost pull away from the vision. Where my
body is, I'm probably rolling my eyes for just a moment. I have heard those words before.
Another person who claims to have heard a message from the Great Queen has said a

similar thing. I have disagreed with how they have used it, not so much the core of the words themselves, but that they have been used to further discord among an already divided people and have encouraged hate and violence. I almost want to say to the Queen, "Why are you telling me this?"

Then I feel it. I feel anger, rage, a storm of madness, of poison, infecting everything it touches. Poison, so much poison in the world. It seeps out of people like sap from a tree, sticky and thick, attaching to everything it touches. It twists inside them like dark serpents, full of venom.

"They do not understand what it is," she says. "It is within." I see one of the shadow people she watches writhe, shouting and fighting against another shadow person, while the poison surges through his or her veins, devouring and rotting everything it touches. I see their hearts twisted with snakes. I see some ripping at their hearts and tearing the serpents from their own chests to be rid of them. Black oily poison spills away from them as they rock back and forth waiting for all the poison to drain away. It makes me think of an addict fighting through withdrawal, trying to make it through the shakes to get clean. Others let the poison flow through their blood, the serpents growing larger, and call it strength.

"They must ride it to the end," she says. "It's their own poison they fight against. They must let the poison run its course, to see if they survive, if they are still standing at the end."

She looks away from the writhing shadows, her chess pieces, and looks directly at me. It strikes me that in the impenetrable dark she is the only light.

"Gather your ravens. Be the calm in the storm. A haven, the eye of the storm. Give them shelter. Take strength in one another. Weather the storm.

"Survive. Thrive. Heal.

"Do not go blindly into the whirlwind."

———

This visionary experience happened abruptly. I was sitting in front of my altar as I normally do. I made offerings and was doing my daily devotions like any other day, then *bam*, I was swallowed by the experience. It was almost like an out-of-body experience. One moment I was in my house, the next I was in the Cave of Cruachan. It was like being instantly teleported from one place to another, then back again. Visions don't always come when you want them to.

When the gods wish to speak, they speak, and it is usually when you don't feel like you need to know anything. I wasn't facing any difficult challenge in life at the time, but the intensity of the message led me to explore what my own poisons were and the Morrigan's relation to this idea of releasing poison.

The *Dindshenchas*, a collection of lore concerning Irish place names, tells us that the Morrigan had a son who was plagued with serpents within him. The story goes something like this:

The Morrigan's son, Meiche, had three hearts. Three hearts plagued by three serpents. The serpents twisted within him, their poison seeping into his blood and into the air he breathed, until it was clear that unless the serpents were killed they would grow so great that they would devour all of Ireland. Because of this, Meiche was killed by Mac Cecht, and the three hearts and their three serpents were burned, their ashes thrown into a river. Even in death the poison of the serpents was powerful. The river waters boiled as the ashes were thrown into them, and all the living things in the river died. Because of this, the *Dindshenchas* tells us, the river is named *Berba*, meaning "dumb waters."[38] Another meaning for the name *Berba* is "seething," coming from the verb *berbaid*, which means to "boil" or "cook."[39] Isolde Carmody also connects the etymology of Berba to "silent" or "stammering."[40]

Today the Berba is known in Ireland as the River Barrow. It is the second longest river in Ireland. Interestingly, mirroring the three serpents and Meiche's three hearts, the Barrow is one of a grouping of three rivers called the Three Sisters. The Three Sisters also include the River Suir and the River Nore. After winding through six counties, the three rivers eventually join together, flowing into Waterford harbor and into the sea. Another layer to the story to consider is that many winding rivers and many lakes in Ireland have a long history of folklore connecting them to *péist* (pronounced *PAY-sht*). *Péist* were monstrous serpents or worms. The serpentine paths of many rivers were said to be dug out by their giant bodies or carved during battles between the worms and

38.   Whitley Stokes, "The Prose Tales in the Rennes Dindshenchas," *Revue Celtique* 15 (1894): 305.

39.   Mark Williams, *Ireland's Immortals: A History of the Gods of Irish Myth* (Princeton, NJ: Princeton University Press, 2016), 115.

40.   Isolde Carmody, "The Dindshenchas of the Barrow River—Berba," May 29, 2013. https://storyarchaeology.com/the-dindshenchas-of-the-barrow-river-berba/.

the heroes or saints who drove them away. Some would argue that the Loch Ness monster is a *péist*. In a different version of Meiche's story it was Dian Cecht, the Irish god of medicine, who slew Meiche.[41] In this version, which also revolves around explaining the origins of the Berba, Meiche is described as taking the shape of a serpent. Dian Cecht is said to have battled other serpents, so it is no surprise that this serpent or great worm motif is continued in the version where he is the one battling Meiche. Considering the absence of snakes in Ireland, the monstrous size Meiche's serpents are feared to be able to grow to, and the connection to a river, it is likely that what is being referred to is a *péist*. Either Meiche will turn into one or the serpents in his hearts are *péist*. Although, in at least one variation the serpents are described as alders.

I have often contemplated this story. For such a short story, there are many layers to look at. I am a devotee of the Morrigan, I am her priestess, but I also consider myself a child of the Morrigan. Looking at the gods as divine parents from the heavens can be problematic. It can inspire us to wrongly assume they will sweep down from the heavens and fix all our messes. But when I call the Morrigan *Mother*, I think of her not as a divine parent, but as the source of what I am made of. She is the force that has shaped me. Something about her calls to me, and something about my being calls to her. She is not a mother goddess, yet still when I speak with her, *Mother* is the term I often use. It has more to do with my own relationship with her than it does with her being "motherly." With that being said, I have often thought about the fate of her divine child Meiche. What caused these poisonous serpents to infest his many hearts? Does part of being a child of the Morrigan, a devotee, a worshiper of the Great Queen mean we must fight off similar poisons within our own hearts? And if we don't, are we destined to the same fate as Meiche: to be destroyed by the poisons within us?

One of the hang-ups many worshipers of the Morrigan encounter is focusing on the battles outside themselves. There is a lot wrong with the world, and of course we want to take on those battles. But if we ignore the small battles, the things within ourselves we must change, the truth is we won't be able to make any meaningful change in the worlds around us. Of course, recognizing that we need to fix ourselves and face our own demons isn't very

---

41.   Edward Gwynn, trans., *The Metrical Dindshenchas*, vol. 2 (Dublin: Royal Irish Academy, 1906), 63.

appealing. We avoid it, saying that other battles are more important, but I can tell you they are not. We can't help others until we help ourselves. Going off to battle is only a part of what the Morrigan is. She is also the force that rips the poison out of our souls, lest it taint everything around us. The war on the outside is a distraction. The real lesson is to learn to fight the battle within ourselves and win.

I think sometimes people assume that if the Morrigan shows up in their lives, it means she is hiring them as a soldier of fortune to fight the world's ills. We so very much want to be the heroes to shape the world, yet we avoid shaping the most important part of the world: ourselves. We want to be Mac Cecht and fight monsters. But sometimes we don't realize the monster we are fighting is ourselves. In my own experience, the Morrigan is far more concerned with us healing the broken parts within ourselves than sending us out into the world to do her bidding. I think that changing ourselves and how we interact with the world is far more likely to cause real change than us fighting battles outside ourselves while we are carrying around festering poison.

Connecting with Meiche

As with many topics in this book, we are going deep into the realm of UPG here. Meiche's story is short, and it is the only time his name is mentioned in Irish lore. I can tell you what I have experienced with Meiche, but perhaps you will connect with him differently.

I connect Meiche very strongly with rivers, in part because the ashes of his hearts are put into a river and change the character of that river. If we see him as a serpent deity or a *péist,* he is also a shaper of rivers. Offerings to him can be left in bodies of water or thrown into the waters of a river. Just be mindful that your offering will not hurt any wildlife and that it is safe to be put into a river. The Morrigan as the Washer at the Ford also is seen by river fords and bodies of water, and it is in conjunction with this aspect of her that I find my own work with Meiche to be the most meaningful. Meiche, who was poisoned within, and the Washer Woman, who stands at the river's edge ready to cleanse us of what no longer serves—together they are powerful allies in healing ourselves and releasing pain and trauma.

The serpent aspect to this story is important, but let's take a step back for a moment and look at Meiche before the serpents took residence in his hearts.

Why are we given this imagery of three hearts? Certainly, he doesn't need two extra ones. He could have just as easily had a single heart infested with serpents. But three is a number that has significance in Irish mythology, and I doubt it's an accident. In the context of the story, I see these three hearts as the three centers to Meiche's being. You could see them as mind, body, and soul; id, ego, and superego; or land, sea, and sky. Regardless of what you want to call them, I see them as the three major pieces that make up Meiche's essence, his very being. Meiche asks us to look at the different centers of ourselves. What poisons those places within us? How did this poison—the poison we have ourselves put there and the poison the world has placed there—take root, and how do we cleanse it? We wash it away. We give the poison to the waters, like the ashes of Meiche's hearts, and we call to the parts of the Morrigan that rule over such cleansing waters, and poisons, to aid us.

The Venomous Wives of Neit

The Morrigan's son is not the only connection the Morrigan has with poison. We have only to look at her more obscure faces to see that there is a theme here. When we look to Nemain, we again find poison. Nemain's name means "venomous," coming from the Proto-Celtic *nemo* meaning "dose of poison."[42] Although Nemain, as we have already discussed, has a separate parentage than the three sisters Anu, Macha, and Badb, she is still often mentioned alongside Badb. Both Badb and Nemain, as well as the obscure goddess Fea, are all named as the wives of the war god Neit. In some cases the two wives of Neit are listed as Fea and Nemain, and in others they are Badb and Nemain. It is fairly clear that there is a connection between Badb, Nemain, and Fea. They are equated with one another often enough, and their names are used interchangeably in connection to Neit.

Nemain can be terrifying when you first encounter her. When I see her, she is naked, covered in blood more often than not. She has an aura of either madness or silence, the kind of silence in the eye of a storm. She exudes a deep self-knowing. You have to know yourself to be calm and collected in the eye of chaos. She is venomous and can be the battle fury, but she also knows how to survive the venom, to suck it out of our veins and not let it affect us anymore.

---

42. Ranko Matasovic, *Etymological Dictionary of Proto-Celtic* (Boston: Brill, 2019), 288.

The poison is, after all, in the dose. Too much chaos destroys, while too little leads to complacency.

In general, I often work with Badb and Nemain as a dyad of sisters, which I suspect they once were, with Badb later merging into the grouping we now know as the Morrigan. Fea, about whom little is known, could also be seen as a face of Nemain or as forming a triad with Nemain and Badb. Their three names are never listed together as a triad in the source material, but one can easily work with them as such.

Fea's name means "hateful" or "death."[43] While in her dissertation Angelique Gulermovich Epstein relates *Fea* to the Irish words *fee* and *fe*, meaning death as well as the measuring rod for graves, she also relates her name to the Latin *vae*, meaning an "exclamation of woe."[44] There are several connections here I find interesting. Badb as the Washer at the Ford is often seen wailing and mourning over her bloody laundry. She has often led me to use the practice of keening in my work with her. Fea's name, if Epstein's conclusions are correct, means an "exclamation of woe," which is an appropriate description of keening, a practice that is not just giving one's grief a voice but also a releasing of that grief. Releasing the things that poison us isn't always just washing them away. Sometimes we have to acknowledge them in a visceral way. Through calling on Fea and the power of keening, we can release the poison and sorrow within us.

When I encounter Fea, she appears as a pale woman in gray, looking very much like a phantom or what most of us would imagine a banshee to look like. At first she would not speak to me. There was only the keening, the wailing sounds of sorrow that I heard from her. Through her I would learn that I had to give voice to my grief, rather than staying silent. Giving an emotion a presence in the physical world through sounds can be a powerful tool because our sorrow can be like a phantom, there but unseen. To release it and acknowledge it is real, valid, and legitimate, we have to give it form in the physical world. Keening isn't supposed to be pretty; it's supposed to be unnerving and raw.

---

43. W. M. Hennessy, "The Ancient Irish Goddess of War," *Revue Celtique* 1 (1870–72): 35; Angelique Gulermovich Epstein, "War Goddess: The Morrigan and Her Germano-Celtic Counterparts" (PhD diss., UCLA, 1998), 32.

44. Epstein, "War Goddess: The Morrigan and Her Germano-Celtic Counterparts," 32.

Together Badb, Nemain, and Fea have formed a separate kind of trio in my work as a priestess. The lore is obscure, and only so much can be extrapolated from it. The rest comes from my own experiences as a priestess with them. But I can say that Meiche's story and my search to connect with him led me to working more deeply with these three. For me, they embody poison and madness, seen in Nemain and her venom. Keening, recognizing, and giving voice to our sorrow are represented in Fea, and last, the washing away of that poison is in Badb as the Washer at the Ford.

This idea of washing away poison, of cleaning the soul, resonates very strongly with how I view the wives of Neit, who may or may not be the Morrigan. The things that poison us differ from person to person. They might be grief, anger, or sorrow. Badb as the Washer at the Ford has filled this role for me for a long time. The Washer at the Ford is often seen as an ill omen of doom and death. She can be just that. Certainly, the lore is filled with the Washer at the Ford's appearance predicting the deaths of those about to go into battle. But omens are only good or ill depending on the action we take upon receiving them. In most cases her warnings are ignored and the warriors stubbornly march onward, not altering their course of action, and of course that doesn't go well. She has appeared very strongly to me in times when my life was about to fall apart, and I think listening to what she said to me in those times is in part what helped me weather those storms.

A Prayer to Meiche

Meiche
Son of the Morrigan
Poisonous heart
Serpents twisting, writhing within
Teach me to
Let my fears and anger drain away
To not let my own poison taint me
Let it be washed away
As the ashes of your own hearts
Were washed away
By the silent waters
May I be whole and healed

A Prayer to Nemain

Nemain

Poisonous one

Venomous one

The eye of the storm

Silent and waiting

Help me release what no longer serves

Cleansing, wrathful storm

Wash away

Make me strong

Wash away

Let me be renewed

Transformed

A Prayer to Fea

Fea of the sorrows

Fea of the keening

Wailing, mourning, bitter one

Mourn with me

Help me release

What weighs down my heart

To release what poisons my spirit

Wail with me

Keen with me

Chapter 10
UPG and the Morrigan

*I*t is the day before Samhain and we are on pilgrimage in Ireland, visiting sites connected to the Morrigan and the Irish gods. We stop to visit the holy well of Ogulla.
There are Christian statues around the well and an abused hawthorn tree that we take
some time to remove the clooties from. Tying strips of cloth around the branches of
sacred trees is an old tradition, but most of the things tied around this tree are modern fibers and plastic ribbons that can't disintegrate naturally, as the older tradition
intended. The unintended end result is the trees being strangled and in some cases dying.
The tree grows right at the base of the well, which is really a natural spring rather than
what Americans would traditionally think of as a well. I can see where the waters flow
farther down, forming a small channel, but the well itself is hidden. Layers of some
kind of water plant form a thick blanket over the spring, and if I wasn't careful I might
have thought it was solid ground.

As we did for the hawthorn tree, our group begins cleaning the water weeds out of
the clogged well. Our work is our offering to this sacred place. Sometimes I find that this
sort of work ends up being the most meaningful part of visiting a sacred place, tending
and caring for it, rather than just taking and not giving anything back.

The water weeds we are pulling up become a heaping pile, and soon we can see the
sandy bottom and clear water of the actual spring. Some of us put waterproof boots
on that we planned on using later that day in Oweynagat and wade knee-deep into the
water, pulling up assorted garbage from the sandy bottom.

As we work, a car pulls to the side of the little road and parks. An older man gets
out of the car and walks to the area where the waters form a little channel away from
the springhead. There is a Celtic cross erected there, and he dips his hand in and very
reverently crosses himself with the water. I remember that it is Sunday. He speaks to

our guide for a few minutes and then, after assessing that we aren't damaging the site or doing something unsavory, gets back into his car and is on his way.

As I pull up CDs, tea lights, and other garbage from the well, I think about what this obviously Christian man might get from visiting such a site. There are Christian statues and even a little chapel-like building next to the well erected for a past visit from the Pope. Yet it is still an ancient Pagan site. Like so much in Ireland, Christian and Pagan influences blend together to form something uniquely Irish. The well's history reflects that as well. It is said Laoghaire, the last Pagan king of Ireland, had two daughters who came to the well to bathe. A Christian priest (or St. Patrick himself, depending on the story) came upon the women and converted them after telling them about his god. He baptized them in the well waters, and they were so full of longing to see this god he spoke of that they died on the spot from the power of their faith and their longing to see god in all his glory in heaven. I think it is more likely that the women were slain rather than converted.

Ogulla has a very quiet feel. Not quite sad. It is a place where different religions still cross paths and in some ways clash, while in other ways get along. Some attempts have been made to cut down the sacred hawthorn growing next to the well, deeming it too Pagan. Yet today both a Christian and a bunch of Pagans visit this site, and both honor the spirit of this place in their own way without conflict.

My friend calls out, holding up a small iridescent seashell she has found in the well. A gift perhaps for pulling up all the weeds and garbage. The shell also has a particular meaning to the beings she worships, and all around it seems a good omen to her. Next to me, my partner also pulls up a gift from the well: a hunter's discarded shotgun shell. Given the gun laws in Ireland, this is a rare find. But also a deeply meaningful one, since we are going to visit the home of the goddess of war in a few short hours, and part of his own devotional practice includes training with modern weapons to honor the Great Queen. We laugh that they both found "shells," very different sorts, yet both with deep meaning in each's spiritual practice.

I find it interesting how the spirit of this place speaks to all those who come here to honor it. From the Christian crossing himself on Sunday morning in the holy waters, to the Pagans who pulled up gifts from the well that had meaning to their distinct Pagan paths. I know all of it in the end is unverified personal gnosis. That each person here has been given a message, and in some cases a gift, that only has meaning to them. These messages and gifts even span religious boundaries. What is undoubted in my mind is that Ogulla is speaking to those who visit its sacred waters. It makes me think about how the gods speak to us differently as well. Messages aren't always meant to be universal; sometimes they are just for ourselves. I think about how often we fight over such messages due to our need to be right and find universal truths. Just as I'm sure the king's daughters probably found themselves at odds with the message of the priest who happened upon them in this very place. A difference of opinion likely caused their deaths. I think about how a Christian felt it necessary to harm a tree that Pagans felt was sacred, when both groups called this place sacred. Messages from the divine have power. They can be deeply moving, yet as always, we must know how to interpret the message and remind ourselves that there is room in the world for multiple meanings. What we need from the divine isn't always the same. Yet sometimes there are places of convergence, like Ogulla.

———

Much of this book is personal experience. Whether in the form of visons, words the Morrigan has spoken to me, or things I have experienced in ritual and in trance, all these things fall under the category of unverified personal gnosis (UPG). It is only fair that we take a look at what this term means in connection to the worshiping of the Morrigan.

Simply put, UPG is information we receive directly from the gods or spirits. *Gnosis* is a Greek word meaning "knowing," so it is a kind of knowing or knowledge imparted to us from outside of ourselves. This could be something we experience, hear, see, or feel during journey work, dreams, ritual, or a vision. The catch, of course, is that when you relay this information to another person, they have no idea if it is truly divinely inspired or if you made it up. Sometimes the person who experiences this imparted knowledge may question if it is legitimate or their own imagination. Generally, in the Pagan community if you say you were told a message by a god or goddess, it's taken at face value to be true. I believe the gods are real and they speak to us, but realistically I have to accept that the imagination and ego are powerful things too. Sometimes UPG is just someone's ego talking or just something created whole cloth to serve someone's agenda. It's sad but it is an unfortunate truth.

When you stop to think about it, a good chunk of modern Pagan practice is UPG, as is the majority of a priest's work. After all, people seek out priests because they have a strong connection with the divine. The problem is if you don't take the time to understand how personal gnosis works, the more easily the messages of the divine can be misunderstood or, worse, be twisted. UPG by its very definition is unverifiable, which can lead to all sorts of problems. What we experience when we invite gods like the Morrigan into our lives can be profound and life changing. Compared to other deities, the Morrigan is very straightforward. If we are open to hearing her voice, she will speak to us. Other gods can be more mysterious and less forthcoming. But with any spiritual experience we must be able to take a step away from the experience itself and analyze and understand what occurred to fully understand a message's meaning and validity. It's perfectly okay to have a mind-blowing encounter with deity and still stop to consider if there are any factors that might discredit your experiences. A little skepticism is healthy.

When it comes to the Morrigan, there are quite a lot of modern examples of UPG found within the Pagan community and on the internet. They include personal experiences, apocalyptic predictions, and gnosis that is used to connect her to foxes and other animals traditionally not associated with her. Most of this UPG has been spread so often on the internet that I often see some treating it as if it comes directly from actual folklore. When someone points out that the lore doesn't support what another person feels the Morrigan has shown them, well, then it usually turns ugly.

So how do we handle UPG with the Morrigan? What happens if she shows us something that isn't in the lore? How can we know how to process our own experiences and discern the value in the experiences of others? Let's look at a few examples I've encountered.

Raven-Haired Queen

Perhaps the most common kind of personal gnosis you will find about any deity is how their worshipers see and experience them. In general UPG can be broken down into two categories. The first is information about a deity's appearance and temperament. This can be what they look like and their likes and dislikes, as well as information about how they want to be worshiped. In the Morrigan's case her worshipers tend to report seeing her as a tall woman with black, raven-colored hair. The second most common description is a tall woman with red hair. Most devotees will also tell you that they feel she asks for whiskey as a common offering. None of these things can be verified as truly coming from the Morrigan, but how often people who do not know each other pick up on the same imagery and information on this shared gnosis tends to lend credence to the information. This type of gnosis often does have meaning to people other than ourselves. It is in many ways a shared experience.

Rewriting the Lore

The second type of gnosis is messages that pertain to your personal development or only to you as an individual. This type of UPG, unlike the first, usually will only have meaning to you. It may be information related to where you are in your life at the current moment, or it could be information in a symbolic language that you personally will understand. The majority of UPG I see about the Morrigan fits into this category.

For example, a young man contacted me to ask about the Morrigan's connection with deer. He had encountered the Morrigan in a dream where she appeared beside him with a stag. He was a little upset when I explained to him she had no associations with stags and that she was probably speaking in symbols he would understand to convey her message. I also noted that his avatar on social media, through which he had messaged me, and background pictures were all images of stags and deer. Clearly, deer had a personal meaning to him. Instead, he decided that the Morrigan must have had some ancient long-forgotten connection to deer, and she was telling him this secret knowledge so he could tell others. I think this reaction is in part because he believed that if the Morrigan didn't have this association, then he wasn't really talking to her. To make his experience valid, he needed to prove the imagery had a meaning in the wider world, rather than just having meaning to him.

Foxes are another animal some internet sources will claim have a connection to the Morrigan revealed through UPG. But, as with the other example, these claims are all born out of a personal experience someone had that probably really just had meaning and relevance to them. Many people receive messages from the Morrigan that don't quite fit her mythology or traditional associations. This doesn't make them any less valid, but we have to take a step back and ask ourselves, is this message only for me? This is the most dangerous part of UPG. If it doesn't fit the lore, then people tend to try to rewrite the myths and lore of a deity to fit what they experienced. There is a whole lot of missing information about the worship and stories of the gods. Not everything about the Pagan practices of the past has survived. UPG can be a tool for us to recover missing gaps in how the gods wish to be worshiped. But at the same time, we have to look at what we experience with a grain of salt. Is this what I want to hear? Does this fit into what I know about her mythology? Is this message relevant to anyone else? What is the Morrigan trying to tell me? What could the images I'm seeing represent? These are all important questions.

What tends to be a stumbling block for most folks with this kind of UPG is that it only pertains to themselves. For many, that lessens the experience. On some level this can be due to ego. We all want to be the chosen one the gods reveal their secrets to. Or they fear that they were imagining the whole thing. People tend to seek outside confirmation to validate that what they have experienced is legitimate. We don't want to be seen as crazy people who hear voices. If the message or knowledge revealed isn't something for the masses, then they tend to feel like the experience had little value. If the message is just about your own personal growth, then it means you actually have to do something about it, like make changes in your life or face difficult things. If the message is just something to be relayed to others, and you are just the mouthpiece, then you have no responsibility to do anything except tell others. When other people point out that the message may just be meant for the person who experienced it, not a great dire warning for the entire world to hear, then people start fighting and digging their heels in, insisting that their gnosis is a great revelation given only to them.

Not all gnosis needs to be shared. There are many experiences I have had that I am reluctant to share. Not because I fear they are a product of my imagination, but because they are deeply personal. They speak to my own purpose and path. If they are shared, it is only because I feel someone can find value in my experiences, rather than a need to validate the information. There are some experiences and gnosis that I will never share because they only belong to me and are supposed to. If you have a visionary experience, you aren't required to share it and shouldn't feel pressured to do so.

Close Encounters of the Vulture Kind

Several years ago a woman contacted me with much the same question as the man with the stag, only the animal she was encountering the Morrigan through was the vulture. At the time part of my weekly routine was to hike a trail through a local park close to where I worked. It was a kind of walking meditation. I let go of the stress of the day and listened to my playlist as I walked among the trees and huffed up the hills before I went home for the day. On one particular day the woman's question was on my mind. I didn't doubt her experience, yet there was no connection in the lore between vultures and the Morrigan. I felt like I was going to disappoint her when I replied to her message.

I continued on the trail, thinking about the experience she had detailed in her email. It's not hard to zone out a bit when doing a walking meditation. In a way, it is the point. As I hiked down a steep trail, being careful not to trip over some tree roots poking up along the path, I suddenly realized I was not alone. Something brushed over the top of my head. Understandably surprised, I shrieked at the top of my lungs and ducked down. There were no trees overhead. I had just come into an open area, and there were definitely no branches that could have brushed the top of my head. Branches didn't feel like that, like something alive. I looked up and saw a turkey vulture circling above me. It swooped down one more time before circling higher. Then I heard a crow call out, as if laughing at me. In truth I'm pretty sure the Morrigan was laughing at me. "I am a shape-shifter," I felt her say. "I will appear as I like."

In that moment, I understood it didn't really matter how the Morrigan appeared, only that she showed up in the first place in our lives. She would speak as she wished, through whatever means she wished. Yes, she had no connections in the lore to vultures, but that wasn't the point. Whatever she was trying to tell this woman, vultures had some kind of relevance to that message. In the end it had nothing to do with the lore and everything to do with the language of symbols the Morrigan was using to speak to the woman. Not everyone hears the voices of the gods in words. Sometimes it is through symbols and omens. The language of symbols is vast. We aren't just going to encounter animals and symbols connected to the Morrigan. After all, what would that really tell us except that she was there? I already knew she was there, and I think the woman I was chatting with via email already knew the Queen was walking with her too. There were messages in the images she was showing this woman, a kind of visual language. When I channel, sometimes I see an image or have an intense feeling, and that is the message, not specific words. What the woman really needed to learn was how to speak the Morrigan's language, to decipher the language of symbols the divine was speaking.

Bullets and Blood

Offerings are an important part of my relationship with the Morrigan. Whether they are something given during my daily devotionals by my altar or during a ritual, offerings are a vital part of how I honor the Morrigan. What is offered, and how it is offered, to the gods is important. We can choose offerings because of their associations and properties, but in the end offerings usually reflect the tastes of the person making the offering and, yes, their UPG. Offerings should be something of value and significance to the person making the offering, something precious they are gifting to the divine. Precious is relative. It might be a beloved piece of jewelry or your last sip of coffee.

Most Pagans will tell you they felt directed by deity to offer a certain thing or certain kind of drink. Deciding what offerings should be given falls under the practice of UPG. Sometimes offerings may be picked because they are historically accurate, but I can confidently say the vast majority of my offerings have all been things I decided to offer based on gnosis. Just because the Morrigan, or any god, asks for something doesn't mean you have to give it to them. But in general, I find that the Morrigan will ask for things that have meaning to both her and me. Some of these things are not physical things. Many of the offerings I have been asked to give, and have offered, were doing a certain task: an act of bravery, hosting a ritual, or an event in her honor.

Just like when someone is given a message that you disagree with from the gods, one person might be directed by the Morrigan to make offerings another devotee finds repugnant. Just like messages obtained through UPG can pertain only to oneself, what one devotee is told to give in offering to the Morrigan may not be considered valuable or have significance to another devotee.

Bullets tend to be the most volatilely debated offering among Morrigan devotees. A quick Google search will supply you with a whole host of blogs both in support of and against this offering. I do have a few bullets on my altar. Two of them are from WWII and have been carried through real combat. Near them, against the wall, is a bayonet that my grandfather brought back from WWII. Because I have two great uncles and a grandfather who all fought in and survived D-Day, these all have meaning to me. There is a modern bullet there too, alongside the WWII relics, sitting beside offering bowls for whiskey, swords, spears, a drum painted with a raven, and multiple statues. Bullets are not what I offer on a daily basis, but they're something I have felt called by her to leave on her altar. My altar to her is a reflection of all her aspects, not just the ones I like the best. She is still a goddess of war—not just Iron Age war or war that involves swords. Modern weapons belong to the goddess of war too, in my opinion.

Also, I own modern weapons and have devoted learning how to use them for my own self-defense as an act done in her honor. There is something very empowering about knowing that if someone is bigger and stronger than you, you can defend yourself. That you can even the odds. Similarly, I know a few members of the military and police force who offer similar things, including their range time, as an act of devotion to the Morrigan. This is what I am comfortable with and what I have been directed to learn by the Morrigan. But that's my UPG, and I'll be the first one to say no one is required to agree with me. If it's something you are not comfortable with, then don't do it.

Online, this debate boiled down to many people's discomfort with modern weapons versus ancient weapons. Swords, which many people use in both their Witchcraft and in honoring the Morrigan, are weapons whose sole purpose was to kill. Swords were expensive weapons to buy and make. No one was commissioning a sword to chop firewood. Perhaps because of our modern romanticized notions of swords, knights, and glowing elvish weapons from fantasy movies, which dispatch enemies bloodlessly off screen, we don't connect them to anything negative, as we do with modern weapons.

Similarly, you will find many people on different sides of the debate on offering one's own blood to the Morrigan, be that menstrual blood or a few drops from a finger pricked by a lancet. Again, you have to decide what you are comfortable with. Personally, I have been instructed by Badb that I *must* offer her a few drops of my own blood before doing any work or ritual involving her. The few times I have forgotten I somehow got accidently cut by something. I once scraped myself on a briar bush in the woods before realizing my error because I had been rushing to get ready for a ritual. Another time I cut my foot on what I can only guess was a rock because one moment I was fine and the next moment I was bleeding. But this is something she has directed *me* to do. It doesn't mean she will ask the same of someone else.

Maybe you share my UPG, maybe you don't. It's okay to recognize that what one person is directed to do in their worship, their UPG, and what you are directed to do are both different and at the same time valid. Different doesn't instantly equal wrong. It's just different. I think we all really want on some level for there to be universal truths, one set of directions that works for everyone and shows the right way to do something when it comes to the Morrigan. There just isn't one right way. The sooner we realize that different isn't an attack on your gnosis, the less fighting there will be in the community.

An additional thing to consider is that what you plan on offering when in a group setting or a public space should be mentioned ahead of time to all participating. For example, someone in recovery may not be comfortable consuming or being around alcohol, even if it's just being poured on the ground. If you feel there is something you absolutely must offer to the Morrigan because your UPG demands it, that is between you and her. Doing so privately before the ritual is a good idea. Blood can be a health risk, and while there are plenty of public rituals I have done for Badb, my offering to her is done privately at some point during that day in preparation for the ritual, rather than during the ritual itself. The key is respecting the gnosis of others and not assuming our gnosis will be shared or imposing it on others.

Tongues and Curses

A few years ago, a friend tragically passed away at the hands of her former partner. I and others who knew her were reeling from the news. Our friend had been active in one of the Morrigan groups I am a part of, and we all decided we wanted to honor her with a prayer written for her and individually light a candle for her at an appointed time. While we were organizing this, one person on an online message board suggested that we curse the spirit of her deceased boyfriend as punishment. The person hadn't known our friend in life but felt that since the Morrigan was a goddess of justice, clearly the Morrigan would want us to curse this man's spirit. They also detailed a way to do it involving a cow tongue nailed to a tree. Now don't get me wrong, I'm all for a good old curse when the situation legitimately warrants action. But this wasn't the time. We were mourning. The person who had caused this harm was already dead. His spirit was already in the hands of the gods, and their judgment was enough for me.

When we asked if the person felt that the Morrigan had told them to do this or if they felt it was at the direction of our friend's spirit, they insisted it was because of the type of goddess the Morrigan was. Clearly, this is what a goddess of war and justice would want. Why bother asking the Morrigan? Herein lies the danger. It's easy to let our ego take the reins and convince ourselves that we know what the gods want. Or to think that because we are angry, they would want us to act in a certain way, because we want that to be the answer they give us. I was angry and sad, but this wasn't the right action to take.

Although I was pretty certain ego had a lot of do with this person's suggestion, I followed my usual course of action when trying to verify UPG. Whether it's my own or someone else's doesn't matter. I did divination, first to see if this was something our friend's spirit wanted. No. Then to see if this was something the Morrigan wanted. No, again. I spent time at my altar connecting to the Morrigan and asking for guidance, and everything I felt was pointing toward mourning my friend. "Send your blessings and love to that which has been lost." So that is what I did.

Things to Consider

While UPG by its very definition is unverifiable, there are a few things we should take into consideration when trying to verify the unverifiable.

Which Morrigan am I talking to?

When it comes to UPG and the Morrigan, the biggest issue I see folks running into is figuring out whom they are talking to. The Morrigan really isn't a single being. A message from Badb is going to have a whole different feel and tone to it than a message from Anu. I'm really not surprised when someone says, "Well, the Morrigan told me this," and then someone else immediately stands up and says they were told something completely left field of the first person's impressions. Of course, it's always important to remember that a message may simply be for the individual rather than a wider audience. But my first gut reaction is to ask, "Which Morrigan were you talking to?" For that matter, some consider Nemain, Fea, and a host of other goddesses to be part of the Morrigan triplicity. That's a whole lot of personalities to contend with. It is only to be expected that we will get different messages and answers when we are talking to such a variety of beings.

Did you do divination?

This is an important one. If you want clarification on a message you received or you just want to confirm it's not a product of your own ego, this is an excellent way to get some outside confirmation. You could pull cards or ask someone else to pull cards for you. Other less formal versions of divination will work just as well. For example, you could ask the Morrigan to send you an omen to confirm or clarify your message. It is okay to say, "Hey, I don't understand what you are telling me. But I'm listening. Help me understand." Compared to other deities, the Morrigan is pretty direct and to the point in my experience. She isn't shy about giving you an answer. Whether or not you will like the answer is another story.

Is this exactly what I want to hear?

This is the hardest part of UPG, since it means we have to be really honest with ourselves and keep our egos in check. If it sounds too good to be true, then it probably is. That isn't always the case, but the vast majority of my own vision-ary experiences and messages have been hard truths I had to face and certainly didn't want to hear.

Ego doesn't necessarily mean you are arrogant. We all have egos. We all have at some point jumped to a conclusion because we couldn't look past our own perspective. Loss of ego is something every priest needs to cultivate.

Not all gnosis needs to be shared gnosis.

It's okay if you receive one answer from the Morrigan, and I receive a totally different one. Not all gnosis needs to be universal. Some things are just going to pertain to the individual. Sharing gnosis with others isn't something you have to do. Deep and transformational work with the Morrigan will lead to very personal messages. Just because the Morrigan reveals something to you doesn't mean you owe anyone else the telling of that story. Some things are not meant to be shared. On the flip side of that, when we hear someone else share their gnosis, we have to remember that we don't have to agree with it. It might not mean anything to you, but it might have great relevance to someone else's path, and you can both disagree and be respectful at the same time.

We all have different marching orders.

It's important to keep in mind that the Morrigan, and really all the gods, are interested in us for different reasons. Our work and our purposes for incarnating on this earth are all different, so the work and direction the gods give us in life will be different too. I think we are sometimes too fast to discredit the experiences of others because they don't mesh with our personal views or the things we care about. Just because we don't agree with someone's UPG doesn't mean it isn't a legitimate experience.

Do you trust her? Do you trust yourself?

This is really important and not something that is going to happen overnight. You have to be able to trust yourself enough to be able to sort out what is your ego talking and what is a real experience. To me the nudges I get from the Morrigan have a very particular feel to them. I know what her voice and energy feel like because of how long we have had a relationship. Learning to be confident in that took time. Learning to just trust the information took even longer. It's something you have to find for yourself in your own time.

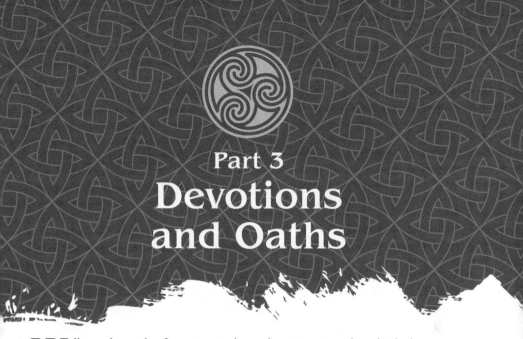

Part 3
Devotions and Oaths

Walking the path of a priest is about devotion. I used to think that meant that you didn't forget to make routine offerings, that you remembered to speak a certain prayer on a certain day. Devotion was reverently uttered words and expressions of awe. It was something hard to pinpoint past that, so I started there. Daily devotions, offerings, prayers.

Eventually, I realized devotion was more than that. It was in the things I did. Hosting public rituals. It was in how I lived. It was in the oaths I kept to her. It was so much more than whispered words and poured whiskey. Sometimes just holding space and listening to someone can be an act of devotion. It's all about living your connection to the Morrigan, weaving it into the everyday and making it a part of all that you are. That is no easy task, but it is worth the effort.

Later my devotion took the shape of promises and oaths I made as part of my relationship with the Morrigan. I experienced initiations that changed how I viewed my path and the Morrigan herself. I stepped from being a devotee to being a priest, and my relationship changed with that oath. Navigating these experiences changed my devotion and how I practiced my spirituality. They challenged me to deepen my devotional work and evolve in my practices.

In this section we will look at the nature of both devotion and oaths, and how they impact our relationship with the Great Queen. I'll discuss not only how to go about building a meaningful connection to the Morrigan but also how to navigate this process and the difficulties you might encounter along the way.

Chapter 11
Initiations

*T*wenty years ago ...

I've spent about an hour hiking to a place I know I will not be disturbed. My ritual tools have been carefully packed in a bag and I take them out and arrange them around the area that will be my ritual space. I take my time to make it perfect, because at this point in time, I still think I need the "right" tools and the "right" setup for my magic and devotion to "work." I say the words of the ritual I have written, I call to the Morrigan, to the Great Queen, and she answers. Her presence is lightning sharp and so very tangible. I am in awe of it every time I feel it. There is no one there to initiate me as a priestess except the Morrigan herself. It is more than enough for me, more mean-ingful in many ways. I have chosen this path, and she has been calling me toward it. I speak my oaths, and I feel they are accepted. I make offerings. When all is done and I begin my journey home, I stupidly think it is all done now. The initiation is over.

———

Eight years ago ...

After our ritual, everyone else has gone off to take care of the many tasks that still need to be done for the day. We chose to do this ritual in honor of Macha in the after-noon, as many of us will be leaving for home before the end of the night. The copse of trees is quiet, and the sunlight streams down between the tree branches, warming me, as do the last burning embers of the fire at the center of the area. We have set up a simple altar by the fire. A horse skull I have painted in Macha's honor, apples, and a wooden bowl for pouring offerings sit beside it. Throughout the ritual, I have been having my own conversation with Macha. That is why I have stayed behind. I have felt lost, so much upheaval in my own life. There are lessons the Morrigan has needed me to learn, and I have been stubbornly avoiding them. She has been quiet, oh so quiet. Part of her still feels distant, except for Macha. Of the three daughters of Ernmas, of the three Morrigans, her voice remains.

I sit by the altar and leave my own offerings, and we speak. It is through Macha I will learn these lessons. If I accept, now is the time to deepen my work with her. Oaths are made and accepted. And I become not just a priestess of the Morrigan, but a priestess of Macha, and I am surprised to find there is a very distinct difference between those two things.

———

Four years ago …

I have never loved small, dark places. But I am just about jumping out of my skin to crawl down into one right now. We stand at the entrance to the Cave of Cruachan, the home of the Morrigan, on the eve of Samhain. All I want to do is drive down into the dark and unknown. Something calls to me in a way I can barely understand. I have felt the Morrigan's presence before, but this … this is different somehow. We are not calling her presence to a place but rather going to the place she dwells, a place she naturally inhabits. She is already down there, no invocation needed.

I am surprised at how big the cave is. The passage is so small that some feared they would not be able to fit through it, yet after we have crawled down into the earth, the cave opens to a large cavern, vagina-like in shape almost. When we turn off the flashlights, it is so dark I simply close my eyes, because when I open them, I cannot tell that they are open. It is more than slightly disorienting. Almost immediately, I feel myself slipping into trance. I sit with my hand against cool stone, and the Morrigan speaks, a familiar voice within me.

Almost everyone else has left, but there are things I must say, things I must understand. I feel unable to move or leave until that communication between me and her is done. I think back to when I first became her priestess. How so much has changed, how my understanding of her has evolved and deepened. I say the words I spoke so long ago to her again, here in this place. I did not come to the Cave of Cruachan to be initiated, but it has become a kind of initiation. A reaffirming of old vows and making of new ones. When I finally crawl back up to the world above, I feel light and elated. I feel altered, and I have ever since. They say when you enter a faery mound, you come out dead, mad, or a poet. The Cave of Cruachan is an entrance to the Otherworlds, a sidhe in its own right.[45] *I feel a new conviction and direction in my work with the Morrigan. I have come out of that cave, but part of me has not, the shadows and pain of the past have been left behind. Painful lessons, but lessons that shaped me. Now it is time to move onward.*

———

Two years ago …

I am alone, sitting by the fire and making an offering when I feel her presence. When the Morrigan first showed up in my life, Badb was all battle fury, wild and frenzy. Then there was a time when I was not listening to what she was trying to tell me, and Badb's voice went silent. It took a long time before I felt Badb's presence again. But I kept showing up. I kept doing the difficult work I had been avoiding. I made Badb offerings and actively sought out her presence. I strived to do better. Now her familiar voice returns, but it is a different side of her. I had learned what I could from Badb the fury. Now it is Badb the seeress who has become a presence in my life. It is this aspect of Badb that I feel with me in the woods.

A new agreement is struck, a new deepening to the work I will do with and for her. It is unexpected, but I am realizing more and more that these sorts of things often are. She calls me her priestess, then says, "Now you belong to all of us."

It was a simple statement but one that would shape my understanding of the Morrigan. I thought about my first initiation as a priestess, when I felt the presence of the Morrigan accept me as her priestess, and how I had felt the echo of that, a reaffirming of that long-ago initiation, in the Cave of Cruachan. I thought of how years after that first initiation Macha claimed me as her priestess, another spontaneous initiation, marking me clearly as hers. And now Badb had made her own unseen mark of claiming on me. The Morrigan, Macha, and Badb had all claimed me in their own ways, acting individually and independent of the rest. I think of how complicated the gods are. I think of how being a priestess is an ongoing process. Initiation is never really over.

———

45.   The word *sidhe* can refer to a faery being and also a faery mound or an entryway into the Otherworlds.

Before we entered the Cave of Cruachan, our guide spoke to us a little bit about the site itself. That it was probably used as a place of initiation. The power of the place itself and the utter pitch blackness within the cave could and probably should frighten anyone. It is a very disorienting and frightening feeling to open your eyes and find that it is just as dark whether you keep your eyes open or closed. Then there is the fact that it is more than just a cave but also an entrance into the Otherworlds. In Ireland, Wales, and Scotland there is a long folk tradition that tells us that those who sleep on or stay overnight in a place held sacred by the Fair Folk will leave it dead, mad, or a poet. In this sense "poet" can mean someone of spiritual genius of some kind, although the musical talents of many famous bards have been accredited to such an Other-worldly encounter. Poets in Ireland were said to have prophetic gifts, so there is that element to it as well.

When I entered the Morrigan's cave, I felt as if I had in some way fulfilled all those points in some way. We were entering the cave on Samhain, a day when the veil between the world of the living and dead is thinnest. Later when I returned to the world of the living from the depths of the earth, I felt as if I had shed something of myself. I was altered, changed—the me who walked out of the cave was different fundamentally somehow, and that was a kind of death. Before we entered the cave, we talked a bit about how some people have very strong reactions to the cave and to being underground in the dark, as well as what to do if you felt panicked or needed to leave. There was one person who at the last minute did opt out. Oddly enough, for someone who does not like tight dark spaces, I was beyond ready to dive down into this deep dark hole I had never been in before. It was a kind of madness almost, a good kind, from my perspective. This place was calling to me, the Queen was calling to me; all I wanted was our guide to be done with the explanations and let us go down there. I felt like the cartoon character that is suspended midair in a diving pose, ready to dive off a cliff or into the unknown. I have never felt such a pull before or after. What I experienced in the cave, the words the Morrigan spoke to me, and my answering ones have altered both myself and my work as a priestess. Yet it was a long time before I realized this was an initiatory experi-ence. I had already been initiated, hadn't I? I had already made my oaths to the Queen and that was it, wasn't it?

When I first began my spiritual path, I thought initiations were fairly straightforward. We experience many initiations in life, and most of them are created with intention. When we graduate from school, we wear a cap and gown. When we get married, we have a certain ceremony. When we get to a certain skill level in a martial art, we earn a belt. When we join a tradition or gain a certain level within a magical system, there is an initiation ceremony performed either by the group or in a solitary ritual. In most of these cases a task has been completed and the initiation marks this completion. We move on to a new level of study and understanding. In these cases, you know what is happening. It's not a surprise. But that is not always how it goes.

When initiations come from the gods or spirits, more often than not, we get blindsided. We forget that when it comes to the gods, the Morrigan included, we can't force their hand. We can't guarantee they will give us what we want or even be present when they don't wish it. It is not unlike when we pour an offering. Simply pouring the offering doesn't mean it's instantly accepted. For true reciprocity, the gods must be willing to give as much as we are willing to receive and vice versa. Initiation works the same way, even when it is spontaneous. We have the choice to either accept or turn down what is offered, but it will change us. As a good friend once told me, initiation is like a job offer. You don't accept the job and not show up for work the next day.

Only my first initiatory experience with the Morrigan was initiated by myself. All the rest have been spontaneous and very unexpected. Each time has heralded a change within my life and my work as a priestess. Each of her many faces has chosen to claim me at different times. It had been happening for years, but it didn't really click until I felt Badb's claws dig into me and proclaimed that now I belonged to all of them. It wasn't like I didn't have a relationship with Badb already. I certainly did. But her claiming of me as her priestess—not just a priestess of the Morrigan, but a priestess of Badb—started a chain of events that made oracular work a stronger focus in my work for the Morrigan as a whole. Taking on this work and accepting her leading me through the process came with conditions—a price, if you will. A *géis* that was willingly taken on.[46] Her words made me realize that the process I had started twenty years ago wasn't

---

46. *Géis* is an Irish term for a type of taboo or spiritual prohibition. This can be not eating a certain food, not cutting one's hair, or any number of things. Breaking one's taboo usually results in disaster or death within mythology. See chapter 13 for more information.

over. I had put things into motion, but it has continued as both I and my understanding of the Morrigan changed.

Part of what makes being a priestess scary is that in many ways you are bound by your oaths to that deity. You are their representative in the world, and as you take part, the process of that work changes you. The Morrigan, like any god, is vast. She lives in a space beyond limitations and her sight reaches farther than my own. From that vantage point, she can see when the right time and the moment to instigate change has come. These are when the Morrigan thrusts initiation on us. This is when she asks us to choose: Move forward or not?

The thing is I can't see the way ahead. Not as far or as clearly as the Morrigan does, anyway. I don't think any of us can outclass a goddess of prophecy. When the Morrigan thrusts initiation upon us, it is a leap of faith. Each time it has forced me to ask myself, "Do I trust her?" I know the answer probably sounds obvious. But faith is something Neopagans can have issues with. There are a few reasons for this. I think in part it is because *faith* is a word we connect to the religions we might have grown up in, in which blind faith in scripture was a requirement. But faith is a component of any religion, Paganism included. Belief is easy; faith is hard. Faith requires trust. As a magical community, we are used to having the mindset that we don't always need the gods. Our fate is in our own hands. We have magic, after all, so we can create our own futures and destiny, right? We don't like giving up the control. Being a priestess inherently means giving up some control over to the gods you serve. Faith requires that we trust that the gods can see a clearer picture and that the direction they are pointing us in is the right one. The thing is you really have no way of knowing if it is all going to work out.

I think when it comes down to it, most people would say no. They don't trust the gods enough to put their life in their hands. And that's okay. It's not a requirement of worshiping the gods, but it is part of being a priest. Therein lies both the price and the blessing. To gain greater knowledge of a deity, to go farther down the rabbit hole, you have to give up some of your control.

The Morrigan has given me many choices, many chances to choose whether I trusted her and let her guide me to where I am supposed to be. Each time has been a leap of faith. Sometimes there were soft landings and rewards, and other times I hit some rocks along the way down and learned some hard lessons. But each leap of faith, each initiation, led me to greater understanding of my work. It has taught me what true service to the gods is like, and that serving the goddess of sovereignty and war has both its costs and its blessings.

If we believe the warning that those who seek to be changed by the Otherworlds will either come out of the experience dead, mad, or a poet, then we have to accept that there is an element of danger to initiation. Being in service to the Morrigan has changed me more times than I can count. There is no guarantee who we will be when we come out the other side, or when we emerge from the faery mound. All we can do is have faith and trust. Who knows where the next leap of faith will take me? Dead, mad, or a poet?

Navigating Initiation

Initiation is innately personal. Perhaps you will find similarities in your initiation to my own, both the chosen and the spontaneous ones. Or your experiences may be vastly different. While initiation is personal and fits with the path each person is walking, there are some common themes that are important to keep in mind when initiation presents itself.

What Is Initiation?

Initiation, put simply, is both the beginning and the end of a phase of development. It marks that you have reached a certain point in your development or work and are undergoing the process of both marking that developmental stage and starting a new deepening level of work. What I can't emphasize enough is that initiation isn't leveling up. It doesn't make you a better priest, devotee, or magical practitioner. It's just the beginning of a new phase of spiritual work. Initiation is about you and your path and your connection to deity. The experiences you have may not even be ones you will tell others about or share with anyone, instead serving as personal spiritual mile markers. It's not about showing how spiritual you are to someone else. It's all about you and your path.

Change Is Part of the Bargain

Initiatory experiences do not come without a cost. Giving something up is usually part of the bargain. When you graduate from school, you are giving up your life as a student for an adult life and beginning a career. The devotee who becomes a priest most likely will give up some freedoms and become bound to certain vows and agreements with deity. Most of the time this is the thing we let go of and the thing we don't mind giving up. We are excited to move on to a new phase. But it is important to recognize that all beginnings start with something ending.

Know What You Are Getting Yourself Into

I don't think that I really knew what I was getting into when I went out into the woods and offered my vows to the Morrigan. I knew I wanted to do it, that I felt called to do so. But I could never have imagined where it would take me or how much it would change me. Any initiation, whether it is one you initiate or one that is spontaneous, requires a lot of thought. Consider that the promises and words you speak will shape you for far longer than you expect.

Sought-After Initiation versus Spontaneous Initiation

There is nothing wrong with self-initiation. I certainly have done this and felt my oaths to the Morrigan were accepted. In many ways you have to be the first one to start off the process. Not all the time, but we do have free will, and I think taking the first step on the path is our choice. From my own experiences, I can say that it is only a first step. The initiations the gods place before us aren't always expected, but it is our choice whether or not to accept them. I think knowing that this process happens and that the unexpected should be expected at some point softens the blow a bit. In my case, I felt like I was playing catchup, only putting the puzzle pieces together later on instead of just realizing that this was a natural part of the process of working deeply with deity.

I see many devotees of the Morrigan talk about how she challenged them at certain pivotal moments or how after they did deep personal work, she just showed up out of the blue in a different aspect, which heralded them starting a new phase of their spiritual work. We acknowledge that these events happen, but we just don't call them what they are: initiatory experiences.

You Can Say No

Yes, you can say no to a god. Really, you can. Just because a god calls to you or decides they want you to take on a particular work or task doesn't mean you have to do it. The choice is still yours to make. If we didn't have free will, the gods wouldn't be asking us at all anyway. Negotiation is something you can do as well. You have a say in the terms of an agreement, even with the divine.

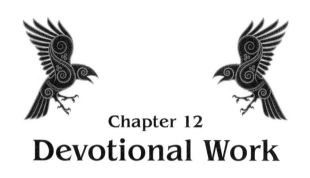

Chapter 12
Devotional Work

Some part of me understands I am dreaming. I am walking toward the edge of a cliff. Little grows here, but there are little shoots and patches of grass sprouting up in the cracks of the gray stones that make up the cliff's edge. The sky has a hazy twilight feel to it, and it is filled with crows. I wonder if it actually is twilight or just looks that way with so many of them in the sky. Some distant part of me is concerned that I am not afraid of being so close to the edge. I don't like heights; I should be afraid. But I'm not. Quite the opposite: I feel drawn to something. That something is a hooded figure that stands on the edge of the cliff. It is hard to look at her and make out any details, because she is constantly changing. She is both a woman and the swirling mass of black birds at the same time. I am drawn to her so strongly. Like a moth to flame, I want nothing more than to be closer to the source of energy that is this being. She feels like power and strength and home. Dangerous and comforting at the same time. "Who are you?" I ask, and she replies, "The Morrigan." The name is unfamiliar. Then I wake up.

I never expected to have a patron deity. I'm only a few years into my journey as a Pagan, and of course I already think I have a solid handle on things. I'm just going to work with all sorts of different gods and not be so locked down to one. Of course, that's not what happens.

I dream of the woman who turned into crows the night I tell the group of women I've been working with that I don't plan on taking a patron deity. But now I am not so sure. I feel a little blindsided. So I make an altar. I find a beautiful black silk altar cloth. I find a small statue, the only one that seems made for this "dangerous" goddess everyone warns me not to talk to. I pick out just the right incense I feel is appropriate. I arrange the statue just so. Everything is perfect.

I sit in front of my altar and I'm at a loss for what to actually do. I built the altar. Something is supposed to happen, right? I just sit there and somehow that connection just happens. Except it doesn't, and I'm panicking, thinking I've done something wrong. I try to imagine her before me. I wonder what exactly I am reaching out toward. The energy of the being I felt in my dream? How am I supposed to welcome the Morrigan's presence to my altar, to my life, when I don't even know where she is or how to locate that feeling of connection? Where does the Morrigan dwell, and how do I pinpoint that godly GPS location?

I light the candle on the altar and worry that I am doing this wrong. At a loss, I just start talking to her, or no one—I'm not sure yet. "How do I find you?" I ask. I am more than a little surprised when there is an answer: "I am no further away than the beating of your own heart."

———

Sometimes the hardest part of public priesthood is keeping your own personal connection to deity well nourished. It's easy to get lost in tending to the needs of others. I know the Morrigan well enough to be able to be that bridge and help facilitate that connection to her for others. I can call on her during ritual, in which the focus has everything to do with what the other person or people around me need. But the focus in all those things is other people. Those leading the ritual will always have a different experience than those simply attending. It's no less moving or sacred, but you are making sure the energy moves in a certain way, that things happen at a certain time. You have your psychic ear to the ground, listening to what the gods want. In every ritual, no matter how planned out it is, something unexpected always happens. Sometimes it is something small. The Morrigan wants me to say a certain thing or do a certain thing a different way than we initially planned. It's the nature of ritual. We are calling out to the gods to honor them, so it's only natural they might guide our hands for part of it. But again, my focus as a priestess is outside of myself.

More often than not, I have to remind myself to tend to my own relationship to the Morrigan. It's easy to say that my service to others is part of that relationship—it is—but it's not the whole of it. It is easy for serving others to become something all consuming. We don't have clergy whose sole focus is the spiritual. Unless you find someone who is independently wealthy, we really ask for all the benefits and services of clergy without feeling the need to pay for the time, effort, and living expenses of that clergy member. That means almost all Pagan clergy will divide their time between their religious calling and making a living in other professions, as well as spending time with their families and the rest of the business of a busy life. And somewhere in there, they carve time out for a personal relationship with deity. That's a lot. Taking time for oneself, and a relationship to the Morrigan, can be trying at times. If one is hosting several public events and rituals and running a group, organizing all those things can become all one focuses on. Then somewhere along the line you become burnt out and exhausted, before you realize that you have spiritual needs too. You need time to do your own personal work.

When I forget that lesson, the Morrigan is the first to remind me that she isn't just interested in what I can do for her, but she is interested in me and my own intrinsic value. In many ways, we are taught from a young age our value is in what we can do or can be for others. It's a hard lesson to unlearn. It is important to remember that the gods are interested in us for who we are, they see us fully, and something about us resonates with them, just as something within the divine resonates with us. Being a priestess doesn't mean being a slave. I would still be the Morrigan's, even if I wasn't her priestess.

Personal connection sounds easy, yet it is often the hardest thing we can do. Most books suggest making offerings and standing in front of your altar to seek a connection. I suggest the same. But I also remember taking such advice and standing in front of my altar wondering, well, what do I do now? How do I know it's working? Is something wrong if nothing happens? After all, we are trying to connect with something intangible. How do we know we are making the connection? Where does the Morrigan dwell? How do we find and feed that inner connection with her?

Building the Bridge

The honest truth is it doesn't matter where you decide to stop and open yourself up to the Morrigan. It is more about taking the time to do so on a regular basis. It could be in your car, on the couch while drinking your morning coffee. It could be out on a trail while surrounded by nature. It could be a quiet moment at your desk at work during a really bad day. It doesn't really matter, except that you do it. The trick to opening that line of communication is that it can't always be about asking for things. It is just about the connection and reaching out to the presence of the Morrigan. Then, after a while, things will start to flow through that connection. All too often we just don't give the gods a word in edgewise. There is so much going on in our lives and so many things we need that we get caught up in asking for those things or asking for help. There is a place for that, but you need to build a connection to the Morrigan first before she can help you with those things. You must learn to hear her voice first. You have to build that bridge between her and yourself.

It's actually pretty hard to sit in front of an altar or try to talk to a god and not ask for something. I often catch myself when I do so. It's like clearing your mind to meditate, but while you do so, your "to-do list" for the day starts going through your head. Before you know it, your mind isn't clear anymore but planning out the rest of the day. It's important to remember the Morrigan is a goddess, not a cosmic vending machine. Don't get me wrong. There are plenty of times I ask her for things, pray fervently for things, and make offerings to her, asking for her aid. But if I didn't sit still and listen, if I didn't take the time to hear her voice, then so much of my relationship with her would be silent and empty. It would be a one-way conversation. There is power and awe in simply experiencing the gods, and having that line of communication well-tuned is vital to being a priest.

A good starting point is to take a few minutes a day and just sit quietly and connect to the Morrigan. Don't ask her for anything. Just spend the time reaching out and touching her vast presence. What does that presence feel like? Does it have a feeling connected to it, a color, a sound? What defines that presence for you? The more you do this the more it will become second nature. At first you might not feel anything. Don't give up. Simply keep showing up, keep doing the work, and eventually, you will find her voice and presence. It is not a contest: it doesn't matter if it takes a few days or a month or a year to get to that point of connection. All that matters is the effort and devotion you are offering.

Responses and Silence

Many of us put a lot of focus on learning how to hear the Morrigan's voice, but building a devotional relationship is more than just opening a phone line.

What comes through that line of connection and what we do with it are important too.

You will often hear devotees of the Morrigan talk about how she can show up and turn your life upside down. This is certainly true. But remember, the point is to learn to be able to listen to her, hear her voice, and understand her messages so she doesn't have to turn your life into a tornado to get the message across. The problem is these big shake-ups are validating. It's proof of the reality and existence of the Morrigan and the gods themselves. Sometimes that validation can be addictive. For some, that will mean they don't start listening to the messages they receive until the Queen starts stirring up some chaos.

Silence is also another thing to consider. When you start out, it may be a long time before you hear the Morrigan's voice, and that is okay. Connection doesn't come instantaneously; you will have to work at it. But when you already have that connection and there is a sudden silence, that can be daunting. Continually ignoring messages will probably lead to a point when she stops talking, because the gods will only repeat themselves so many times before they hold up their hands and say, "Fine, don't listen. You're on your own." It doesn't mean the silence will be forever, but it does mean you have to make amends and try to rebuild that connection again. In many ways I think this stems from our concepts of the gods and divine parents. Yes, I've called the Morrigan *Mother* many times, but our mortal concepts of parental responsibility include that they will always be there and that the relationship is *obligatory*. In contrast, the gods aren't obligated to us. We can choose to welcome them into our lives, or we can choose to push them away. It is possible to drive them away or turn our backs on them if we are hardheaded enough. This doesn't mean you have to do everything they say. But if you keep asking a question, get an answer, and keep on asking the same question because you don't like the answer, eventually she will stop talking. It's a scary thought that the gods might not always be at our side to help us simply because we exist and made some offerings several years ago. The point is that it's a relationship that needs tending like any other. It is one that, like any relationship, can end if you don't nurture it.

Daily Devotions

If you have a busy life, daily devotions can be difficult. Even carving out a few minutes can be hard to do. For some, scheduling a certain time of the day to do devotions is helpful.

What works for me is committing to doing something each day. What that something is varies. Sometimes is it more complicated, and sometimes it is something very simple and quick. How much time I have in a given day might vary a lot depending on what I am doing or how many times I hit the snooze button in the morning. What is important is that I do it. It might be a devotional prayer and a half hour meditating when I get home in the evening, or on a busy night it might be spending a few quick moments silently communing in front of my altar. I'm also honest with myself. I'm a night owl, and no matter how much people tell me doing their devotion in the morning is the best thing and it sets up the day for them, it just doesn't work for me. When I arrive home in the evening, relaxing and recollecting my thoughts just works best to recenter myself to my connection with the Great Queen. Find what works for you. If you feel you cannot stick to doing something every day, pick a particular day of the week that will be your day to do devotional work.

Be creative in your daily devotions. They can be something as simple as a prayer that you have written for the Morrigan. It might be spending a few minutes connecting to the Morrigan and focusing on what your personal connection to her means for you. It could be making a small offering. Or it might be a specific action you do in honor of the Morrigan today, an act of bravery or doing something that has scared you in the past. It doesn't have to be a grand gesture. Sometimes having a difficult but needed conversation with someone can be an act of bravery. You will likely find many more things to add to that list. The point is don't limit what devotion can be.

Morrigan Daily Devotional

The following is a daily devotion I use often. It can be something you do in front of your altar but doesn't have to be. I've used it before rituals or before making an offering to help myself focus on the connection between myself and the Morrigan, but it can be done anywhere.

In this devotion you will be vibrating the names of the Morrigan. Vibrating a name will be different for everyone. It can require a little bit of practice, especially if you are like me and are musically challenged. When you vibrate a name, you are stretching out the vowels and elongating the name or word. Morrigan, for example, would be *Moooor-eeeee-gaaan*. You should feel this in your diaphragm when doing so. The pitch one can hold a note for the longest will differ from person to person. Take some time to find where your voice is the most comfortable.

Stand comfortably and bring your hands above your head. Form a triangle with your fingers so that your index fingers and thumbs touch, and so the point of the triangle is facing upward. Then vibrate:

An Morrigan[47]

Keeping your arms straight, sweep your arms down and around the sides of your body, as if you are drawing a giant circle around yourself. Continue to vibrate her names as you move your arms.

Anu

Macha

Badb

---

47.   *An* means "the" in Irish. If you are more comfortable saying *the* instead of *an*, then do so.

You do not have to make the circle with your arms quickly. You are doing this devotion with intention; nothing should be fast. I begin to vibrate *Anu* as my arms reach shoulder level, *Macha* when they are parallel to my waist, and *Badb* when they are parallel to my hips. As you vibrate, see her power and presence encircling you and surrounding you. Complete the circle by bringing your hands together to form another triangle over your groin, this time with the thumbs and index fingers pointing toward the ground.

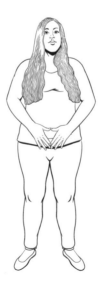

Next you will bring your hands toward your chest, and as you do so, twist your thumbs around one another with your fingers out to either side. This gesture will look a little like what you would do to make a bird shadow puppet with your hands, or in this case a "raven." Bring your hands in this raven gesture to rest on your chest over your heart, saying:

> *May I be encircled in your presence this day*[48]
> *As Macha's brooch encircles the land*
> *As Badb's wings encircle her warriors*
> *As Anu's sovereignty encircles the mighty*
> *May it be so, today, tomorrow, and forever*

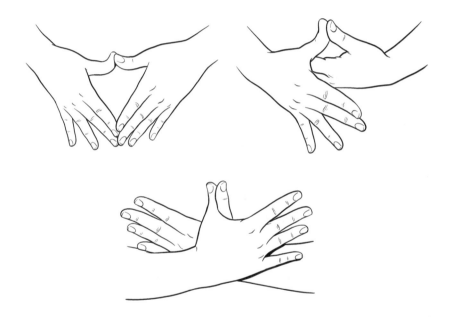

Morrigan Lesser Banishing Ritual of the Pentagram

The following is my own version of a Morrigan-based Lesser Banishing Ritual of the Pentagram (LBRP). Many ceremonialists and students of the Kabbalah will know the LBRP can be a powerful tool both in magical work and as a daily magical practice. You do not need to be familiar with Kabbalistic practices to

---

48. This can be tweaked depending on the day or your preferences. *Presence* could be replaced with *protection*, *divine grace*, *wisdom*, *wings*, *magic*, and so on.

be able to use this in your devotional practices. It is simply the same magical technology filtered through a different lens. You could do this in a group setting if you liked, with all participants intoning or with a single person leading the exercise and doing the intoning. In my own practices I use it in the morning or evening prior to making offerings at my altar. I have also used it to clear a space of disruptive energy prior to doing ritual work. Other days when I feel my own energy is off balance, I use it to cleanse my energetic field.

The LBRP calls upon angelic beings connected to the compass directions and involves vibrating the many names of God in Hebrew as a way of banishing negative or unwanted energies and beings. Instead of using the traditional Kabbalistic Cross, we will be using pieces of the Morrigan's prophecy from *The Second Battle of Moytura* as well as vibrating the various names of the Morrigan. In place of the archangels, we will use the four treasures of the Irish gods and the gods connected to them:

- Claíomh Solais, the sword of Nuada, which no enemy could escape
- Undry, the bottomless cauldron of the Dagda that never was empty
- Gae Assail, the spear of Lugh that never missed its mark
- Lia Fáil, the stone that cried out when the rightful king touched it

Of the four, the Lia Fáil has no deity specifically connected to it. Since it is connected to the land, I have used Ériu as the deity called upon for this item. Ériu is another daughter of Ernmas, like the Morrigan, and a goddess who has lent her name to the land of Ireland. While I use the English translations for lines of the Morrigan's peace prophecy, you could just as easily say them in the original Irish if you prefer; the same goes for the names of the four treasures.

You will need a dagger or athame, but if you don't have one available, using your hand to draw the pentagrams is just as good.

Begin by standing with your feet slightly apart. Imagine a brilliant white light descending from above to touch your forehead. Raise your left hand above your head as you intone:

Peace as high as the sky

Hold your right hand pointing down to the earth, palm out. See the white light continuing down through your body and to your feet as you intone:

Sky to earth

Bring your hands together over your heart to form a triangle with your thumbs and index fingers touching and pointing up, palms facing outward. Intone:

Earth under sky

Hold your hands outward to either side. See another brilliant ray of light descending to fill your right hand. Intone:

Strength in everyone

See yet another brilliant ray of light descend to fill your left hand. Intone:

A cup overflowing

Take a moment to breathe in this light, then intone:

May it be so nine times eternal

Facing the east, draw a banishing pentagram in the air with your finger or athame, then vibrate:

Morrigan

Imagine that your voice echoes across the universe, banishing negative or unwanted energy. See the Morrigan standing in front of you proud and strong.

Tracing with the athame from east, turn toward the south. As you move the athame, see a brilliant white light following to form a circle. Facing the south, draw a banishing pentagram in the air with your finger or an athame, then vibrate:

Macha

Imagine that your voice echoes across the universe, banishing negative or unwanted energy. See Macha standing before you: regal, a torc around her neck, and sword in one hand.

Continue tracing a circle with the athame, moving from the south toward the west.

Facing the west, draw a banishing pentagram in the air with your finger or an athame, then vibrate:

Badb

Imagine that your voice echoes across the universe, banishing negative or unwanted energy. See Badb standing before you, her river ford in the distance behind her, raven hair flowing down her shoulders.

Finally, continuing to trace the circle with your athame, turn toward the north. Facing the north, draw a banishing pentagram in the air with your finger or an athame, then vibrate:

Anu

Imagine that your voice echoes across the universe, banishing negative or unwanted energy. See Anu standing before you; the hills that bear her name, the Paps of Anu, are behind her.

Trace the last part of the circle as you return to the east, completing the circle of brilliant white light. Instead of calling upon angels, we will instead call upon and surround ourselves with the four treasures of the Tuatha Dé Danann and the gods who wield them. You can point your athame at each direction as you say the following, or simply see each of the treasures in the appropriate place around you with their associated deities. See the deity next to or holding the magical item. They shine with brilliant light, their strength, power, and protection flowing into you as you vibrate the god names. Say:

Before me the sword of Nuada (NOO-ah-da)
Behind me the cauldron of the Dagda (DAG-duh)
At my right the spear of Lugh (LOO)
At my left the stone of Ériu (AIR-oo)

Take a few more moments to clearly see all the treasures and gods around you, encircling you in their light and protection. When you are ready, say:

About me shine the pentagrams
Within me shines the strength of the Morrigan and the Tuatha Dé Danann
May it be so nine times eternal

Finally, you will repeat the opening (our replacement for the Kabbalistic Cross) to finish. Raise your left hand above your head as you intone:

Peace as high as the sky

Hold your right hand pointing down to the earth, palm out. See the white light continuing down through your body and to your feet as you intone:

Sky to earth

Bring your hands together over your heart to form a triangle with your thumbs and index fingers touching. Intone:

Earth under sky

Hold your hands outward to either side. See another brilliant ray of light descending to fill your right hand. Intone:

Strength in everyone

See yet another brilliant ray of light descending to fill your left hand. Intone:

A cup overflowing

Take a moment to breathe in this light, then intone:

May it be so nine times eternal

Prayer

Prayer is another vital way to connect to the Morrigan or any deity. Prayer has a bit of a bad reputation in Paganism. We think of it as something we left behind from the religions we might have grown up with, but prayer is a vital part of all religions. It is simply another way to connect and commune with the divine. For many people, prayer helps them get into the mindset where they can open themselves to deity. Prayer invokes images and traits of deity as well as their titles and various names. It's a way to remind yourself who and what you are trying to connect to, while praising the deity at the same time.

Many people have trouble sitting down and instantly connecting. Before I was able to do that, I started to use prayer when I sat in front of my altar. I figured I shouldn't just sit there and wait for the Morrigan to do something. I needed to start the process off by telling the Morrigan I was trying to connect to her, that I wanted to honor and thank her for her many gifts. Prayer was my way of being able to "dial in" to the Morrigan. By speaking her name and reminding myself of the things she did in her myths, I could find that thread of energy and presence I recognized as the Morrigan.

We don't have any surviving ancient prayers that honor the Morrigan, although we do have a noteworthy mention of someone praying to the Morrigan in *The Bodleian Dinnshenchas*. The druid Tulchaine prays to the Morrigan, asking her to steal a cow for him so he could win the hand of his Otherworldly love, Dil. Apparently the faery woman is very attached to a particular calf born in the same hour as herself and will not come out of her mound to be with Tulchaine because she is saddened at the idea of being separated from her favorite cow. The druid's solution is to ask the Morrigan to take the cow from the *sidhe* mound and bring it to a field that he owned: "Tulchine was unable to carry her off until he took the ox with her. The Morrigan was good unto him, and he prayed her to give him that drove."[49] The faery woman can have her favorite pet, he can have her hand, and everyone can be happy. I find it rather amusing for someone to pray to the Morrigan to basically commit theft

---

49.   Whitley Stokes, ed. and trans., "The Bodleian Dinnshenchas," *Folk-Lore* 3 (1892): 471.

for him—in the name of love, of course. All the same, it is fascinating to have a record of someone praying to her and for it to be for something other than war.

Modern devotees are only left with modern prayers. Nothing survives from the past, and that is okay. I find that writing my own prayers can be an act of devotion and connection in itself. The following are some of the prayers I have used over the years. You can use them as is, change them to your liking, or create your own. Also included are a few prayers from fellow devotees I work with.

Macha Prayer Cycle

On my altar I have different statues and pictures to represent the different faces of Macha. After each stanza is spoken, an offering is poured or given to that face of Macha.

Macha, Mighty Queen
Woman of sidhe
Who brings blessings to those who are kind
And curses the wicked
Macha of the sidhe, be with me this day
And always

Macha Mong Ruad
Battle Crow
Fierce Queen
Whose brooch spans the track of Emain Macha
Macha Mong Ruad, be with me this day
And always

Macha of the Tuatha
Weaver of spells
Clearer of plains, builder of mounds
Who teaches us to create anew
You who know the cost of sacrifice
Macha of the Tuatha, be with me this day and always
Macha, fierce raven queen, may your blessings be upon me

Prayer to Cath Badb

Badb, lady of the battlefields
You who claim your portion of the dead
Badb, whose words echo across the din of battle
You who both proclaim the peace
And incite bloody frenzy
Badb of prophesy
Who sees all that has been and will be
Your sister Nemain at your side
Screaming fury
Blood-red women
Lips stained with gore
Keening in sorrow, wailing war cries
Poisonous women, keening women,
Walking the battlefield, choosing the dead
May we know what is worth fighting for
And pursue it with your fierceness
May I mourn my losses but know how to move past sorrow
May I see with raven's eyes my way through danger and hardship

Prayer to Macha Mong Ruad

Macha Mong Ruad
Fierce raven woman
Bring me courage in dark times
May what I hold dear be in your keeping
May I stand strong against hardship
May I not give in to fear
May I know when to rise up
And when to stay my hand
Guide my steps, Macha
May you be a shield against harm
May you be a sword ready to defend
May you be a voice of wisdom
To guide me in troubled times

Prayer to Morrigan of Cruachan

Oweynagat is the name of the Cave of Cruachan, the Morrigan's cave. If you visit the Cave of Cruachan or look at a picture of it, you will notice there is a hawthorn tree growing over the entrance.

I have met you at Cruachan
Lady of Oweynagat
I have felt you in the racing beats of my own heart
Lady of madness and battles
I have seen you in the watchful eyes of the black birds
Lady of ravens, mother of crows
I have heard you in the wind
Lady of keening and sorrows
I see you in the ancient landscapes, hidden, secret
Lady who lives under the hawthorn tree
I know you by many names
Anu, Macha, Badb
Queen, warrior, poetess
Morrigan

Prayer to the Washer Woman to Let Go of the Past

Prophetess
Singing spells of power
Weaving men's fates
Red-mouthed Badb
Who washes at the ford
Wife of the Dagda
Keening one
Mourn with me
Weep with me
Wash the poison from my veins
Let the blood wash away
Let the sorrow wash away
That I may see the value of difficult lessons

That I may heal
That my heart may be whole
That I may pass through your waters
Cleansed and restored

Prayer for the Morrigan
by Ruth Doyle

Dark Mother, Great Phantom, Queen, we call you!
I am your teeth and claws
I am your soft fur
I am your wings and raven eyes
I am your scales and shedding skin
Through you I see all and feel all
You are my comfort in dark places
You are my sword and shield in battle
You are my fire and passion in love
I am of you and you are in me
May I be ever worthy of carrying your presence in the world

Prayer for One Who Has Passed
May the Morrigan wrap her wings around you
May Anu guide you on your journey
May Macha give you strength
May Badb bring you across her river to rest in peace

Prayer for Jaime
by Karen Storminger, Stephanie Woodfield, and Gina Martini

This prayer was written for a friend who passed, but you are welcome to adapt it to honor someone you have lost. *Sister* can be substituted with *brother* or a name, or it can be said to remember and honor all women who have lost their lives to domestic violence.

Badb, we come to your river
You are the primal force; your river runs through our lives
Taken too soon from us, our sister crosses the river
Wash her soul
Help her embrace your healing waters
Pour out her pain and fears and the ugliness of this world into the current
Let it flow to you
Let sorrow no longer touch her
Badb, we come to your river
We keen for our sister, for all women taken in violence
Wash her soul
She is remembered
She is loved
Her life touched us all
We keen at the river's edge for the loss of her shining soul
Her kindness, her smile
Badb, we come to your river in sorrow
In prayer, loss in our hearts
Guide our sister across your river
Let her spirit flow with the current and welcome her home

Prayer to Badb
by Karen Storminger

Jet black wings that caress my face
Your glossy mantle enveloping my soul
I call to you, Phantom Queen, and hear you whisper my name
You who wash away the blood at the river's edge
Crimson tears streaming down your face at the sorrow of it all
I come to you, and you pull me down into your cool embrace
Ripping and tearing away that which does not serve me or you
Claiming what is yours with flesh and bone
Cradled in darkness, released, we rise together
Wrapped in blackest wings of night, Badb! Hear my voice, hear my call!
Together we dance upon opposite shores, separate yet connected

I hear your call returning mine, your voice whispering in my ear,
your shriek upon the wind
With you I am never alone; be with me now
Always at my back
Always at my side
Always in my heart
May it be so nine times eternal!

Prayer to Macha in Times of Pestilence

This can be altered to be used in battling any illness but was specifically written in response to the COVID-19 pandemic.

Macha, daughter of Partholon
You who have faced plague
With the sons and daughters of the second invasion
Macha, daughter of Ernmas, one of the Morrigna
Great Queen of the Tuatha Dé Danann
Who fought alongside Nuada
With your sisters weave the magic of protection and battle
Strike down the unseen enemy
Drive out from these shores all contagion and fear
Give us strength to overcome this hardship
Give us healing, as you did Cuchulain, and make those who suffer whole
Give us your mighty protection against all harm
Great Queen, stand between us and all malady

Chapter 13
The Halidom of Macha: Oaths and Vows

The candles flicker in the small room, a gentle glow that illuminates the polished bronze of the sword pointed at my heart. I should be afraid, but I'm not. The bite of its point against my skin feels so welcoming, and I would impale myself upon it if I could. Not in a real sense—I have no death wish—but there is power there, flowing from the woman who holds it fast in her hands. The priestess is fully possessed by the Morrigan. The energy is palpable, and I would soak it in. I would let it fill me, no matter the danger. I hold my arms out welcomingly, and I lean toward the danger, because I am not standing before a mortal woman anymore, but a goddess.

This is the first year of the Morrigan's Call Retreat, a crazy idea that I didn't real-ize would eventually almost take up a decade of my life and my work as a priestess. Gathering her devotees together was something she has called me to do. So I did. After a devotional ritual to Macha deep in the woods of Massachusetts, the rest of our com-panions had returned to their cabins and tents, while I and two of the priestesses who facilitated the ritual returned to the temple we created to the Morrigan and her many guises for our stay in the woods. The little building is used as the camp's yoga studio. Most of the walls have large screens to keep out the bugs but also let the open air move through the building. It stands apart from the rest of the camp, up high on top of the mountain. This is where we have dutifully hauled our altars, swords, and statues for the Great Queen. I'm not even sure how we managed to make it up the small dirt path in the dark, but we did. We jokingly call it a "goat trail" as we navigate it, in the dark, after an exhausting ritual. Nothing is easy with the Morrigan, at least not at first.

During the ritual, one of the priestesses channeled the Morrigan in her guise as Macha, and we had called for those who wished to speak to Macha to come forward to meet Macha's challenge and offer her their oaths if they wished. I felt the need to go forward but resisted. When the ritual is over and all the participants have left for their cabins, I see my friends waiting for me by the edge of the clearing.

"Why didn't you come forward?" the friend who was channeling asks. I've been asking myself the same thing. I was helping facilitate the ritual after all. I was there to help the others move through the ritual. It wasn't about me tonight, was it? That is how we end up here, in her temple, just us three priestesses in the dark. There is more to say and more to be heard. I won't ignore the Morrigan a second time. The ritual isn't over. Not until the Morrigan says it is.

We light candles on the altars and pour offerings. There is no electricity here, and it is pitch black outside, the candles our only light. The wind blows gently through the large screened-in windows. Everything seems timeless. When I look into my friend's eyes, they are not her own. There is a vast wild depth to them. I am almost afraid to be caught too long in their gaze, but I resist looking away all the same. Her voice has a new familiar edge to it. I have heard that voice in my dreams. She seems taller, and it is perhaps the only time I have ever felt short next to my friend, who is easily a head shorter than me. She points the sword at my chest. Not just any sword: a sword forged just for her by a smith who specializes in reproductions of Bronze Age swords. A sword blessed in a holy spring in the UK and forged during a storm. Macha's sword.

"Say your oath," she says.

Those eyes look at me expectantly, and I say my oath—three, in fact. Three promises that would shape the course of my life and practices for the next several years, and I have no doubt they will continue to. Once said, an oath can't be unsaid. It's as binding as steel. Then the Morrigan speaks, and there is truth and warning in her words.

Afterward we sit exhausted on the wood floor of the temple. My friend is drained but back in possession of her own body again, the bronze sword returned to its sheath. The sounds of our friends' laughter farther down the hillside call us back to the normal world. I couldn't remember hearing their laughter or voices before. When we traveled up the goat path, everything had been silent except for the wind and our own banter. It is like we have stepped into the Otherworlds for that time, and now that the Morrigan's presence is gone, we are back in the mundane world. I still felt her in the temple, but it is not the same as someone holding part of that vast presence in their physical body. We start to make our way back down the mountainside, toward the voices of our friends. But the Morrigan's words stay with me. The feel of her blade pressed against my breast remains, as do the words of my oaths.

In *The Cattle Raid of Cooley* Fergus, the great warrior and lover of Queen Maeve, swears he will have vengeance and calls on *"macha mind,"* which he says is the point of his sword.[50] As with most Irish words, *mind,* which can be translated as "halidom," has layers of meaning.[51] It can also be translated as "blade" or an "oath."[52] Since I have in many ways changed the course of my life by taking an oath—an oath given to Macha, no less—at the point of a blade, I find this fascinating. In many ways oaths are like a blade to the chest. Once they are spoken, there are consequences to not holding true to them, just as the point of a sword holds consequences depending on its use.

It would not be until a few years after that I fully understood all of what the Morrigan had said that night or the path that my own words would set me on. That night in the woods I made a vow that was both heartfelt and one that I foolishly thought I could easily keep. I stood before the Morrigan and vowed to fight for my own happiness. Simple, right? Well, I thought so. I wasn't happy with many of the circumstances or people in my life. And some part of me felt if I just did the right spell, asked the right deity to help me, it would be easy to fix. All the puzzle pieces that I was desperately trying to force to fit together would magically connect with ease. Or perhaps my perspective would change. I couldn't really be unhappy with my life, right? I was just looking at it the wrong way. I could learn to be content. Of course, that wasn't the case. What I had to accept was that what I had to do was turn my life upside down, burn parts of it to the ground and remake myself out of the ashes.

I also made some unpopular choices, but ones that were for my own good, even if others did not like them. I left a long-broken relationship. I found one that nourished and fulfilled me. I moved and found a better job. I pulled the dead things out of my soul and realized I couldn't please everyone. That I didn't need to. Deep, powerful magic doesn't come without a cost. Healing festering scars doesn't happen until you choose to tend the wound instead of ignoring it, burning out the rot and letting it heal over. The process isn't easy,

---

50.　John Strachan and J. G. O'Keefe, "Táin Bó Cuailnge," *Ériu* 2, supplement (1905): 36.

51.　Morgan Daimler, "The Story of the Sword," *Living Liminally* (blog), July 16, 2014, https://lairbhan.blogspot.com/2014/07/the-story-of-sword.html.

52.　Daimler, *Irish Paganism,* 66.

nor is it without pain. Nor does it happen without criticism. Yet I don't regret it. I chose to fight for myself that night. I put myself first. Not everyone was happy about that, but I chose to stop placating people, to do what was right for myself despite the opinions of others. It felt like I was burning down the life I had built around me, but with the intention of rising up from the ashes, of building something stronger. Fulfilling my oath required it. At the time, I had no idea if I would succeed or not, just that I couldn't keep on going as I had been. Upholding my oath taught me that I could survive losing people who don't really care about my best interests. It taught me that I didn't have to settle for a life without joy and fulfillment. All of that was the result of holding true to something I thought was going to be easy.

I often wonder what shape my life would have taken if I hadn't spoken that oath. If the Morrigan hadn't for the most part commandeered a priestess to make absolutely certain I offered her that oath. It's not like she forced me to say those words. They were my words, after all. But I don't know if I would have done the things required to seek my own happiness if it was just simply something I wanted instead of something I was oathbound to stick true to. How many times would I have said, "Later, I'll take care of that some other day"? Would I have been able to be honest with myself about being unhappy? That something had to be done about it? I don't know if I would have, and that's a scary thought. Some part of me believes the Morrigan knew this, and knew that if I spoke those words to her, it would set into motion a certain chain of events. She is connected to prophecy, after all, and in my experience, she always knows the right time to poke or push us to set certain events into motion. Like any good chess player, she is always ten steps ahead of us.

An oath isn't something we say once and forget about. It is something we are constantly reaffirming. Something we are constantly challenged to hold true to. Upholding our promises is a constant reaffirming of our devotion to the gods and ourselves. They can be something meant to be fulfilled within a certain amount of time or something lifelong. But oaths are often treated casually. We think of them as grand pronouncements that sound good in ritual, nice-sounding suggestions that have no real-world consequences, not unlike a New Year's resolution, and we know how good people are at keeping those. How many times have you made such a resolution and failed to fulfill it? What would it be like if once the oath was spoken, you had no choice but to fulfill it?

That is what an oath to the gods is like. Perhaps even more so to ˈ
since she tends to show up in her stories to test heroes and kings,
will break their oaths when temptation is placed before them.

Oaths versus Geasa

Where the Morrigan is concerned, many times the concept of an oath and a
géis are confused. The main difference is that an oath is voluntary. It is something you decide to offer to deity, and it can take many forms: "I will do XYZ
for you," "I will do a certain thing as an act of service to you or in your honor,"
"I will travel to this place," or "I will give you an offering every Tuesday for the
next three months." Whatever your oath is, you are the driving force behind it.
No one forces you to take an oath other than yourself. The same can be said
for an oath of priesthood. You are choosing to take up the role and all it entails.
Even if the Morrigan called you to such service, you still had to say yes. There
is an element of free will involved.

A *géis* (also sometimes spelled *geas*; plural, *geasa*) is not something you
choose. A *géis* is a kind of taboo or sacred prohibition. Also, unlike an oath,
which is usually a promise of something you will do, a *géis* instead revolves
around actions you promise *not* to do. This could be not eating something, not
going to a certain kind of place, or not doing any number of prohibited actions
or activities. The terminology is Irish, but the concept of spiritual prohibitions
is found in many cultures. In mythology a *géis* was put on a hero or king by a
deity or Otherworldly being. Usually, at some point a divine or Otherworldly
being also arrives to test whether or not the person will be true to their word
and not break the prohibition. The Morrigan herself does this several times. In
most cases breaking a *géis* resulted in a person's death or great calamity around
them. Irish lore is filled with many examples of kings and heroes dying because
of breaking their prohibitions.

In a modern practice a *géis* isn't very different from what we might read in
mythology. It prohibits a behavior and is not something you specifically take
up. Something you choose would be an oath. A *géis* is given to you, whether
it be by the Morrigan, the *sidhe*, or another deity. In my experience it is something that is usually given when taking on a new level of spiritual work. This
information regarding the prohibition could be transmitted through a channeled experience, a dream, journey work, or something deity relates to you

during ritual. It has been my own experience that the terms of the *géis* have to be acknowledged and accepted by the person having the *géis* placed upon them. You can always say no. There will probably be some consequences to that, perhaps not progressing on with certain work, but you do have the right to say no.

Usually, a *géis* is inconvenient. It's not necessarily something you want to have, especially given the dire consequences of breaking it. Neither is it meant to be something impossible to keep, just simply something you would have to make a conscious effort not to do, even when it puts you in precarious situations. It might be not cutting your hair or not eating a certain type of food. It could be not doing a certain action or not being able to enter a certain kind of place. It complicates life. Not having a *géis* is far from a bad thing. It doesn't mean you aren't a good enough priest any more than it makes a priest with a *géis* a better or more important priest.

For example, my partner has a *géis* from the Morrigan that forbids him to kneel in submission before man or god. This sounds easy, right? How often does one need to kneel before anyone? If you think a *géis* is easy, just wait, because the gods will prove to you why it is not. One night we attended a ritual whose focus was various historical and divine queens. Even though it wasn't supposed to be part of the ritual, there was a point when everyone just started spontaneously kneeling when Macha Mong Ruad was invoked. One person did it and then everyone quickly joined. There were seats in the room, so my partner was faced with the choice of sitting, kneeling, or standing. He figured sitting in the presence of a queen would be considered rude, so that was out. He could kneel like everyone else and break his *géis*. Kneeling would have been the easiest thing to do and the option that would not have made him stick out, but he would be breaking his word to his goddess. So he stood. His agreement with the Morrigan was more important than what a group of strangers would think about him. Let's just say that it is super awkward when you are the only one standing in a large room with fifty other people kneeling and you aren't going along with the crowd. Afterward, we ended up chatting with those hosting the ritual to explain why he needed to stand so the reasons behind it would be understood. Again, a *géis* isn't supposed to be easy. By keeping it, you are keeping faith with the Morrigan or whatever deity has placed such a prohibition on you. And the gods have a way of putting us in situations we would have never expected to have been in where we need to prove we will be honorable and uphold our promises.

Both oaths and *geasa* remind us that our words mean something. The upholding of our word is a show of our character. While they are similar it is important to understand where they differ. That element of testing is something I do not find as prevalent in oaths. A *géis* seems to have the tendency to be tested by the being who laid the prohibition in the first place, while an oath is up to you to carry out. Both have consequences for being broken, but you are somewhat left to your own devices to work out the keeping of an oath. Oaths tends to have a time limit on them in some, but not all, cases. Once the task or time period requirements are fulfilled, the oath is completed. A *géis* generally is lifelong. In the myths removing them usually involves breaking them and bringing on disaster. In a modern practice I would approach a *géis* as something intended to be permanent. The deity could lift it completely or lift it and place another one in its place, but again the deity has the majority of the control.

Elements of an Oath

As we have already established, an oath is something you choose to offer and choose how to craft the wording of. A *géis* is given to you whole cloth, and you aren't writing the terms or the rules. As always, the fine print in any contract is important. There are several things to take into consideration when offering an oath to the Morrigan.

Time Limits and Specifications

Learn from my mistakes. Not that I regret the oath I gave the Morrigan in the slightest, but I was definitely not thinking when I made it. It came from the emotion of the moment. That isn't always bad, but it can get you in a lot of trouble. If you haven't already noticed, I didn't specify a time frame, so my oath still stands now. It's something that I will always be working toward fulfilling because I, not thinking, made it an indefinite promise.

I have a friend who offered a grand oath to the Morrigan that she would visit Ireland by a particular birthday. That birthday came and went, and she ended up not having the money to go on the trip by the appointed day. Lo and behold, things started going crazy in her life. A few cases of bad luck turned into an unending string of bad luck. You might think this sounds petty. Okay, she couldn't afford the trip and she didn't plan ahead to be able to make sure she had the funds to go. Life happens. Shouldn't the Morrigan give her a break? Life does happen, but it wasn't really about the trip. It was about her saying she'd do something to a god, then she didn't do it. It's a breaking of trust. We expect the gods to keep their words to us, so we need to be just as accountable. I think if she had renegotiated with the Queen and made a very worthy offering in place of the trip, it would have gone more easily for her. But she didn't. It was like she was sneaking home after curfew and tiptoeing with her shoes off, hoping not to get caught out by the Morrigan. Maybe she'd just forget that silly thing I said? Nope. So my friend made offerings. She started saving up money, and the next year she went on the trip she promised. Not surprisingly, the string of bad luck ended the moment she bought her ticket.

Being specific is a good idea when making an oath. Have a specific time frame in mind. Don't leave things open-ended. If you leave something open-ended, deity may take you up on completing whatever you have offered them sooner than you expected. Also don't make it an impossibly grand task. You don't have to impress the Morrigan with something grand; you just have to follow through.

Whom Are You Offering It To?

I have made different oaths to different goddesses that form the Morrigan. What I have promised Macha is very different from what I have offered Badb. It is a good idea to understand the temperament and personality of which of the Morrigans you are making an oath to. There are certainly sides of her that are more forgiving than others, so it is important to understand who you are dealing with.

Negotiate

In one visionary experience, the Morrigan specifically told me not to be afraid to negotiate with her. There is some historic precedence across cultures for oaths being taken on when asking for a boon from a deity. In my current practice, when I do take an oath, it is usually this kind of oath. It is a kind of reciprocity. I will offer you this boon if you, in turn, grant me a boon. The catch, of course, is you have to fulfill your side of the bargain regardless of whether or not the deity chooses to fulfill the boon you are asking for.

When Oaths Are Broken

Sometimes we mess up. Sometimes we don't mean to break an oath and we do. In mythology we see kings and heroes meeting untimely ends when this happens. What can we do to make amends when we break faith or mess up? Of course, the best safeguard is keeping your oath, but there are things you can do to try to make amends. Making a significant sacrifice as recompense is a good start. For many, a sacrifice is wine or burnt incense. These are offerings, but they are things we can fairly easily obtain. Something personal and meaningful or something that takes great effort to create or find would be the kind of offering that is appropriate when trying to make amends. It doesn't have to be a physical item. It can be something you do as well. Throwing a precious ring you have had for years that has personal meaning instead of a handful of incense into a fire, for example, is a real sacrifice. The value of what is being offered needs to exceed the offense given.

Part 4

Sorcery and
Ritual Craft

The Morrigan is referred to as a sorceress more than once in her mythology. Sharpening our magical skills comes with being a devotee of the Morrigan. A very large part of the work of any public priestess will be crafting group rituals. Whether you are only working with a small private group or leading a ritual at a Pagan convention, public event, or private gathering, there are many things to consider when creating a dynamic and meaningful ritual experience. All too often group rituals are treated as larger versions of solitary rituals, an approach that rarely works well. We will look at how to honor the Morrigan in group rituals and take a look at some of the rituals I have created for group work over the years.

Ritual craft is only one aspect of the magic we can weave with the Morrigan. When the Morrigan uses her magic in her mythology, it is to transform others and herself. She chants battle magic and weaves curses. We will explore what is at the core of the Morrigan's magic and how curse work can be a practice to restore justice. Although a somewhat taboo topic to modern Pagans, curses were not so taboo to our ancestors. Cursing is also not something one should undertake without a certain skill set and understanding of the mechanics of magic.

Whether it is the magic woven together in group ritual or solitary sorcery, magic is a vital part of a devotion to the Morrigan.

Chapter 14
She Sung Spells of Power: Curse Work and the Morrigan

*W*e are celebrating a birthday, and as we all give our food orders to the waitress, I try to pay attention to my friend with senses other than my eyes. Something feels wrong. Her health has been a problem, and stress in other areas of her life seems to be piling up. Something is always happening to her, and it seems like an unusual onslaught of bad luck.

I see threads around her, knots upon knots, weighing her down. It feels like a dark, angry force is at the edge of her aura syphoning energy away. Another of our friends notices it too, so we ask her about it. Every time we ask her about what we are sensing, it's as if she forgets, another topic is brought up, or she seems to feel ill. She isn't avoiding the topics. Instead it's like something is making it difficult for her to talk about it, to concentrate on it.

A family member of our friend uses magic in destructive ways. They are not a practitioner of any particular path but someone who likes to use magic to get their way, to harm, and to settle petty grievances. We all think the family member has done something to our friend. It may not even have been intentionally harmful, or perhaps it was. It doesn't really matter. It is clearly causing all sorts of problems. Something needs to be done about it.

We all return to my house and go to work. It's fairly simple, our curse breaking, our driving out of whatever is sucking on her like an energetic leech. We run an egg over her body to absorb the energy we are breaking and banishing. I run my hands a few inches above her body. I feel the Morrigan's presence flowing through me. Badb stands on one side and Macha on the other. I call on their power to cut the threads of the curse, to send it back to the person who has woven it. I feel Macha's strength and strong countenance, and with it I drive out the evil. I feel Badb's fury and whirlwind of shrieking energies; it helps me rip and break the knots.

Later we have our friend throw the egg out the window of her car at a crossroads. Slowly, things start getting better for her. She takes other measures to protect herself as things improve. This is how it goes with curses. More often you are breaking one than laying one on someone. But magic is magic, and not understanding baneful magic is like tying a hand behind your back and hoping for a fair fight. I have called on the Morrigan for justice, both in the making and breaking of curses. This will not be the first time or the last time I will do so.

———

There is no argument that the Morrigan possesses powerful magic. She and her sisters rain down fire and blood on the enemies of the Irish gods, she transforms those who anger her into features of the land, and she curses the Ulster men for their disrespect. Although only the last is outright called a curse, it can be argued that all the magical feats mentioned here are kinds of curses, or a form of baneful magic that follows a particular type of pattern.

In the *Dindshenchas*, which recounts tales explaining place names, there is a story about the woman Odras and how she was transformed by the Morrigan's magic into a river. Odras has a penchant for falling asleep at inopportune times. She falls asleep while watching her husband's cattle, and while she sleeps, the Morrigan comes and takes her prized bull named Slemon. Slemon's name means "slippery," which is amusing since Odras can't seem to keep hold of him, and he will keep slipping between her fingers as the story goes on. Upon waking, Odras sets out to steal the bull back from the Morrigan. Probably not the best idea in the world. She almost reaches the Cave of Cruachan, which she knows is the Morrigan's home, when she decides to take another nap. The Morrigan of course takes this opportunity to thwart the woman's attempts to take back the bull. While Odras sleeps, the Morrigan sings spells over the woman and transforms her into a small river: "The horrid Morrigan out of the cave of Cruachu, her fit abode, came upon her slumbering. . . . The owner of the kine chanted over her, with fierceness unabating … every spell of power: she was full of guile. The forceful woman melted away toward Segais in a sleepy stream."[53]

There are several interesting things here. The Morrigan is referred to as the "owner of kine," or cattle, insinuating the Morrigan had a right to take the bull. When she transforms Odras into a river, she does so by singing spells of power. We might think of this as nothing more than descriptive detail to the story, but this fits well with how the Morrigan uses her magic and could very likely indicate she is using a specific type of Irish magic.

There is a great deal of poetry spoken by the Morrigan in Irish lore. The prophecy she speaks after *The Second Battle of Moytura*, when she predicts peace followed by hard times, is referred to as a poem, and she recites a poem elsewhere in the same text when she incites the kings of the Tuatha to fight fiercely in battle. To modern eyes they seem like long poetic speeches or monologues, but they are a very specific kind of poetry: the *rosc*. As we have already discussed, the Irish believed poets to have certain kinds of magic. There were prophetic poetic practices, but there was also poetic magic that could be used to bless or curse. We can also see this use of sung spells and poetry reflected in the Gaulish *cantlos*, which is a kind of magical song sung for the use of enchantment.[54]

Rosc poetry is a type of magic that utilizes recursive speech or chanting. There are a couple of key factors that distinguish a *rosc*. First, it is spoken in present tense, as if the speaker is in the future and the actions described have already happened. Occasionally, it is in future tense, but the idea is the same. Saying something is so, or will be so, is a way to focus our magical will to manifesting the desired result. I say it will be so, so it is. *Rosc* poetry also has a repetitive nature and a very descriptive quality. Most of the spell is a long description of what one is willing into existence. It doesn't need to rhyme but instead relies on the repetition of certain words or lines. In the Morrigan's peace prophecy (see page 62) we see words mirrored from one line of the poem in the line below it. For example, "sky to earth" is followed by "earth below sky" in the

---

53. Gwynn, *The Metrical Dindshenchas*, vol. 4, 198–99.

54. Bernard Mees, *Celtic Curses* (Woodbridge, UK: Boydell Press, 2009), 20.

next line.[55] The lines are describing how great the peace will be, that it reaches to heaven. But the style is clear. Sky and earth are mirrored from one line to the next, and the pattern of other words being repeated from line to line continues in the rest of the poem. The repetitive nature also appears in the mirroring of words or ideas in both the first line and the last. Depending on the example you are looking at, in general a *rosc* draws power from the person speaking it, although there are some that call upon a higher power to enact the desired result described in the poem.

The *rosc* was used for various purposes. The druids were said to be able to use this form of magic to heal, to interpret dreams, for blessings, and for curses.[56] When used in battle, it is referred to as *rosc catha. Rosc catha,* meaning "battle magic," is in essence a curse. You want your enemies to fail and their luck to falter. This is clear when Lugh uses the *rosc* in *The Second Battle of Moytura.* He does this while circling his own men, magically reiterating that his men will win the battle, and also cursing the enemy to fail. While saying the poem, he closes one eye, puts one hand behind his back, and hops on one foot, a posture associated with cursing. Interestingly, one of the meanings for *rosc* is "eye."[57]

The Morrigan's Curses

Now that we have established a kind of magical pattern used by the Morrigan, it is important to look at why she takes the actions she does. The curse she lays on the men of Ulster is the most straightforward. In one story Macha takes a mortal husband. It is never really clear if she is just disguised as a mortal woman or if she is presumed to be a woman of the *sidhe,* or a faery woman, in this story. She warns her husband not to boast about her, but of course he does so. When the king hears her husband boast that his wife can run faster than the king's horses, she is forced to prove her husband's boast and race the king's horses while heavily pregnant. When she asks for this task to be done after she delivers her children, she is denied this mercy. Furthermore, no one speaks up

---

55. Morgan Daimler, "The Morrigan's Peace Prophecy," Irish-American Witchcraft, *Patheos Pagan* (blog), November 17, 2015, https://www.patheos.com/blogs/agora/2015/11/irish-american-witchcraft-the-morrigans-peace-prophecy/.

56. Dáithi O hOgain, *Myth, Legend, and Romance: An Encyclopaedia of Irish Folk Tradition* (New York: Prentice Hall, 1991), 76.

57. Niall Ó Dónaill, *Foclóir Gaeilge-Béarla* (London: Colton Book Imports, 1997), 211.

for her among the Ulster men. She of course wins the race and afterward delivers twin children at the finish line. She dies as she speaks her curse, inflicting the debilitating pain of childbirth on the men in the hour of their greatest need for nine generations.[58] Although divine, the Irish gods often die in one story only to reappear very much alive in another story. While Macha isn't any the worse off for her "death," the curse on the Ulster men remains and plays a pivotal role in their ability to defend themselves in other stories.

We can see why Macha delivers this curse. She has been wronged and curses the men who would not offer her kindness or mercy. She also curses future generations of Ulster men, stating the curse will remain for nine generations. An injustice is done, and her curse is repayment for that injustice. A kind of balance is struck, and the Ulster men learn their actions have consequences, not only for themselves but for their children's children.

Arguably, Odras's transformation is also a curse. Odras tries to act against the Morrigan, who the story hints had some right to take the bull. Odras has a choice to pursue the goddess or forfeit the bull. It's not like she asked to be turned into a river, so in this case the transformation is both a punishment and curse. Although not related to the Morrigan specifically, in another Irish story, the children of Lir are turned into swans by their jealous stepmother, again a forced transformation from a curse.

When the Tuatha Dé Danann arrive in Ireland, the Morrigan and her sisters go into the Fir Bolg camp to delay them, calling down a rain of blood and fire. It's quite apparent that this is a kind of battle magic. Although we are not told how they accomplish this feat, if it follows the Morrigan's other use of magic, it is likely a form of *rosc catha* was used. That the rest of the Irish gods sent the trio of Morrigan sisters specifically to do this task also testifies to their clout among the Irish gods for being particularly skilled at magically inflicting harm.

What does that tell us, then, if almost all the Morrigan's historical uses of magic are curse work? Really, the only example in which she uses the magic of the *rosc* for something other than a curse is her peace prophecy. But this is more prophecy than magic, and it also may be related to *dichetal do chennaib*, a kind of spontaneous spoken form of prophecy.[59] She also uses her magic to heal

---

58. Kinsella, *The Táin*, 6–8.

59. See chapter 6 for more about this kind of Irish prophecy.

Cuchulain after their battle at the ford in *The Cattle Raid of Cooley*. Disguised as a hag, they offer blessings to one another and are mutually healed. This is very fitting, as one who is skilled in curses should also be skilled in blessings and the breaking of baneful magic. In many cases most magic only needs slight modification to be used for either blessings or cursing. This fits with what we are told about the *rosc*, that it could be used for blessings as well as cursing and battle magic. What can bless can curse and vice versa.

Cursing as a Modern Practice

If we can take anything from the Morrigan's use of baneful magic, it is that cursing was not taboo. It was simply another type of magic, one that the Morrigan and many of the other Irish gods engaged in. For modern practitioners, cursing is usually regarded as something distinctly different from the rest of the magic they practice. It is something forbidden and not very understood. We get much of our ideas about curses, morality, and the belief that all curses will backfire on us from a modern misunderstanding of the Eastern concept of karma. Westerners usually view karma as something that has an instant return: you do something good and good comes back to you fairly quickly; do something bad and you will quickly get something equally bad coming in return. The problem is this isn't karma as it is understood in the Eastern religions. Furthermore, Hinduism and its many branches, Buddhism, Jainism, Sikhism, and Taoism all have their own versions of how karma might be enacted in this and other lives, and the majority of them view this as something that will influence future lives and not this one.

Additionally, we have to consider that good or bad is all about perspective. There are many types of "good" magic that can have harmful results. Is it still good magic? Good intentions can very easily cause harm. You can find a more detailed discussion on those topics in regard to curse work in my book *Dark Goddess Craft*. I will not rehash those concepts here, but suffice to say, I do not believe in instant karma or the rule of three. It is also pretty apparent that the Irish didn't either. In fact, many historic peoples engaged in curse work. Archaeology alone proves that. Numerous curse tablets and other artifacts have been found across Europe and the British Isles, proving curses were a regular magical practice, perhaps even the most common type of magic practiced. It is also worth noting some of these tablets were used to curse a disease in order to cure a person of it. The idea is that the curse would only kill the disease or illness, and with the affliction being destroyed the person would become well again. A curse doesn't necessarily have to be done with ill intentions in mind or the intention of righting a wrong but can have multiple applications.

I think it is time we recognized that magic in all its forms is a manipulation of reality. It is neither good nor evil. It's what you make of it. The universe isn't going to punish us for using it. There can be backlash and unforeseen consequence in any magic, even things we see as positive magic, like healing. Thinking that magic can be put into neat little boxes of "good" and "bad" is not only morally lazy, it's also dangerous. If we deem certain magic inherently good, we won't stop to think about what we are doing or what the consequences of our "good" magic might be. We don't consider all the possibilities or outcomes our actions could create in the world. Bad things can come from good magic, and it is our responsibility to consider all the outcomes. We must use it with the understanding that all magic reshapes reality, and the ripples of what we manifest can and will cause things we did not intend.

If anything, seeing no distinction between curses and other magic teaches us to use our magic wisely, to truly consider what we are doing, and in doing so craft our magic with more care and mastery, because we understand the consequence of not crafting it well and with proper intent.

I have used curses when necessary and have no regrets. In those cases, not doing anything would have been the greater evil, in my mind. Curses should never be used for petty reasons—really, no magic should be! Magic is a tool, and there is no reason why it should not be used to even the odds when injustices are done. Sometimes magic is one's only recourse to take such actions if all other options in the mundane world are blocked. We all know that the good guys don't always win and bad people get away with misdeeds more than we would like in this world. Curses at times can be the only avenue for justice for the disenfranchised.

I don't believe I'm going to be punished for such use of magic; I simply will be responsible for the outcome, as with all my magic. Someone who believes they will be punished and will bring about horrible consequences for using such magic is basically manifesting their own belief. If you believe you will be punished, for doing something wrong…well, you are essentially writing that into your magic and helping make it manifest.

Like any magic, curse work takes skill. It is not something that a beginner should try. You need to have a very solid foundation in the mechanics of magic before you take on this kind of work. The wrong wording, the wrong implementation, and the wrong intention can each cause undesirable results. Even those who are skilled should make sure they are not using this kind of magic in the heat of the moment. Like any well-woven magic, it should be thoroughly thought out. Divinations, determination of wording and timing, consultation of deities or spirits, and many other considerations should all precede any such work, just as they all should precede any magical working that you wish to be successful.

Before we look at how to call upon the Morrigan in modern curse work, we first need to look at some of the elements of Irish curses and magic we can use in this work.

Eels and Cursing Stones

An interesting connection can be found between Irish curse work and the Morrigan's transformation into an eel. In *The Cattle Raid of Cooley*, the Morrigan promises to thwart the hero in various animal forms. When he is fighting in a river ford, she twists around his feet in the form of an eel. On the surface this doesn't look like a curse at all, but we can find some interesting similarities in another story. *The Siege of Knocklong*, or *Forbhais Droma Dámhghdire*, describes an invasion of Munster by the high king to collect tribute by force. It's a fantastic account if one is looking for descriptions of Irish magic. Druids on both sides of the conflict use various kinds of magic. The culmination of the struggle between the two forces comes when the druid Mug Ruith uses a spell that has the repetitious qualities of the *rosc* to enchant a special stone. The stone is then tossed into a river ford and turns into a giant sea eel that wraps nine times around Colpa, one of the high king's druids, binding him and destroying his weapons, thus allowing the Munster men to defeat their enemy. Here's part of Mug Ruith's spell:

> *"Bring me my poison-stone, my hand-stone, my hundred-fighter, my*
> *destruction of my enemies." ... He proceeded to put a venomous spell*
> *on it, and he recited the following rhetoric:*
>> *I beseech my Hand-Stone—*
>> *That it be not a flying shadow;*
>> *Be it a brand to rout the foes*

In brave battle.
My fiery hard stone—
Be it a red water-snake—
Woe to him around whom it coils,
Betwixt the swelling waves.
Be it a sea eel—
Be it a vulture among vultures,
Which shall separate body from soul.[60]

In his book *Celtic Curses*, Bernard Mees connects this to the Morrigan taking the form of an eel to bind Cuchulain.[61] Certainly, there is a similar theme here, conflating the magical qualities of eels for binding one's enemies.

That Mug Ruith uses a stone to cast his curse is also interesting. There is a long history of cursing stones, or *bullán* stones, in Ireland. *Bullán* means "bowl" and refers to a stone with a circular depression in it. Some are quite large, others small and semiportable. The number of depressions varies from site to site. A *bullán* may have one depression or several. In some cases, another round stone is placed in the bowl-like depression, and depending on the direction that stone is turned, it can either curse (counterclockwise) or cure and bring blessings (clockwise). In other cases, one would make a fist, put the fist in the depression, and turn the hand in the correct direction for ill or good. One could physically turn the *bullán* stone itself. Similarly, another kind of stone that has a hole in it is a hag stone, although the hole goes completely through the stone rather than being just a depression. Hag stones also have a reputation for being protection against curses.

The belief in the magic the *bullán* stones possess is still prevalent in the not so recent past. Around the end of the nineteenth century in County Cook, a dispute between a beggar woman and a farmer who'd attacked her involved a local *bullán* stone. The farmer "put forward as his defence … that 'she swore to turn the stones of Kilmoon' against him. It was believed that, if a person went

---

60. Seán Ó Duinn, trans., *The Siege of Knocklong/Forbhais Droma Damhghaire* (Cork, Ireland: Mercier Press 1992; Electronic reproduction by Corpus of Electronic Texts, transcribed and edited by Beatrix Färber and Ivonn Devine Nagai, Cork, Ireland: University College, 2014), 77, https://celt.ucc.ie/published/T301044.html.

61. Mees, *Celtic Curses*, 140.

fasting to the place and did seven rounds 'against the sun,' turning each stone in the same unlucky direction, the mouth of the person against whom the stones were turned would be twisted under his ear and his face permanently distorted."[62] Because belief in the stone's power was so strong, the magistrate agreed that the farmer had been acting in self-defense and recommended he pay the woman "a sum of money" for her damages.[63]

A modern practitioner can take several of these themes and ideas and modify them for both cursing and curse breaking.

Curse Posture

Corrguineacht is a magical posture usually connected to cursing. The person using it stands with one eye closed or covered and one hand behind their back, while standing on one leg. Lugh uses this posture while using rosc catha, or battle magic, when fighting his grandfather in The Second Battle of Moytura. In The Destruction of Da Derga's Hostel, a story detailing King Conaire's reign and how he subsequently broke all of his many geasa, we see Badb taking on this cursing posture when goading the king to break the last of his géis: "On one foot, and (holding up) one hand, and (breathing) one breath she sang all that to them from the door of the house."[64] Conaire does break his final prohibition, and it results in both the hostel being burned down and the king being beheaded.

Knowing When You Are on the Receiving End of a Curse

It is important to recognize when something malicious has been set against you. In many cases you might sense that something is wrong, but circumstances keep cropping up that prevent you from doing something about it. You get busy with work, or there is an emergency that takes your attention away from doing something about the bad feeling. When this happens more than once, it's a fair sign that something may be going on. A long string of bad luck and multiple coincidences of bad luck can also be a sign that something is

---

62. Thomas Johnson Westropp, Folklore of Clare: A Folklore Survey of County Clare and County Clare Folktales and Myths (Clare, Ireland: CLASP, 2000), 36.

63. Westropp, Folklore of Clare, 37.

64. Whitley Stokes, trans., "The Destruction of Da Derga's Hostel," Revue Celtique 22 (1901): 59. Parentheses are Stokes's.

wrong. In general, the longer it goes on, there is a kind of snowball effect, and things begin getting exponentially worse until something is done about it.

Calling on the Morrigan for Curse Work

I think there is power in using the words of a god, and you will see the Morrigan's poetry reflected in many of these curses. These words have been repeated and empowered over the ages by countless people in her name. I have used them for blessings, and I have used them for curses, as the Morrigan herself has done in the lore that remains to us. Weaving baneful magic doesn't have to be done by using the Morrigan's poems or by following the pattern of the *rosc,* but I find it effective.

You will also see the themes of curse stones, curse posture, and variations of the spells used in the *Forbhais Droma Dámhghâire.* Presented are my own preferences and techniques, which can be easily modified to your own tastes and style.

Timing

Although most of the curses that follow do not specify a time or simply imply that the curse is permanent, curse work can have a specific time frame to it. Usually, if it targets someone who wronged you, the timing could be until they make amends or pay back a debt. Again, any of the workings can be modified to accommodate a specific time frame or a task to be completed for the curse to be lifted. Sometimes wrongs can be righted, sometimes not. But in many cases, it is a good idea to add such a clause in.

Additional Things to Consider

More often one is called on by others to break curses. It is a good idea to be well versed in unraveling and breaking magic as well as building up one's own personal protections. Curses can be an avenue for the oppressed and wronged to bring about justice, but we also can't forget that many folks who use magic use it for petty reasons. Just because you have morals doesn't mean someone else does or that a person can't look past their own emotions to see that they are causing harm for the sake of harm. Not all magic users are specifically Pagan; there are many branches of magic, all of them attached to different systems of ethics.

Not understanding how curses work or how to use them only opens one up to attack from others. A skilled magic user should know both how to lay down a curse and how to break one. They should be skilled in protective magic and have magical defense in their home or on their person. Protective magic is used not only to reflect any ill magic sent against you, but also to avoid other harmful influences and energy you might come in contact with in the world. An entire book can be written on the subject of protective magic alone, but suffice to say if you practice curse work or curse breaking, it would be in your best interest to become well versed in protective magic as well.

Basic Bullán Spell Format

This basic format can be used for several different workings when combined with a spoken chant or on its own. I personally like the use of stones in cursing or the use of a cursing posture while speaking particular words. One can even combine the two by taking on a cursing posture while moving the stone in the correct direction.

You will need a bowl or mortar, preferably one made from stone, and a fairly round stone. Try to find a bowl or mortar that the stone fits well in, without there being too much room for it to move around. In a pinch one could use the pestle as the stone and move it in the desired direction to do the working. Most mortar and pestle sets are made of soapstone, and this is perfectly suitable to the task. If you can find a portable stone with a natural depression in it, even better, but as this might be hard to come by, I find using a stone bowl is just as effective.

Most *bullán* stones collect water, since they have depressions. I like to add water from a particular place that has meaning to me or a cooled tea with herbs that are meaningful to the working. You do not have to have any liquid in the bowl, but it does also aid in the turning of the stone.

You should spend some time charging the stone you use in your work. It doesn't even have to be specifically for baneful work. *Bullán* stones were connected to both casting or removing curses and to blessings. Think of it like a battery you are charging to enact whatever your will is when used. Once you have your stone and bowl in place, speak your curse or spellwork while turning the stone counterclockwise for cursing or clockwise for curse breaking or blessings. For curse work you could also turn the stone while standing in a cursing posture.

This whole procedure could be done alone or as a working within a larger ritual. Intent and your ability to focus energy toward your will is the key here, as in any kind of magic.

A Hag Stone for Protection against Curses

Hag stones are stones with holes that have been formed from the natural erosion of water. It is thought that when looking through the hole, one can see through illusions and into the realm of the faery folk. They are also well renowned for protection against curses. I have been lucky enough to find a few hag stones in the wild, a favorite one while on pilgrimage to Ireland, but you can also find hag stones in some spiritual stores and even online through eBay and Etsy. The stone can be worn on a necklace looped through the hole, or it can be kept in a pocket or in the home as a blessing and deterrent.

To bless the stone hold it in your hands, seeing it forming a protective force-field around you, your home, or whatever you want to protect. See any negative energy reflecting off the protective field. Say:

Morrigan
Curse maker, curse breaker
Be a shield to me, turning away all harm
Be a cloak of feathers to me, hiding me from harm's sight
Be a boon to me, a blessing and protector
Turn all ill and calamity away from me and mine
Curse maker, curse breaker
Morrigan
Be a shield, be a cloak of feathers, be a boon unto me

A Charm for Curse Breaking

The following is based on a spell used by Mug Ruith in *The Siege of Knocklong*, with the idea of "turning" meaning the breaking and bending of magical work done maliciously against you. If using the curse stone format, you would turn the stone clockwise, a motion of blessing and curse breaking.

Macha, curse maker, curse breaker
In your care I turn, I re-turn
I turn back that of darkness
I turn, I re-turn all ill spells
I turn all speckled spells
I turn all ill done in deed and word against me
I turn poison to purity of form
I turn high, I turn mightily
I turn that which is my adversary
I turn and twist and break to subside
I turn and twist and break to subdue
I turn and twist and break to reform and reshape
Ill fortune and poison, set upon me
Turn and twist and break
Return, return, you I now unmake
In the presence of and through the will of
Macha, curse maker, curse breaker
Twist, turn
Break

The Morrigan's Eel Cursing Stone Charm

This curse is based on the spell Mug Ruith speaks to transform the stone into a monstrous eel in *The Siege of Knocklong*. Offerings should be made to the Morrigan in her guise as a shape-shifter. As you turn the stone and say the spell, visualize the Morrigan in eel form twisting around the person in question, binding them, preventing them from causing further harm, and draining away their strength and vitality.

I beseech thee, stone
Be you a flying shadow
Be you a brand, a spear, to rout my foes
Be you a red water snake, a monstrous eel
As the Morrigan bound Cuchulain,

So too bind those who move against me
Be you a sea eel of nine coils
Which shall rend power from evil men/women
Woe to him/her around whom you coil
Nines times you wrap around my enemy
Nine times you sap their strength
Nine times you gnash your teeth
Tearing, destroying their evil
Nine times you bind their limbs
Nine times nine, a curse
Bound like the honeysuckle round the tree
That no deed or hand may be raised against me
That their deeds shall be made to fail
Be you an eel of the Morrigan's making
Be you a flying shadow
I beseech thee stone

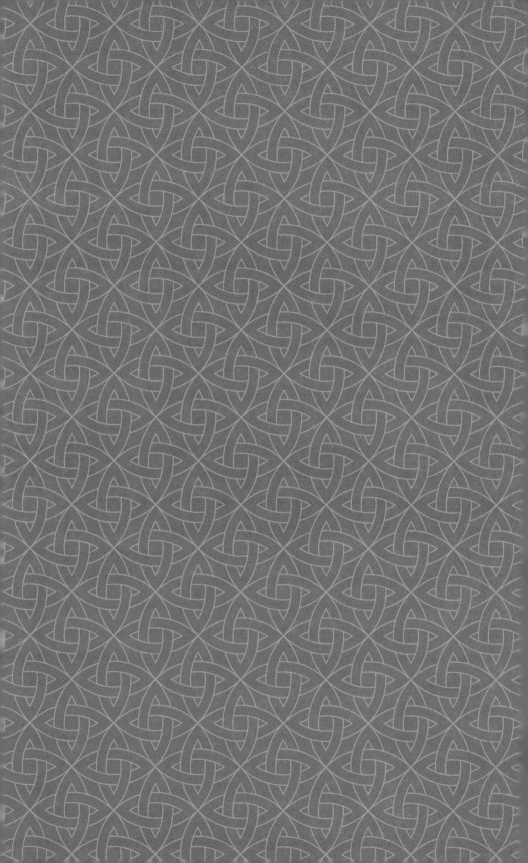

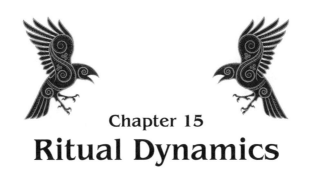

Chapter 15
Ritual Dynamics

We will be hosting a ritual for a large gathering at a conference, and my group and I have decided we need to do a practice run. All the furniture is pushed back in the living room, and we plan out who will be standing where and what will be done when. We find a few flaws—a place here where it takes too long to do a certain thing, another place where it takes too much time to place a veil on our heads—so we change things and eliminate other things.

We also practice something none of us have done before. Keening is something we have read about and people know existed, but not something many people actually do. We find one recording online of what someone thinks keening might have sounded like. We find another video of modern women practicing their own version of keening at a protest rally. So we have been practicing in our spare time, in the car, in the shower. When we all wail together, the power this ritual could carry becomes apparent. We can feel the heart-wrenching emotion behind it. As we do this in our practice ritual, my cat bolts out of her hiding spot in the bedroom. She looks at us wide-eyed, as if trying to find the source of our pain. She comes and rubs against everyone's legs and licks our hands, all motherly cat concern. She seems confused by our lack of injury and looks at us like she isn't sure if we are all sane before returning to her hiding spot. We all laugh and comment that it will be an interesting ritual.

One member of our group also tells the story of how her neighbor was watching her while she was outside making some of the rags we will use for the washer women in the ritual. She has taken a clean white sheet and splattered red paint on it with a brush to make it look "bloody." She tells him it is for Halloween, even though Halloween is months away. The description of the look on her bewildered neighbor's face makes us all laugh.

So much of what ritual is, is in the preparation. This ritual ends up being an amazingly powerful experience. But it is a group effort, one that takes lots of planning, practice, spooked neighbors, and concerned cats to create.

———

A priestess serves not only the gods but also the community. When you take on the mantle of priesthood, you will soon find there is a distinct change in your ritual practice. In my early practice my rituals were solitary, I filled all the roles, and most of the intent was focused on my own connection to deity and my personal spiritual development. A priest's focus is different. You are the bridge between the divine and the community. You become a vessel for the divine. The ritual is no longer focused on yourself but on those attending. Your experience in ritual changes as a priest. It is still rewarding, but the reward is that you are facilitating an experience for others. You become a vessel for the divine for others to experience.

The mechanics of group ritual also differ greatly from the needs of a solitary ritual. While I do some small personal rituals for myself, as a priestess the majority of my public ritual work is creating ritual for large groups. If it is a local ritual, it might be anywhere from fifteen to forty people. At some of the larger retreats and festivals that I organize or attend, I am consistently creating rituals for anywhere between ninety and 150 participants. Nothing can be further from a solitary ritual than a ritual where you have to keep 150 people focused and occupied for any given period of time—and on top of that, have them leave feeling like they have engaged in a spiritual experience.

All the rituals you will find in this chapter have been test-driven and used. Some work well for small groups and others for larger groups. Although you will find several parts to be filled in each ritual, most rituals can run smoothly with one person filling more than one role if need be. You can use the rituals as they are or change them to suit your own needs. I hope that they offer you a road map to creating your own group rituals in honor of the Great Queen.

Basics of Group Ritual

Before we look at the rituals themselves, let's talk about some best practices for group ritual. I have certainly botched rituals in my time, some quite spectacularly. Everyone does. It's how we learn. Here are some of the key things that have helped me over the years.

Triage

While I think triage is something to keep in mind for any ritual, it is especially important for those invoking the Morrigan. Ritual shouldn't just be a collection of gestures and pretty words. The whole point is to foster a meaningful experience with those participating in the ritual and the gods, as well as properly honoring the gods themselves. No one ever had a meaningful spiritual experience while bored to death. A deeply moving experience will invoke emotions within people that range anywhere from ecstasy to rage to sorrow. If someone has an emotional moment, there needs to be someone other than the priest or priestess leading the ritual that is there to care for that person. Before any ritual, it's important to assign someone to spiritual triage for your ritual. The larger the group ritual the more people you may have to put on this task. Being up-front with those participating beforehand and explaining what the ritual will entail can help your participants prepare mentally and emotionally for what will happen in the ritual.

Memorization

I know, it's not fun to memorize lines. But it's mandatory for the rituals I lead. There is nothing worse than someone looking at a cue card and jerkily delivering their lines during a ritual. It's an energy buzzkill for those watching. For the priest delivering the line, doing something like reading takes them into a completely different headspace. When you have to concentrate on reading something, you aren't keeping your mind in the headspace where you can connect and draw in deity. Trust me, memorizing your lines will lead to a smoother ritual and keep your connection to the divine more open and fluid. Also, if you memorize the ritual, you already know where you need to be and when. You don't have to check your notes to see which part is happening next.

Don't get me wrong, memorizing your lines for ritual doesn't mean the ritual will happen how you wrote it. I don't think I have ever done a group or public ritual in which lines didn't change or something happened differently than we intended. And you know what? All those rituals turned out ten times better because of it. Part of memorizing a ritual is allowing yourself to be in that headspace where you connect with deity. More often than not, deity will lead you to do whatever is needed. It may be something you never would have thought of but fits perfectly and adds depth to the ritual. Different wording to an invocation or a speaking part within your ritual by divine inspiration isn't a bad thing. Anticipate this happening and don't fight it. It's a sign that something is going right, not that something is wrong. Having a good ritual team is also key. If you are working with a group that is energetically in sync and knows each other's strengths and weaknesses in ritual it becomes easier to roll with any on-the-spot changes that happen.

Give Them Something to Do

In any ritual over twenty people, giving them something to do is key. People lose focus, get bored, and in general have short attention spans when they aren't doing anything. If you have ever gone to Disney World or any of the larger theme parks, you will notice that in the queue to get on the ride there are interesting things to look at, games built into the scenery, and aspects of the environment you can interact with. All of this is designed to make your wait time seem shorter because you are occupied and engaged in an activity. The same things are true in ritual. You need to keep everyone engaged in what is going on. Make them an active participant in the ritual, so instead of just watching the ritual, they are adding their energy and intent into the work you are doing. You want them to feel like they aren't watching a performance but instead are part of something.

There are many things you can have participants do during a ritual. For larger group rituals, you might want to decide on the activity elements first and then craft the ritual around them. If chanting is your audience participation element, try a test run. How long does it take for the chant to become monotonous? See if you can come up with more than one chant to rotate through. If you have a different kind of active element, try it out with your group and see if it runs smoothly before using it. Most importantly, make sure it's clear what you want the participants to do in the ritual. Just because you understand what's going on or what the meaning behind something is doesn't mean that they will instantly get it. For chanting, it helps to have a printout of the words on small pieces of paper to be handed out to the participants, so they don't have to memorize the chant (that's your job). Having plants in the ritual also helps people understand what they need to do. This can be a priest with a minor role in the ritual who is free to be the first one someone hands an item to when audience participation occurs and can either show or direct others in doing the task.

Do a Test Run

You don't want to work out the kinks of a large ritual the first time you are doing that ritual. Do a test run. Ask witchy friends to be ritual test subjects or have some of your ritual team play the role of a participant rather than a priest in a dry run. Ask them for honest feedback. However you do it, trust me, it is always beneficial to try out a large-scale ritual on a smaller group first. You can see what works and what doesn't and tweak things that you will be kicking yourself over later on. When you are putting words on paper and imagining things in your mind's eye, it will seem like it will run perfectly. How could it possibly go wrong? Then when you try it in real life, you realize something was too clunky there, someone tripped over that item, or no one understood the audience directions and they kept asking their neighbor in circle, "Is this what I'm supposed to do?" in a hushed whisper.

I like rituals that are meant to be done several times. Maybe it's just once a year or something you only pull out for certain a group or public work, but the more you do a ritual, the better it will become over time. Each time will be different, but it takes on its own life and your precision in executing it will only get better.

How Long Is Your Ritual?

The length of time a ritual takes is just as important as the flow. Make a ritual too long and people will get bored and the energy will fizzle out. Make it too short and people will feel like they didn't get the deep experience they were looking for. It can sometimes be hard to find a sweet spot in between. Doing your test run will help you feel this out and help you adjust it. Making a ritual fairly simple with as few moving parts as possible will also help. The majority of the time the simplest rituals are the most successful ones for a large group.

Mobility

Whether you are doing ritual indoors or outdoors, there will more than likely be someone in your audience who has a mobility issue to take into consideration. For my rituals, there is almost always someone assigned to lead the participants into the ritual space. This person should be in charge of not only giving the participants an overview of what is about to happen and running through any chants that will be used, but they also should have anyone with mobility issues come to the front of the group that is processing into ritual space. This way they can set the pace instead of being left behind in the dust. This also allows the person leading everyone into the space to be near those folks so they can grab a chair for them or help them get settled. Alternatively, you might ask those with mobility issues to enter the space ten or fifteen minutes before everyone else so they can get situated and any arrangements that are necessary for them to attend can be arranged.

Divination, or Does Something Feel Off?

Most people think of divination in terms of divining the future to see if they will get a new job or what will happen in their love life. But divination should be your go-to tool in your ritual practice as well. Divination can be a starting point in crafting your rituals. All the rituals you will find in this book started with divination work asking the Queen what she wanted from the work we intended to do. It is also the way I decide what the yearly theme for the retreat I organize in her honor will be. When creating ritual with the intention of honoring deity, it is a good idea to see what the deity wants to have done in the ritual. The energy of the ritual will be more connected and in sync with deity. In the Morrigan's case ignoring what she wants is usually a sure way to make her not show up energetically for the rite in question. The gods want to speak to us; let them guide you and show you the best way to open that channel ritualistically to them. If you fight against the current, as it were, things can go dramatically wrong.

For example, each year at the Morrigan's Call Retreat we have three big rituals that all interconnect with the theme over the course of three days. A lot of time is spent creating the rituals, and by the time we get to the retreat, we have set this intention in motion for the better part of nine months. One year, the first two days went off perfectly, but by the day of the last ritual, almost everyone who was participating in that particular ritual had something happen that caused them to leave the campground for some reason. One person was fine the day before and woke up with a sore throat. Another person got called in for an emergency at his job, which ironically would only be for the time we were due to have the ritual. Parts were reassigned, then re-reassigned. It's not abnormal to have to make some last-minute changes in a ritual, but the number of people out for the count was growing, so much that I realized I would have to either rewrite the ritual (literally twenty minutes before it happened) or assign the parts to new people, all of whom would have to read the unfamiliar lines off a script, and it would probably flow horribly. I almost considered the latter. But when I stopped trying to "manage" the problem and opened my awareness, I realized there was nothing wrong with the ritual, but it wasn't the ritual the Morrigan wanted for whatever reason. Maybe it had been what she wanted nine months ago, but something had shifted. I needed to shift with her.

I sat quietly. I did divination and connected with the Morrigan and asked what she wanted. Using the impressions and nudges I was shown, I mentally rewrote the entire ritual in my head, and we did that ritual instead. My ritual team seemed pretty terrified by this, but we used our regular opening and closing, which they all already knew, so they didn't need to relearn anything. When we came to the working, I took charge, doing what the Morrigan showed me in my divination. And you know what? Everything was great. The energy flowed and after the ritual someone came up to me to let me know that something in the ritual had a very specific personal meaning for him in relation to his own work with the Morrigan. That he had been told receiving a specific item would signal when it was time to work more closely with her again. The token I had used for that ritual was not what I originally intended to use and was felt out during that last-minute divination twenty minutes beforehand. I took it as a sign that I did the right thing. Trying to force our original plan for the ritual just wasn't what she wanted. I was doing the ritual in her honor, after all. I had to honor her wishes.

I often wonder if our original divination months prior to the ritual was accurate. Had we read the signs correctly? Had something changed between the time we did the divination and the day of? All possible. But my gut tells me it was a lesson from the Morrigan. Was I willing to listen to her? Or would I just stick with my plan no matter what because it was what I wanted to do, and, damn it, it was just going to happen the way I wanted it! That's not priest work. The work of a priest requires flexibility. You have to listen to the whispers and nudges from the gods. We have to be able to see and feel the subtle pushes so they don't become a hard shove when we ignore the little things. It made me more confident in listening to those nudges, in trusting that sometimes I would need to play it by ear and that was okay.

Whatever your go-to divination is, it would be wise to use it in crafting your ritual, before the ritual, or at the end to determine if offerings were accepted, and so on. Feeling a nudge from deity is a kind of divination or omen in itself. If you feel that nudge, let it guide you. Don't be afraid to listen to deity's voice. After all, the whole point of ritual is to connect with the divine. When the divine speaks, listen. And when the Morrigan speaks, absolutely listen.

Basic Morrigan Ritual Opening and Closing

The following is a basic opening and closing for all the following rituals you will find in this book. It is a system that was inspired by the Morrigan herself and one that I use in almost all my personal and public rituals.

At this point in my spiritual practice I very rarely cast circles. Did I in my early practices? Sure. Depending on the type of work I am doing, it's still in my bag of tricks. If you feel called to do so, is something wrong with that? Absolutely not. We don't know what specifically the druids in Ireland did in their rituals. We have bits of myth and folklore, but no solid notion of what their ritual practice looked like. We do know that the concept of casting a circle, usually to protect or contain a summoned spirit, comes to us from ceremonial magick. There is nothing wrong with the practice, and it certainly works well. For my own work with the Morrigan, I both wanted something different and felt that she was leading me to create something else for her. I didn't want something that drew on a practice that wasn't part of the Irish way of looking at the world. This ritual is my own interpretation of that, and I'm sure it doesn't resemble what the Irish druids did any more than casting a circle and calling the quarters does. But when I felt my ritual practice was turning stale, I asked her what she wanted, and this is what she showed me. It works well for me and my group, and I hope it will for you as well. If it does not, I encourage you to create your own. Think outside the box and see what the Morrigan inspires in you. Or use the opening and closing that work best for you from your own tradition. All that matters is that you find the style that energetically works for you.

The more work I do the more I like the idea of seeing all space as sacred. The circle isn't sacred because you cast it. The ground beneath it, you, and the items in it were already sacred before you started. Mostly, you are just acknowledging this out loud so you remember to see the sacredness all around you. Once that clicked for me, I started casting circles less and less. I do cleanse an area before I work if I feel it is necessary, but more than likely I will make offerings to the spirits of place before I do ritual work in that area. This is done more easily outside, but buildings have spirits of place too; you just have to tune in to sensing them.

While I do not cast circles, there is a lot of evidence in Irish and Scottish folklore that walking in a particular direction to circle an area or object had significance. This could be walking around a mound, a sacred well, or a house, for a particular purpose. Movement clockwise was done for blessings, while movement counterclockwise was done either for cursing or breaking a spell and was in general connected with faeries or the Otherworlds. In the ballad of "Childe Rowland" a boy walks counterclockwise around a church in an effort to enter the Otherworlds and rescue his sister, who was taken by walking the same way.[65] While I do not cast a circle, walking in a particular direction throughout all the steps in this opening and closing has significance to me. It is more about the significance of the directional movement than marking out a boundary. It may change depending on the purpose of the ritual, but in general I use a clockwise, or blessing, motion for all the moving elements in the ritual.

Most of what you will see in this opening/closing involves making libations or offerings. In this case, we make them to the spirits of the land (or spirits of place), the *sidhe,* and the ancestors. This is to both ask for their blessings on the work and to set up the energetic working space you will be using. For me, these three represent the layers of the Otherworlds. First, we have the land, the earth we are standing upon, the physical realm where we reside. The Otherworlds are connected to the land. They are the invisible layers that lie on top our own. The realm of the *sidhe* is just one step deeper into the realm of the Otherworlds. The Morrigan's cave is a *sidhe,* or entrance into the Otherworlds, both in the lore and, as I experienced there, quite literally. Many of the places connected to the Morrigan in Ireland have a strong connection to the *sidhe,* and I feel it is important to recognize them in my own ritual practice. Giving the *sidhe* proper respect and their due is always a good idea, whether you work

---

65. Lowry C. Wimberly, *Folklore in the English and Scottish Ballads* (New York: Frederick Ungar, 1928), 364.

with them or not. Last, the ancestors dwell in the deepest part of the Other-worlds, the place where gods and incorporeal spirits live. With each offering you are not only asking for the blessing and aid of the denizens of these layers of the Otherworlds but also moving your consciousness deeper into the Otherworlds. When you make offerings in the closing, you will move in the opposite direction, honoring the ancestors and the deepest parts of the Otherworlds first, then coming back out to the land and the physical world.

The Layout

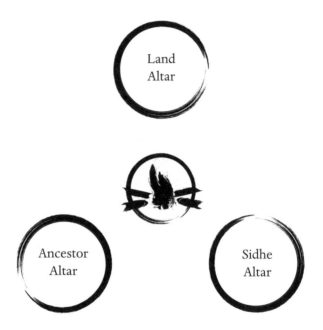

The altars for the land, *sidhe,* and ancestors should be set up to form a triangle within the sacred space. If I am working outside, there might be a fire in the middle, or the center area of the triangle may be left open for the priests to place other items necessary for the ritual. There is a blessing included here for a sacred fire. If you choose to have a fire, this is where offerings or items that might need to be burnt during the main working can be placed. Triangles have been sacred in many cultures. In Western occultism this would be seen as an invoking triangle. I use it to represent the triple Morrigan, the three layers of the Otherworlds, and a symbolical representation of a cairn. Cairns, like faery mounds, were seen as entrances to the Otherworlds, and I have had several very vivid experiences inside cairns in Ireland. How you choose to view it is up to you. Invoking triangle, cairn, triple Morrigan, or all three, there are several layers of meaning to draw from.

Roles

- Land altar priest
- *Sidhe* altar priest
- Ancestor altar priest
- Cup bearer

The Opening and Closing

The opening and closing are ideally done with four priests. If you are short-handed, one person can fill all roles, although the effect is less dramatic. The priests standing at the three altars should have the cup bearer walk the cup from the first altar (land) to the next and so on, finally returning it to the first altar when all the calls and offerings have been made. The priests saying the blessing for each altar remain at their altars for the entire opening or closing. Small bowls as well as other items that represent the aspect of the Morrigan or the powers being called should be placed on each altar. For example, a skull would be appropriate for the ancestors and a large stone or a plant for the land.

The cup bearer brings the libations to be offered from altar to altar so each priest may make offerings and say the blessing for the land, *sidhe*, and ancestors. If one person is filling this role, they would instead walk from altar to altar. The only significance is the direction in which they walk. As we talked about previously, walking in different directions had significance in Irish lore. Unless you are changing it to suit the working you are doing, clockwise should be the direction the priests are walking when doing the opening and closing.

Opening Blessing for the Space

The cup bearer hands the offering cup or horn to the priest at the land altar, who pours the offering on the altar, saying:

Land Blessing

We call to the daughters of Ernmas
We call to Anu

Who is the sovereignty of the land
May we honor the ground beneath our feet
The land that nourishes and sustains us
Anu, may your blessings be on our work this day

The land altar priest hands the cup back to the cup bearer, who walks it to the next altar. The cup bearer hands the offering cup or horn to the priest at the *sidhe* altar, who pours the offering on the altar, saying:

Sidhe Blessing

We call to the daughters of Ernmas
We call to Macha of the faery mounds
Woman of the sidhe
We make this offering to the Good Folk
May there be peace between us
May we be friend, not foe
Macha, may your blessing be on our work this day

The *sidhe* altar priest hands the cup back to the cup bearer, who walks it to the next altar. The cup bearer hands the offering cup or horn to the priest at the ancestor altar, who pours the offering on the altar, saying:

Ancestor Blessing

We call to the daughters of Ernmas
We call to Badb
Washer Woman keening, you who take your portion of the dead
We call to the ancestor and beloved dead
Kindred of blood and kindred of spirit
May your wisdom and sacrifice guide us
May the blessing of the ancestors be on our work this day
Badb, may your blessing be on our work this day

The priest hands the cup back to the cup bearer, who walks it back to the land altar and puts it on the altar, completing the circuit around the space.

Blessing the Fire (Optional)

If you are in an outdoor space and can have a sacred fire, use it to pour additional offerings made during the working or burn certain items used in the working. It is not a requirement and can be skipped over if you are working indoors. Some of the rituals in this book do require things to be burned in a fire and were designed to be done in an outdoor space. With a little tweaking and a firesafe bowl, or by choosing to burn items outside after the ritual, you can accomplish the same intent.

> *We call to the fierce daughters of Ernmas*
> *To help us light the way*
> *To help us light her sacred fires*
> *May this fire be blessed in the name of Anu*
> *In the name of Macha*
> *In the name of Badb*
> *May all that is burned in it be made sacred*
> *As an offering to the Morrigan*
> *May all that is poured into it reach her lips*
> *May any words spoken by it reach her ears*
> *May all that is burned within it come into her keeping*
> *May it be so nine times eternal!*

Working

At this point we have honored the ancestors, the *sidhe*, and the land, as well as asked for the blessings of the three Morrigans. Now any working, celebrations, divination, meditation, and so on should be done.

Closing Blessing for the Space

The cup bearer hands the offering cup or horn to the ancestor altar priest, who pours the offering on the altar.

Ancestor altar priest:

> *We honor the ancestors gone to dust*
> *Ancestors, accept this offering!*
> *Badb, may you accept this offering!*

The priest hands the cup back to the cup bearer, who walks it to the next altar. The cup bearer hands the offering cup or horn to the priest at the *sidhe* altar, who pours the offering on the altar.

Sidhe altar priest:

> *We honor the sidhe in their shining halls*
> *May the shining folk accept this offering!*
> *Macha, may you accept this offering!*

The priest hands the cup back to the cup bearer, who walks it to the next altar. The cup bearer hands the offering cup or horn to the priest at the land altar, who pours the offering on the altar.

Land altar priest:

> *We honor the land the ground beneath our feet,*
> *Spirit of the land, may you accept this offering!*
> *Anu, may you accept this offering!*

The priest hands the cup back to the cup bearer, who walks it back to the land altar and puts it on the altar, completing the circuit around the space.

Final Offering to the Morrigan

In general, this last offering should reflect the specific work or celebration you have done and can be tweaked depending on the ritual you are doing.

> *Hail An Morrigan!*
> *We make this offering in gratitude for _____!*
> *And so we say this rite is done,*
> *May it be nine times eternal!*

Chapter 16
Group Rituals

All the following rituals consist of only the "working," or main body of the ritual. You can use the opening and closing in the previous chapter or one from your own tradition. I and those I work with have used all these rituals. If you feel the need to change or tweak parts of these rituals, you are welcome to do so, or use them as inspiration to create your own.

A Ritual of Keening

Roles

- Badb 1
- Badb 2
- Badb 3

Supplies

- Large cauldron or bowl
- 3 veils or head coverings for the Badbs
- White cloth
- Red or red-speckled cloth
- Tokens to be given at the end of the ritual to the participants

The focus of this ritual is the releasing of grief and sorrow. It calls upon the Washer at the Ford to help us release and cleanse ourselves so that we may move on toward healing. Cleansing oneself is also necessary when a person or group is preparing for deeper magical work, in which case this could be used by a group to cleanse in preparation for other magical work the group will take on in the future.

Keening, or ritualized wailing, was practiced by both men and women in Ireland. We know little of the art other than it involved wails of sorrow, singing, and even recounting the deeds of the dead or how much their relatives would miss them. There were even professional keeners one could hire when a loved one passed on. What is agreed upon is that the sound of a keening is unsettling and at times even Otherworldly. It is the wails of the banshee and the Washer at the Ford, who keens as she washes her bloody rags. Keening gives a voice to pain and sorrow. It isn't supposed to be pretty. It's the sound of one's heart breaking. It is the sound of regret and anger. When voiced, these things can be released, because we have acknowledged them in this primal way. It is not uncommon to be shaking and weeping when keening. It's something you have to feel in your whole body, but afterward it can leave you feeling cleansed and most of all acknowledged, knowing your pain has been heard and recognized.

In this ritual the three priests who will embody Badb (one person can fill multiple roles) will be keening, and all the participants will be invited to keen with them. It can be a very powerful experience, and a talk about keening beforehand would be ideal to ready everyone for the experience. You will need a large cauldron or large pot big enough to hold the fabric. For the bloody rags, you can take a flat white sheet, cut it into three or four long strips, and splatter them with red paint. Alternatively, you could buy a red sheet to represent the bloody rags of the Washer at the Ford. You will also need a clean white sheet. This will remain at the bottom of the cauldron and will be pulled out "transformed" at the end of the ritual. You will also need three veils or head coverings for the priests to wear during the keening.

The token to be given to each participant at the end of the ritual is up to you. It should be something the participants can use as a kind of omen. You could hand out a printout of a symbol, oracle card, or tarot card or a stone with an ogham written on it. I have found that a small square of white cloth with an ogham drawn on it works well and mirrors some of the symbolism used in the ritual. Whatever you choose, it should be something the participants can use to meditate upon later or use as a guide for further work.

A priest or priestess will lead everyone into the ritual area. Giving a brief explanation of what will happen in the ritual is always a good thing to do. The priest should also teach everyone the chant that will be used later in ritual and should be sung as everyone enters the space.

Morrigan, Morrigan
Lover of heroes, mother of crows
Lady of victory, healer of souls
Great Queen, Phantom Queen[66]

To begin the ritual use the basic ritual opening beginning on page 190, or use whatever system you are most comfortable with. The cauldron or bowl with the red splattered strips of cloth and the white sheet should be in the center of the ritual area. All three Badbs should have some weapon in hand, preferably spears, but swords or athames would work as well. They will put these on the ground at one point in the ritual to symbolize it is now time to direct your focus on healing. Depending on what weapons you use, you should have a plan ahead of time for where to put them so they will not be tripped over or dangerous to the priest or participants as they move in the space.

Statement of Purpose
Badb 1:

Who has the telling of the story?

Badb 2:

There is always a story to be told. The Morrigan is a goddess of war, but she is far more than just that. Tonight we call upon her as Badb and as the Washer at the Ford. As the Washer at the Ford, she stands in the waters keening for the dead, washing their bloody clothes. She mourns the parts of us that no longer serve us, the parts that poison us, yet we refuse to give up.
Badb is the bringer of victory, the mother of heroes. It is she who

---

66. You can of course use any chant you prefer. The tempo here should be drawn out and dirgelike, with Morrigan chanted as *Mor-ee-gan*, the syllables elongated.

proclaims when the fighting begins and when it is over, when it is
time to sheathe our swords and tend to our wounds. Because if we do
not face our demons, if we don't heal our scars, we will not be strong
enough to face future battles.

When we do not seek to heal, our anger, our pain, our hate becomes
a poison. A poison that seeps into our hearts. The Morrigan has a
son, named Meiche. So great was his passion for life that he had not
one heart in his chest but three. But the poisons of the world seeped
into those hearts, and Meiche's fear and anger transformed into three
serpents within his three hearts. The serpents twisted within him, their
poison seeping into his blood and into the air he breathed, until all he
was, was poison. It was clear that if the serpents were not slain, they
would grow and devour all of Ireland. And so Meiche was killed. His
three poisonous hearts were burned to ash and thrown into the water
of the Morrigan's river to be cleansed of their poison. Meiche was
destroyed by his own fear and anger.

Badb 3:

I know your hearts are strong. I know they are warrior's hearts. And
I know they carry sorrow. What will you choose? Will you choose the
healing the Morrigan offers? Or will you let your poison consume you,
as Meiche did?

Are you willing to let go of what weighs you down? Are you willing
to wash it away in waters of the Washer Woman? Are you ready to
accept the victory the Morrigan offers you?

Participants:

Yes.

Badb 3:

Then let us call to the Badb to help us in this task!

Invoking Badb

All three Badbs should stand around the cauldron and face the participants. As each says their invocation, they put their spear or weapon down, turn and kneel around the cauldron, and pull on a veil or head covering. They can also pull some of the paint splattered rags from the cauldron and pretend to wash them in their hands as the other priests finish their invocations.

Badb 1:

> *We call to the Daughters of Ernmas*
> *We call to Badb*
> *Queen of Phantoms*
> *Washer at the Ford*
> *You who wash the gore and spoils of war*
> *Staining the waters crimson*
> *You wash the clothes of those destined to die*
> *You who know sorrow and loss*
> *We seek healing*
> *We seek wisdom*
> *We seek an end to sorrow*
> *Be with us now!*

Badb 2:

> *We call to the Daughters of Ernmas*
> *We call to Badb*
> *Queen of Battle*
> *Lover of heroes*
> *Who dances from spearpoint to spearpoint*
> *Blessing your favored warriors*
> *You who are strength and frenzy*
> *Who delight in the din of battle*
> *You bring victory or doom*
> *Grant us the strength to endure*
> *To be victorious in our trials!*
> *Be with us now!*

Badb 3:

> *We call to the Daughters of Ernmas*
> *We call to Badb*
> *Great Queen, poetess, Lady of Visions*
> *You who see all that is, was, and can be*
> *Your gifts are prophecy and victory*
> *Your blessings balanced on the edge of a blade*
> *Teach us what is worth fighting for*
> *And what is worth letting go of*
> *Be with us now!*

Before turning to face the cauldron, Badb 3 challenges the participants, saying:

> *Are you willing to put your swords down so you can heal?*
> *So you might be strong enough to face the next battle when it comes?*

Badb 3 puts their spear or weapon down as well and faces the cauldron.

The Working

Badb 1 and 2 kneel before the cauldron and "wash" the rags, running them through their hands as if they were ringing out laundry. Badb 3 addresses the participants and leads them through the keening. As Badb 3 speaks, the other two Badbs should pull the "bloody" rags from the cauldron and give them to the participants to be passed around the circle. This works best if ahead of time you assign one of the participants to help hand out the rags to the others. The rags should be long strips, so several people will hold parts of the cloth at the same time. The participants should be encouraged to run their hands over the fabric during the keening or make their own "washing" motions with the cloth as the keening happens while seeing their sorrows flowing into the fabric.

Badb 3:

> *Grief poisons us. Grief for our failures. Grief for the pieces of ourselves*
> *that are no more. Grief for those we have lost. Grief sticks in our guts,*
> *weighing us down. Giving a voice to this grief and sorrow draws it*
> *out. Tonight, we will keen with the Washer Woman. We will draw*

*out the poisons within ourselves. We will mourn our losses and seek
healing from the Great Queen, that we may transform these things to
help us move forward. Wash the bloody rags with us. Pour into them
the things you need to release.*

*The Washer Woman washes your bloody clothing. She sees what
weighs upon your heart. She washes and keens for the pieces of you
that are no more. When grief is witnessed, when it is acknowledged,
when it is seen, it is irrevocably changed. It is transformed! Transform
it with us! Wash it away with us!*

For the keening, it is also helpful to let the participants know ahead of time
that when they hear the line "alone in the dark," it is their cue to begin keening. This will happen three times and can be drawn out as long as you feel necessary. The keening part of this working was created by Sonja Sadovsky.
Badb 3:

> *Weep, ravens, for what we have lost*
> *We gather here to mourn*
> *To witness*
> *To wail into the void*
> *Our steadfast companions*
> *Bright and bold*
> *Have been cut down in their prime*
> *Who will love us, alone in the dark?*
> *(Keen.)*

All three Badbs wail, encouraging the participants to keen with them. Don't
be afraid to let this grow and build for a few minutes.
Badb 3:

> *Weep, ravens, for the peace that has shattered*
> *The trust that has been broken*
> *We have nurtured the ones who have hurt us the most*
> *Our hands have been burned*
> *Our hearts and minds too*
> *Who may we love without fear, alone in the dark?*

(Keen.)
Weep, ravens, for the time we have wasted
Chasing dreams, chasing failures, again and again
For the lies we have taught ourselves to believe
Who will know us truly, know us as we are, alone in the dark?
(Keen.)

Allow the last keen to build. When the keening is at its height, the three Badbs should raise their arms and drop them quickly as a sign to end the keening.

The "bloody" rags should be returned to the cauldron. All three Badbs hold their hands over the cauldron.

Badb 2:

Let us transform this sorrow
Let us transform this grief
We have given it a form and shape with our keening
Now let us release these things
Let there be peace
Let there be victory
May our hearts be whole and healed!

Start the chanting. Begin low and then build it up. Let its pace become faster as the energy builds. While everyone is chanting, the three Badbs should again make the motions of washing, or in this case transforming. The chanting should end when one of the Badbs reaches into the cauldron and pulls out the "transformed" clean, unstained cloth.

Badb 2:

We must remember there is an end to grief
The poison has been drawn out!
It is time to move forward toward strength
Toward healing
These bloody rags have been cleansed
We have been purified!
Pain divided us

Peace unites us
We are one, we are whole!

Badb 1:

We are the Washer at the Ford and we are also the Lady of Prophecy
I challenge you to accept the healing that we offer
We offer you omens to guide your way toward healing, toward victory
May this (whatever the token is) be a reminder that you have let go of what no longer
serves you
The blood is washed away
Let the symbol upon it be a guidepost to you

The three Badbs walk the circle and offer the token to the participants. To close the ritual use the ending beginning on page 195 or a closing of your choice.

Cairn of Macha Ritual

The purpose of this ritual is connecting with Macha as well as community building. I do a version of this ritual yearly, focusing the ritual drama on a different face of Macha each year, depending on what I feel the focus of the coming year will be. It does not need to be a yearly ritual for you, but if done more than once, it does give you the opportunity to explore a different face of Macha in the ritual drama every time.

Since the Irish gods have a habit of dying only to respawn very much alive in another story, there are five distinct incarnations of Macha in Irish mythology:

- Macha, daughter of Partholon. Her father is one of the leaders of the second wave of people invading Ireland after the Biblical flood.
- Macha, wife of Nemed, comes with the third wave of people invading Ireland. She dies after clearing plains for agriculture.
- Macha of the Tuatha Dé Danann, the fifth invading group to come to Ireland, is one of the three daughters of Ernmas. She dies in battle alongside Nuada, which implies she may have been his wife.
- Macha Mong Ruad, a legendary mortal queen of Ulster who goes to war to be able to inherit her father's throne after he dies leaving no male heirs.

- Macha of the *sidhe*, who takes a mortal husband and gives him very specific prohibitions to not boast about her. When her husband breaks his word, it leads to her being forced to race the king's horse and eventually placing a curse on the men of Ulster.

Part of this ritual is for those participating to build a cairn. Simply put, a cairn is a man-made pile of stones. Cairns have been created since prehistory for various purposes, ranging from burial mounds to marking astronomical events. The idea in this ritual is to build something as a community.

All five different Machas of Irish mythology are called upon in the ritual and ideally should be invoked by five different people. A single person could call on all five, but since community is a theme in this ritual, it plays out better when there are more people involved.

Before the ritual, everyone should be given a small stone, something that can easily be held in the palm of the hand. This can be something given to them, or you may want to have them look for a stone that calls to them prior to the ritual. For larger groups, it's a good idea to have a basket of small stones already collected.

Roles

- Macha, wife of Nemed
- Macha, daughter of Partholon
- Macha of the Tuatha Dé Danann
- Macha of the *sidhe*
- Macha Mong Ruad

Supplies

- 1 small stone for each participant
- Libations or offerings

To begin the ritual use the basic ritual opening beginning on page 190 or use whatever system you are most comfortable with.

Invoking Macha

All five Machas should stand back to back in a circle, facing the rest of the participants. Each speaks in turn, addressing the group.

Macha, wife of Nemed:

> *We call to Macha, wife of Nemed*
> *Clearer of plains, lady of vision*
> *Bringer of bounty, sun of womanhood*
> *Raven woman, we call to you!*

Macha, daughter of Partholon:

> *We call to you Macha, daughter of Partholon*
> *You who diffuses all excellence*
> *Raven woman, we call to you!*

Macha of the Tuatha Dé Danann:

> *Macha of the Tuatha, wife of Nuada*
> *Lady of the high places*
> *Fierce in battle*
> *Raven woman, we call to you!*

Macha of the *sidhe*:

> *We call to Macha of the sidhe,*
> *Faery woman, swifter than any horse*
> *Bringer of wealth and curses alike*
> *Raven woman, we call to you!*

Macha Mong Ruad:

> *Macha of the red tresses*
> *Lady of battle, mighty one*
> *Who takes what is hers by right*
> *Raven woman, we call to you!*

Each of the Machas should make an offering. This can be done after each has spoken their part or after all the Machas have spoken.

The Ritual Drama
Macha of the *sidhe*:

Macha wears many faces, has many aspects and many stories
Let us have the knowing of her story

You can take this ritual to many different places, so which story is retold here should be your choice. If you are telling the story of Macha of the *sidhe*, then have the person who invoked that face of Macha come forward to tell the story, and so on. If you are emphasizing overcoming obstacles, you might retell the story of Macha Mong Ruad. If you are concentrating on overcoming injustice, Macha of the *sidhe* and her race against the king's horses would work, or maybe recount Macha, wife of Nemed, and how she cleared the plain so the community would have a place to prosper.

The Cairn Working
Macha Mong Ruad comes forward and addresses everyone, saying:

There are many different kinds of battles. Sometimes fighting means building. Sometimes fighting means clearing away obstacles. Sometimes fighting means being aware of what is worth keeping and what must be let go of, when to pick up your sword and when to put it down. Touch the earth; dig your fingers into the soil. Shaping the earth transforms it, remakes it. What within you are you ready to reshape? What in your life do you need to lay to rest? Macha challenges you to turn the soil of yourself and shape it into what you truly want it to be. Bury in this earth what no longer serves you. See it flowing into the soil. Let it be composted there. Take back the nourishment and strength you need from the earth. The earth takes and the earth gives.

Everyone should be directed to touch the ground, to send their intent down into the earth and to let go of what is no longer necessary, and also to think about intentions they wish to plant and what they wish to nourish and grow. Depending on the size of the group you have, you could do a longer guided meditation, or the person leading the rituals should simply ask everyone to touch the ground and send their intentions into the soil. For a large group simply having them touch the ground and sending out their intentions is enough.

Macha, daughter of Partholon:

> *Cairns have been built for many reasons. There are cairns for letting*
> *things go, cairns to honor the dead, those to bless the living, and cairns*
> *for memorializing. Cairns speak to us in form and power.*

All five Machas put their own stones down in the designated area to start the cairn. They hold their hands over the stones while one of them says the following blessing:

> *Stone by stone, plains are cleared*
> *Stone by stone, cairns are built*
> *Stone by stone, blessing us all*
> *Hand to hand, we stand together*
> *Hand to hand, we find our strength*
> *Hand to hand, we bless each other*
> *May Macha see us standing in strength*
> *May Macha stand with us as we bless each other*
> *May Macha bless us now and always* [67]

Participants come forward and place their stone in the designated area until there is a tiny cairn with stones placed atop stones. Afterward, the five Machas should each pour an offering and give thanks to that aspect of Macha.

To close the ritual make any appropriate offerings and farewells to Macha, then use the closing beginning on page 195 or the format you are the most comfortable with.

A Ritual to the Goddess of Battle

This ritual calls on the Morrigan in her guise as a goddess of battle. Part of the working will be handing out a small stone with a saying on it. Many of the smooth decorative stones sold at craft stores will work well. The goal is not only to work with the Morrigan in her guise concerning battle but also for

---

67.   This blessing was created for this ritual by Morgan Daimler and is used with permission.

each participant to accept and take on a personal challenge. When my group did this ritual, it was with the understanding that the challenge we received in the ritual would be something to work on for a full year with the Morrigan.

Before the ritual, the priests should spend some time meditating and asking the Morrigan what should be written on the stones. These phrases should then be typed and printed on paper in a size that will fit on the stones. They can be attached to the stone with a little bit of glue or spray-on adhesive to seal them to the surface. These should be placed on your altar for use during the working or in an out-of-the-way place. The phrase or words on the stone will represent what the person who picked it up needs to work on. It is the challenge the Morrigan is placing before them.

Roles

- Priest 1
- Priest 2
- Priest 3

Supplies

- Challenge stones
- Libations or preferred offerings

Open the ritual with the example beginning on page 190 or use an opening of your choice.

Invoking the Morrigan
Priest 1:

Let us call to the Great Queen!

Since we are calling on the side of the Morrigan connected to battle, I like to make this invocation to her less formal. The priests should begin the calling. It can be rhythmic or just loudly shouting her name. The idea is to mirror the din and chaos of battle. A room full of people heartfeltly shouting the Morrigan's name can sound like a battlefield but can also raise a great deal of energy. When you feel her presence or feel that enough energy has been raised, one of the priests should lift their arms then drop them as a signal to stop.

The three priests should come forward and walk around the circle, making eye contact and challenging the participants as they speak in turn.

Priest 1:

> *What will you fight for? What is worth laying your life down for? What is worth standing against the multitude for, when all have turned their back on you? I will always challenge you. The world is unjust, life isn't fair, but I would ask you to be strong in spite of it. Each of your battles will be different, fought in your own way, and the things I ask of you, you may not expect. But you will be the better for it.*

Priest 2:

> *You must know which battles to fight and which to leave behind. One does not go to war without purpose or seek justice without having been wronged. The reasons we fight matter. You think you need to go to battle to prove you are strong. No. Fight because you are terrified. Fight because you are broken and scared. Be courageous despite these things. Fight even when victory is not guaranteed, and know when to walk away. The hardest battle may be the one you choose not to fight.*

Priest 3:

> *You fight me, but you are really fighting yourselves. I would raise you up and give you victory, but you cower in fear. You fear taking chances, you fear change, you fear all the gifts I would give you, all the things that will make you strong. Yes, there is pain, and you fear that too, but what is living? How will you know how to fix others if you can't heal yourselves? How can you teach others to fight if you can't fight for yourself? Stand up and make your own lives better.*
>
> *If you would do this, come forward. Take a stone and receive my challenge. But know that you will be bound by it.*

Participants are asked to come forward if they wish. They will take a stone out of the bowl and then return to their place in the ritual space. This would also be a good time to have drumming or chanting until everyone has taken a stone.

Priest 1:

> *Will you rise to the challenge?*

Wait for a response from participants.
Priest 2:

> *Will you overcome what you fear?*

Wait for a response from participants.
Priest 3:

> *Will you be warriors?*

Wait for a response from participants.
Priest 3:

> *Then go forth into the world as warriors,*
> *go forth as kings and queens in your own right!*

Any final offerings should be done now. Then close the ritual using the closing you prefer.

A Ritual to the Dagda and Morrigan

Roles
- Morrigan priest 1
- Morrigan priest 2
- Morrigan priest 3
- Dagda priest
- Chant leader

Supplies
- Large bowl or cauldron
- Libations or preferred offerings
- Small bag for each participant

- Tokens for each altar station (either the ones suggested in the ritual or ones you prefer)

This ritual is based around the idea of calling on the Morrigan and the Dagda for transformation. The Morrigan's and the Dagda's energies balance each other very well. Both are warriors and both are leaders, but where the Morrigan is harsh, the Dagda tempers her with his laughter and bold joy for life. Using these two complementary energies in ritual can be interesting and very useful for transformation and manifestation.

At one point participants will be tossing something into the fire to symbolize what they are letting go of and transforming. This can be a small bag with rock salt and herbs of your choosing. For added effect you can also get small packets that change the color of the fire. These can be found online and usually can be purchased as small individual packets that can easily go into the bags you will be burning. When done in a large group with a good number of these fire color changing packets, the effect is very nice, as everyone can see the change in the colors of the fire and a kind of concrete representation of the transformation asked for in the ritual.

A token is also offered from the Dagda's cauldron in this ritual. You can use a literal cauldron if you have one, or a large bowl can be used to represent his cauldron. What the token should be is up to you. You could have a small stone with a particular meaning, a necklace with a charm, an acorn to symbolize growth and change, or an ogham. As always, the roles can be consolidated or spread out between more priests.

Begin the ritual with the example beginning on page 190 or use an opening you prefer.

Statement of Intent
Dagda priest:

> Tonight, we will call to the Great Queen and meet her challenge, and
> we will call to the Dagda for his strength and steadfastness. Together
> they complement and strengthen each other: the fierceness of battle and
> the strength of endless abundance.
>> Let us call to them!

Invoking the Morrigans

The three Morrigan priests should step forward and walk around the circle, each speaking in turn.

Morrigan priest 1:

> *We call to the Great Queen!*
> *Sorceress, prophetess, Raven of Battle*
> *She is the blade that cleaves flesh from bone*
> *That cuts the old from the new*
> *That reshapes, remakes, redefines us*

Morrigan priest 2:

> *Morrigan, you see past all illusions*
> *You know what is, was, and can be*
> *Above the battlefield you dance upon spearpoints*
> *Seeing us through despair to victory*

Morrigan priest 3:

> *Raven woman,*
> *Together we prepare ourselves to destroy*
> *To reshape, to become anew*
> *To face the challenges you place before us*
> *Not in anger but in strength*

Morrigan priest 3 pours the offerings.

Invoking the Dagda

The Dagda priest should come forward and walk around the circle, addressing the participants.

Dagda priest:

> *We call to the Dagda!*
> *Red God, Great One of Knowledge*

Warrior, druid, King of the Tuatha!
Horse Lord, mover of the seasons,
Speaker of true justice
Dagda, Keeper of the Cauldron
Help us achieve mighty deeds
May we find nourishment
May we find strength
May we find courage
May we find your joy for life
As we face our many challenges!
Dagda, we call to you!

The Dadga priest pours an offering.

Working

The three Morrigan priests should step forward again. They should stand facing the participants. Each should have a sword or dagger to challenge everyone who comes forward. The Dagda priest will be a little bit past where they are standing. Participants must come forward to face the challenge of one of the three Morrigans, and then they can toss their bag into the fire. Afterward they should come to the Dagda priest, who will either be holding a cauldron or have one in front of him, from which he will offer them a symbolic token of renewal and transformation.

Dagda priest:

When we seek transformation, there will always be challenges. True
change within and without must be fought for. They are not the battles
of clashed sword, but they are just as gut-wrenching and bloody. They
are the battles within us. Only you can choose what breaks you and
what shapes you. Only you can decide when you are ready to let go of
the things holding you back. What are you willing to sacrifice to gain
the transformation you seek? We are not shedding what doesn't serve
us. No, instead we will make those things an offering, a sacrifice, to
the Great Queen. In your hand you hold a symbol of what you wish to

sacrifice to the Morrigan. What will you offer her? See it clearly in your mind's eye. See it becoming one with what you hold in your hand.

Morrigan priest 1:

You are not required to step forward.
Accept the challenge the Morrigan placed before you only if you are ready, only if you are willing.

The three Morrigan priests should stand with dagger or sword raised. When a participant approaches them, the Morrigan priest will challenge them. What the challenge is will depend on what that priest feels in the moment, or it can be predetermined. "Will you accept the transformation I offer?" or "Will you transform what burdens you?" are acceptable. Then the participant will throw their offering into the fire and go to the Dagda priest to be given a token.

While people come forward, the chant leader should start the chanting and drumming to keep the energy moving. You can use the following chant or one you prefer.

Chant leader:

Ahhhh Mor-ri-gan
By land, by sea, by sky
Ahhhh Mor-ri-gan
I lift my voice up high
Ahhhh Mor-ri-gan
Your wings embrace my heart
Ahhhh Mor-ri-gan
Your gaze I won't depart
Ahhhh Mor-ri-gan
Come ease this weary soul
Ahhhh Mor-ri-gan
With you I am whole
Ahhhh Mor-ri-gan
By land, by sea, by sky

Ahhhh Mor-ri-gan
I lift my voice up high! [68]

After everyone who wants to come forward has faced the Morrigan's challenge and received a token from the Dagda, a final offering to the Dagda and Morrigan should be made. Additional offerings of thanks should be given to the Morrigan and Dagda, and then you can close the ritual as you see fit.

A Ritual to the Morrigan's Many Faces

Roles

- Chant leader
- Guardian altar guardian
- Altar of transformation guardian
- Altar of challenge guardian
- Altar of prophecy guardian
- Altar of sovereignty guardian
- Altar of victory guardian

Supplies

- Items you wish to place on the altar for each face of the Morrigan
- Small bag for each participant filled with pebbles
- Tokens for each altar station

The focus of this ritual is to see all the many faces of the Morrigan. It also plays on the idea of a descent to the underworld in which the hero receives guidance and tools for their journey. In this case the guidance will come from the various faces of the Morrigan.

For this ritual all the participants will encounter different faces of the Morrigan. Those embodying each of her faces can be male or female. Participants should be gathered away from the ritual space and then be led in. While they are waiting to enter the space, having them chant or sing is a good idea. If you have a large group, it is a good idea to bring them into the space in small groups to go through each station. When one group has finished with one

---

68. This chant was created by Karen Storminger. It is used with permission.

station, then another group can come up to the first, and so on. There should be a central area where everyone ends their journey after visiting all altar stations. This way those who have visited all the stations can meditate on the items they received or chant softly to keep up the energy of the ritual while the rest of the group finishes visiting the altars. I like to set up the altars in a spiral configuration, with them naturally leading to an inner central area, but you can set it up as you like.

As people come to the first altar, the guardian of that altar will hand them each a small bag filled with pebbles. As they visit each subsequent altar, they will have to give up one of the pebbles, which represent their burdens and things they wish to release, and exchange it for a token given by the priest at each altar. Each altar can be decorated with symbols for that aspect of the Great Queen.

Depending on your ritual space, the altar stations in this ritual may be in a separate area from the space you use to open the ritual and make your initial offerings. Since I don't generally cast a circle but instead acknowledge sacred space, I tend to operate in a larger area for ritual. The first time my group did this ritual, we spaced the altars out in a large field, but you can have the altars closer depending on your space.

There are suggested tokens for each station for this ritual, but you can use other items if you wish. Some of the wording may need to be changed if you use a different item.

You can begin this ritual with the opening beginning on page 190, or use one of your own choice. Everyone should be gathered away from the ritual area. The chant leader can lead everyone through several chants and start off sending a few people to the first altar station. Then when they have received their tokens, the chant leader will send the next few people over, and so on.

Guardian Altar

On the altar there should be a basket with small bags. The guardian should have a sword or knife that they hold out in challenge as they approach. They are the guardian of the sacred space. Casting a circle isn't required, as we have already discussed, so the person at this altar not only will be guiding people to enter the space but should also be monitoring the flow of energy for the ritual space in general. Picking someone adept at this work for this role will be helpful.

Guardian:

Do you seek to enter the Otherworlds?

(Wait for response from participants.)

Do you seek transformation?

(Wait for response from participants.)

> *Then know this: there are no guarantees when you enter the Other-*
> *worlds. You must shed your skin and acknowledge that something*
> *about your life, something about yourself, does not work anymore.*
> *Accept that the process of transformation is not easy. It can be painful*
> *and requires sacrifice. And you must know there is no guarantee who*
> *you will be at the end of the process.*
> *Do you still seek the transformation the Great Queen offers you?*

(Wait for response from participants.)

Then enter.

Participants are given the small bags with the pebbles and signaled to move to the next altar.

Altar of Transformation

The suggested token for this altar is a piece of shed snakeskin. You can buy shed skin online, or if you know someone who has a pet snake, you can ask them for some of the snake's sheddings, which can be torn into small pieces to be given out.

As everyone approaches the altar, the guardian speaks and accepts a pebble offered by the participants from their bags and gives them the token in return.

Guardian:

I am release. I am the ripping and tearing. The shedding of skin. I am all that must be let go of. Let go of what no longer serves you, no matter how precious, no matter how painful. Release your pain, your anguish, to me. Let me transform it into something of value, something of beauty. You will remain stagnant no more. My gift to you is snakeskin. Take it and remember your purpose in life is growth. And to grow we all must shed our skins.

Participants are signaled to move to the next altar.

Altar of Challenge

As everyone approaches the altar, the guardian speaks, accepts a pebble offered by the participants from their bags, and gives them a token in return. The suggested token for this altar is an arrowhead or something else representing battle and warriorship.

Guardian:

I will always challenge you. It is not an unkindness. The underworld tests all of us. It forces us to transform if we are to pass through it. I challenge you to heal, I challenge you to be who you were always meant to be. I challenge you to grow. I challenge you to face the unknown within yourself. Be brave, my ravens, and I will see you through all your trials.

Participants are signaled to move to the next altar.

Altar of Prophecy

As everyone approaches the altar, the guardian speaks, accepts a pebble offered by the participants from their bags, and gives them a token in return. The suggested token for this altar is a key.

Guardian:

You are my ravens, and no man or god can stand against my ravens when their hearts are pure. Know that I am always with you. I stand at your side even in the darkest hour. Even when you refuse to hear my voice. Listen. Listen, and I will guide you. Seek my voice, in the wind, in the cries of the ravens, in your own hearts. I am there waiting for you. My gift to you is a key. I have shown you the path. Now walk it. I have given you the tools. Use them.

Participants are signaled to move to the next altar.

Altar of Sovereignty

As everyone approaches the altar, the guardian speaks, accepts a pebble offered by the participants from their bags, and gives them a token in return. The suggested token for this altar is a thorn.

Guardian:

> *A crown is heavy. Whether you claim the sovereignty of self, owning your own skin and deeds. Or if you claim sovereignty for a people, tending to your family, your tribe, your community. Know your strength, show kindness and hospitality when you can. But know you must also defend what you hold dear. Rule wisely.*

Participants are signaled to move to the next altar.

Altar of Victory

As everyone approaches the altar, the guardian speaks, accepts a pebble offered by the participants from their bags, and gives them a token in return. The suggested token for this altar is a black feather or a charm in the shape of a feather.

Guardian:

> *I will break you, but only to remake you. See the beauty in your struggles, in the reshaping of yourselves. I offer you victory. I offer you new beginnings. But my gifts are earned. Know that the path will be difficult, but the rewards are great. Persevere and my gifts are yours.*

Participants are signaled to move to the central area. Before ending the ritual, you can either offer a final round of energy building through chanting or lead everyone through a guided mediation to receive additional messages from the Morrigan. Close the ritual with the closing beginning on page 195, or use one of your own making.

Tarbh Feis: A Ritual of Dream Prophecy

This ritual is a modern version of a *tarbh feis*, or "bull feast." This practice was used to receive prophetic knowledge through dreams. We can see an example of this in the story of *The Destruction of Da Derga's Hostel,* in which one is performed to determine who the next king would be, and it is revealed that the new king would appear on the road to Tara naked. Of course, this comes to pass in the story, and he is made king. To perform the *tarbh feis* a white bull was sacrificed. The person who would receive the prophetic information would eat some of the bull's meat and drink a broth made from the bull's flesh. Then others chanted over the person while they lay in bed. The person had a dream vision, and the images in it predicted who the king would be. The price for giving false information about the dream vision was death.

Many of the elements here can be modified and re-created for modern use. The key thing here is to decide what to use as your sacrifice. Buying a package of meat isn't quite the same as the sacrifice of a prized animal to an agricultural society. It can be argued that you are offering the time it took you to earn the money you use to pay for the meat, in which case I'd suggest getting the finest of cuts and not a cheap one, but I feel that isn't a great enough sacrifice. You could offer something you have created to the fire or something with deep meaning to you. Or think outside the box: offer a poem that you have taken time and effort to craft just for the ritual, or something of that nature. The important thing is you are offering something of value.

Once you have your cut of beef, you can prepare it by boiling it in water and adding any meaningful herbs (ones that are safe to consume, of course). You can make beef stew out of it or some other kind of soup. Personally, I prefer this to just be broth that can be sipped slowly during the ritual. I don't eat beef, so I drink just the broth instead and offer the meat to the fire as an offering to the Queen. If you do plan on consuming the beef, take into consideration health and safety practices. Beef should be cooked to 145 degrees Fahrenheit to be safe for consumption. Allow enough time for the meat to cook safely and properly in your ritual so your participants don't get sick. It is also important to understand that this is not a ritual that is meant to be rushed. Taking your time and building energy is key. Another variation is to use cacao. Cacao has a long history of ritual and trance use and can be a good substitute for a vegetarian.

You can have your beef and broth prepared before ritual, but it's a nice touch if you cook it during the ritual while chanting or raising energy. This of course requires an outdoor firepit. If you don't have access to one, cooking it beforehand will do.

This ritual is fairly straightforward and simple but will also require you to come up with a list of chants you want to rotate through in the chanting part of the ritual. Remember, if consuming the meat during the ritual, you need time for it to cook. You can write your own or find one that works for your purposes. Chanting the same chant over and over gets old quickly. You need to be able to change it up every so often so the energy doesn't die out. It is also a good idea to ask those participating to pick a question they wish to be answered beforehand.

Roles
- Chant leader
- Priest or priestess

Supplies
- Pot or bowl
- Beef broth or vegetable broth
- Cubes of beef to be cooked (optional)
- Something to heat and cook the meat and broth if you do not prepare it ahead of time

Open the ritual using the opening beginning on page 190 or one of your own. If doing this outside, be sure to include the fire blessing on page 195 as part of your preparation of ritual space.

Statement of Purpose and Invoking
Priest:

Badb, who stands at the water's edge
Who stands between worlds
Between what is and what can be
Between this world and the Otherworlds
Guide us toward your water's edge

Let us see what can be seen
We come together seeking wisdom
We come seeking vision
We come seeking truth
Badb, Lady of Prophecy
Guide us

Offerings should be placed in the fire. This can be an offering of your choosing or a portion of the meat. If the beef has not already been prepared, this is when it should be cooked. This can be over your ritual fire using a tripod or other camping equipment.

At this point the chanting should begin. Everyone's focus should be on asking for omens and seeing the answer to whatever questions they have. The following is an example of a chant you could use, but I suggest you come up with a few chants to cycle through, so the energy does not get stale with prolonged chanting.

Badb Catha, Bean Nighe [69]
Battle crow, flying free
Lady of Prophecy
What do you see?
What do you see?

If you have already cooked the meat and made the broth, then chanting should still be done and allowed to build. The priest should welcome up participants one at a time to be given a cup of broth to drink.

When everyone has received a cup, let the chanting slow and then end. The priest can walk everyone through a meditation to find the answers to their questions as they sip the broth, or you can have a few minutes of quiet during which everyone drinks the broth. When everyone is done, move to the closing of the ritual.

Depending on the size of the group and your needs, you can leave it fairly simple. If you are relying on omens to be found in dreams, it is a good idea to gather together the next day to discuss what was seen in everyone's dreams

---

69.   This is pronounced *ban nee.*

and to make an additional offering of gratitude. For a larger group or one that is not working together on a regular basis, going the route of a guided meditation to find answers to their questions would be better.

A Ritual of Unmasking

The idea behind this ritual is that the Morrigan is many things. We tend to see the faces we want to see and forget that there is more to her. This ritual can be a catalyst for later deeper work with the Morrigan for a group, a ritualized reminder to see her other faces.

Before the ritual, all the participants should be given round pieces of cardboard to decorate. These symbolic shields will be burned as an offering later in the ritual. They could be cut from thick construction paper, but I've found the circular cardboard spacers sold at most craft stores to put in between layers of cake work perfectly. Everyone should be given some time to write and draw on their shield. This can include things they are grateful for or things they want to learn about the Morrigan in the future. This is more an offering than something that is burnt to be rid of it. By burning the shield, you are sending it into the Otherworlds as an offering to the Morrigan.

Although they are listed as priestesses, the gender of the three main roles doesn't matter. The important part is that they should be masked from the start of the ritual until the unmasking at the end. Each priestess represents the masked aspects of Anu, Macha, and Badb, although you could rework these to different goddesses connected to the Morrigan if you like. Each priestess should pick a mask that represents the outer surface layer of that side if possible. It could be a skull mask, one shaped like a raven or horse head, or one that gives the impression of wings. You can be as creative as you like. Another option is to make the mask yourself and throw it into your ritual fire as an offering during the unmasking.

As with the other rituals, you can use your own opening or the one beginning on page 190. Since there will be something to burn in this ritual, you will also need a place to make a fire. If you cannot be outside or have no access to a fireplace while inside, you can light a candle to represent the sacred fire and burn the shields outside later.

Roles

- Masked Macha priestess
- Masked Anu priestess
- Masked Badb priestess
- Chant leader

Supplies

- Circular cardboard "shields"
- Markers
- Masks for the three priestesses
- Libations or preferred offerings

Invoke the Morrigan

While lighting the sacred fire, the Macha priestess says:

> *Morrigan, we call to you*
> *Fierce daughters of Ernmas*
> *Shape-shifter, many-faced goddess*
> *We call to you*
> *Be here with us*
> *As we light your sacred fires*
> *May this fire be blessed in the name of Anu*
> *In the name of Macha*
> *In the name of Badb*
> *May all that is burned in it be made sacred*
> *As an offering to the Morrigan*
> *May all that is poured into it reach her lips*
> *May any words spoken by it reach her ears*
> *May all that is burned within it come into her keeping*
> *May it be so nine times eternal!*

Working

The Anu priestess comes forward, saying:

> *When ancient peoples wished to offer something to the gods, they*
> *burned it or broke it. Beautiful treasures, finely crafted swords, and*
> *works of art and value. They broke and burned them to send their*
> *essence into the Otherworlds, to send them to the realm of the gods.*

The Badb priestess comes forward, saying:

> *You hold a shield in your hands, a symbol of your warrior nature. But*
> *it is only part of your nature. A piece of you, not the whole. Think of*
> *the battles you have fought. Think of the scars you bear, the lessons you*
> *have learned. Pour your gratitude for these lessons into your shield. Let*
> *us offer these to the Great Queens. Be grateful for those lessons, hard as*
> *they were. Offer your shields to the fire. Burn them and mark them and*
> *this part of yourself as sacred.*

If possible, there should be drumming or music played for a few minutes as people come to the fire, make their offerings, and say anything they wish as they place the shields into the fire. The chant leader should take the lead here and begin a round of soft singing or chanting.

The Macha priestess comes forward, saying:

> *An Morrigan, may you accept our offerings!*

The Unmasking

As each priestess addresses the group, they should walk around the ritual area.

Anu priestess:

> *The Morrigan is many things. Yes, she is the goddess of war, but she is*
> *far more than just that. And being a devotee of the Morrigan is more*
> *than just being a warrior. We cannot fight all the time. Sometimes*
> *anger must be tempered with mercy. Sometimes the urge to fight on*
> *must be tempered with the need to sit still and seek healing.*
>
> *You are fine warriors. Stand tall knowing you are strong. That*
> *if you need to, you can fight and have fought and weathered many*
> *battles. We have made sacred that part of you that is a warrior in the*
> *fire. But now is the time to lay your swords down, to rest your shields.*
> *To see more than just the goddess of battle. There is more to being a*
> *devotee of the Morrigan than endless battle. And there is more to me*
> *than just war.*

The priestess of Badb comes forward, walking around the ritual area, and addresses the group.

Badb priestess:

> *You know me as the Badb, the screaming phantom, the battle crow, and*
> *bean sidhe.*
> *(The Badb priestess takes off her mask.)*
> *But do you know me as the prophetess?*
> *Do you know me as the weaver of spells, the lady of magic?*

The priestess of Macha comes forward, walking around the ritual area, and addresses the group.

Macha priestess:

> *You know me by the roar and rattling of my war chariot. You know me*
> *as Macha who brought kings low, who cursed the men of Ulster. You*
> *call to me with your swords raised.*
> *(The Macha priestess takes off her mask.)*
> *But do you know me as the wise ruler? Do you know me as a mother*
> *who loves her children? Do you know when to choose peace over battle?*
> *Mercy over anger?*

The priestess of Anu comes forward again, walking around the ritual area, and addresses the group.

Anu priestess:

> *You know me as Anu, you know me as the lady of sovereignty claimed*
> *through battle, claimed by overrunning the enemy.*
> *(The Anu priestess takes off her mask.)*
> *But do you know me as the lady that nourishes the weary warrior?*
> *Do you know when to choose peace over battle? Mercy over anger?*

Badb priestess:

> *Know all of me, not just the parts you want to see. Know all my faces.*
> *This is the challenge I place before you. See the value and lessons of all*
> *my faces. Because if you do not, all I will ever be is battle to you. And*
> *your battles will not end, your scars will not heal, and you will never*

*leave the battlefield to claim the victory you deserve. If you only call
to me as the goddess of battle, I will always be that. Until you have
decided you have had enough. Until you have decided your belly is full
of enough blood. Until you have chosen to see me as more. Until you
have chosen to see yourselves as more. Until you have chosen to take the
victory I offer, to take the healing I offer. Will you meet my challenge?*

The priestesses wait for a response from the participants.

Final Offering

The Anu priestess makes a final offering to the fire. This can be whiskey, a bundle of sacred herbs, or whatever you find meaningful. I don't always like to have something specific scripted here. Your final prayer offered to the Morrigan when giving this offering will probably be more meaningful if spoken from the heart with the energy of the ritual flowing through you.

Closing

Use the closing beginning on page 195 or one that suits your own style better. In addition to closing this ritual, there is a secondary part to ending the rite, which follows.

Macha priestess:

*As we recognized that the Morrigan is more than war, let us acknowledge that there is more to ourselves than what meets the eye. What are
your gifts? What is the greatness of your hearts?*

This closing can be very meaningful, but you will probably have to have a few plants in the group or explain ahead of time how the closing will work so there is no confusion. The three main priestesses should start it, and then let it lead into the rest of the group gathered. If the process is taking too long, a priestess can walk to the middle of the circle and start another chain of this further down the group.

The priestess who starts the closing turns to the priestess next to them, taking their hands. The first priestess says something that is valuable about themselves, such as a talent or specific quality. The second person responds by saying, "I acknowledge these gifts in you." The second person then turns and starts the chain over again by taking the hands of the next person and acknowledging something about themselves. This should continue all the way down the circle until it returns to the first person who spoke, ending it.

When everyone has done this, the Macha priestess says:

> *And I acknowledge all these things in all of you*
> *May it be nine times eternal!*
> *And so I say this rite is done!*

All priestesses:

> *May it be nine times eternal!*

A Ritual of Blessing

This ritual is inspired by Cuchulain's interaction with the Morrigan when she offers him a drink of milk after they have mutually wounded each other. It focuses on the idea of shared blessings: we offer our devotion and blessings to the Morrigan and in reciprocity she offers hers. It is a ritual that can be done when a group wants to offer their thanks to the Great Queen and simply honor her presence.

You will need milk and a cup or horn to hold the milk used for the blessing. Depending on the time of year, you can make this more festive and use eggnog or spiked eggnog in place of the milk. For a public ritual, it would be good to have two horns, one with water and one with milk for anyone with allergies. You could also direct anyone with dairy allergies to pour some of the milk on the ground instead of drinking it.

Roles

- Priest or priestess
- Cup bearer
- Storyteller

Supplies

- Cup or drinking horn
- Enough milk that everyone will be able to take a sip or spill some on the ground

Begin the ritual with the opening that is provided or one of your choosing.

Invoking the Queen

This way of welcoming the Morrigan's presence into the ritual space is a little different. It's fairly simple but works really well. I've used this when visiting sacred sites and doing ritual work in places like graveyards and stone circles, where we can't do very much setup other than using our voices and pouring offerings as the main body of ritual.

The invocation works on the principle that your brain sometimes needs to be overwhelmed before it quiets down and clicks into an altered state. Three people (one or two if you don't have enough people) stand back to back in the center of the space. In this case, they are the priest, the cup bearer, and the storyteller. The rest of the group stands in a wide circle around them. The group standing around them begins to chant:

> *Morrigan, Morrigan,*
> *Mighty Queen, Great Queen*

As everyone continues the chant over and over, the three people in the center begin to speak. Single words or short sentences work best. In this case, it should consist of qualities of the Morrigan or her names. They can just start saying the words together or at disjointed intervals, either works. They should leave a breath or two between words or sentences so it isn't an endless string of words. These words could be something like "Anu, Macha, Badb, sharp sword, prophetess, battle, magic, peace as high as the skies, strength..." These words become a focus for the work. Your brain can't concentrate on the sustained chanting by the group and the words being spoken by those invoking at the same time, and this can very quickly bring you into trance or an altered state. If done correctly, the energy can build nicely quite quickly. It doesn't need to be loud chanting either. It can be as loud or as soft as you like. The three in the center should concentrate on drawing in the presence of the Morrigan as they speak and should signal the rest when they feel her presence has been invoked and it is time to stop.

Statement of Intent and Ritual Drama

This part of the ritual can be done in two ways: you can have the storyteller just retell the story of Cuchulain and the Morrigan, or you can have other participants act out the story as it's being told. Also feel free to change my retelling to suit the needs of your version of the ritual.

Storyteller:

> The Great Queen promised Cuchulain she would come against him
> as an eel, a wolf, and a hornless heifer. She would wound him for his
> arrogance. And she did. Cuchulain did as he promised and wounded
> the Morrigan in turn.
>   It was after the battle that the Morrigan, disguised as a hag, led
> a cow near to where the hero was. A great thirst came upon him. He
> asked the old woman for a drink of her cow's milk, and she granted it
> to him. Each time Cuchulain drank from the cow, he blessed her, one
> of her wounds healing. Two forces that were at odds with one another
> came together. They blessed each other and received healing. We too at
> times ignore the Morrigan's warnings. We too at times stumble on our
> paths. But we always return. We always come back seeking blessings,
> seeking healing, seeking balance. May we too accept the blessings the
> Morrigan offers us, and may our road not be difficult as Cuchulain's.

Priest:

> The Great Queen has given us many blessings, and her blessings are
> hard won. She has touched all of our lives; she has made us stronger.
> At times she has broken us so that we may be remade. She has offered
> us many things; she has blessed us all upon the edge of her blade. She
> knows that all things, even blessings, come with a price. Tonight,
> instead of asking for something, we will make offerings to the Morri-
> gan. Instead of asking her what she offers us, we will show the Queen
> what we offer in return. Whether it be simple thanks, a token of love
> and devotion, or a reaffirming of vows. May we bless her as she has
> blessed us. May we give our gratitude to the Morrigan and be blessed in
> turn.

After the ritual drama is finished, the cup bearer should come forward with
a horn or cup filled with the milk, saying:

> May the person who receives this draft
> be blessed with the strength and might of the Morrigan

May the person who receives this draft be blessed with the healing of the Morrigan
May the person who receives this draft be blessed with the wholeness of this blessing

The cup bearer should move their hand over the horn three times or blow on the milk three times to bless it. They should direct the participants to come forward to be blessed. When they come up, they should be offered the cup and take a sip or pour it on the ground. Before drinking from the cup, they can raise the cup up and offer their thanks to the Morrigan or say their thanks silently in that moment. If you have a larger group, it would be good to have three cups so you can have multiple groups of people coming up to make the process go faster.

Final Blessing

When everyone is done, the priest offers final blessing to the Queen by pouring the last of the milk in the fire or on the ground. It works nicely if everyone repeats each line of the blessing after the priest has spoken it, or you can just have the priest say the whole thing without audience participation. Either works.

Priest:

Washer Woman, cleanse us
Macha, fill us with strength
Anu, open our hearts to one another
I am a sword shining in the dark
I am a spear true to its course
I am a cauldron overflowing
I am a standing stone upon the earth
I am a raven among a tribe of ravens
And we do not stand alone

Closing

Close the ritual with the ritual closing beginning on page 195 or a closing of your choosing.

Conclusion

My path as a priestess of the Morrigan has led me down unexpected roads. There have been trials, stumbling blocks, tears, and heartache, but also joy, fulfillment, and victory. Nothing is straightforward where the Morrigan is concerned. Being in her service has made me not only deepen my devotion to the Great Queen but also learn more about myself than I ever imaged. I hope in these pages you have found something that speaks to your own journey with the Morrigan, something that helps you move further on your own path with her. So much of what is in these pages are pieces of my soul—the wisdom, lessons, and transformation I have undergone as her priestess. Service to the gods changes us. Being a priest is more than a simple spoken vow. It is opening your life up to the power of whom you serve. I think the Morrigan has been kind when she could be and harsh when I needed to learn, but always, always steering me toward healing and victory. Steering me toward a greater understanding of what she is.

The Morrigan walks among us. She is present and real, in this age, waiting for us to call to her. It is up to us to redefine her worship in a modern age, to build new traditions from the old, to learn what the Morrigan wishes us to understand and learn from today's world. I hope we do it well. I hope we become the finest of wolves and the noblest of ravens. Dear reader, I leave you with a blessing. A blessing that your path be smoother than mine, that your soul finds fulfillment and joy as the Great Queen guides you, and that you find victory and fulfillment along the way.

Peace as high as the skies
Sky to earth
And earth to sky
A cup overflowing with blessing,
Strength in everyone
Wisdom when asked for
Healing granted
A thousand victories blooming
May the Morrigan walk with you all your days
A strong shield against all adversary
A cloak of feathers when times are trying
A well of wisdom for a new age
Peace as high as the skies
Sky to earth
And earth to sky
May it be nine times eternal

Appendix
Irish Myths and Resources

I highly recommend reading each of these stories. Reading a myth is not the same as having it paraphrased for you. You might agree with my own impressions from these stories, or you might have your own theories. In many of these texts the Morrigan is not the main focus but appears at pivotal moments or is briefly mentioned. I have listed all the texts by their English names, followed by the Irish and any other alternative names you might find them under. For published versions, the bibliography will be a good resource, although be aware many of these texts can be both hard to find in print and expensive. Thankfully almost all of these can be accessed online in some way, since many of the older translations are public domain. CODECS, the Collaborative Online Database and e-Resources for Celtic Studies (vanhamel.nl/codecs/Home), and CELT, the Corpus of Electronic Texts (celt.ucc.ie), are excellent resources for finding various versions of Celtic-related texts.

I do highly recommend checking out more modern translations, such as works by Isolde Carmody and Morgan Daimler since these are more faithful to the original texts. Just because a translation source is old doesn't mean it is accurate. When compared to the text in its original language, in some cases whole segments are removed because they are problematic for the translator, and in other cases the translator adds things that just aren't in the text. The social norms of the times also color many older translations, with things that would have been seen as scandalous edited out or changed. The aim wasn't always accuracy, while today there is more emphasis on accurate and complete translations. Perhaps part of this shift is because the works aren't just stories from a long-ago past: to many of us these are religious texts. What they accurately say matters more to us, and many of those publishing new translations are them-selves Pagan.

The Book of Invasions

Other Names: Lebor Gabála Érenn, The Book of the Taking of Ireland

The *Lebor Gabála Érenn*, or *Book of Invasions*, is a collection of prose and poems that make up a history of the mythical beings and gods who inhabited or migrated to Ireland. Many of the events are conflated with biblical events by the monks who transcribed the stories to form what they would have thought of as a historical timeline for the events of the story. There are several recensions, or versions, of this work in various manuscripts, including *The Book of Ballymote, The Book of Fermoy,* and *The Book of Lecan,* to name a few. The earliest version of the manuscript dates from the eleventh or twelfth century.

According to the text, the first inhabitants of Ireland are led by a relative of Noah, a woman named Cesair. They arrive before the biblical flood but are killed when the floodwaters strike the earth. Afterward, other groups of people try to settle Ireland, including groups led by Partholon, Nemed, and later Nemed's descendants the Fir Bolg and the Tuatha Dé Danann. The group led by Partholon is killed by a plague. Nemed's people have some problems with the Fomorians, a seafaring race of beings. The Fir Bolg and Tuatha Dé Danann battle to take dominance over Ireland, and later the Tuatha fight and defeat the Fomorians. It seems like the Tuatha Dé Danann have finally taken possession of Ireland until the sixth and final invasion, when the Milesians arrive. The Milesians are often thought to represent the early humans and the forefathers of the Irish people. They battle the Tuatha and then drive them into the faery mounds, although the Milesians do name the island of Ireland after the goddess Ériu of the Tuatha.

For those interested in the Morrigan, the fifth invasion, when the Tuatha Dé Danann arrive in Ireland, will be the most relevant. In this text we also find references to the genealogies of the Irish gods.

Online Resource: CODECS's *Lebor Gabála Érenn* resource page, www.van hamel.nl/codecs/Lebor_gabála_Érenn

The First Battle of Moytura

Other Names: Cath Maige Tuired, Cét-chath Maige Tuired, Cath Muige Tuired Cunga

The *Cath Maige Tuired* is the name of two stories about the Tuatha Dé Danann and their battles against other mystical races for dominance over Ireland. *Maige Tuired* means "plain of pillars" (*Moytura* being the anglicized version of the name) and actually refers to two different places in Ireland. The first battle takes place around the town of Cong in County Mayo and the second in County Sligo.

The story begins with an earlier group of people who inhabited Ireland, the children of Nemed, sailing for Greece. Their descendants became the Fir Bolg, who return to Ireland and rule over it for thirty years. Then another group of Nemed's descendants arrive, the Tuatha Dé Danann. They burn their own ships and attempt to negotiate with the Fir Bolg to split Ireland between the two peoples or meet them in battle. Of course, they choose battle over giving up half the land. The Tuatha send the three Morrigan sisters to distract the Fir Bolg to give the Tuatha enough time to prepare for battle, and the sisters use their magic to rain down fire and blood from the sky.

The two groups meet in a battle that rages on for four days. Nuada, the king of the Tuatha Dé Danann, fights Sreng, the champion of the Fir Bolg. Sreng strikes Nuada's shield, breaking the shield and in the same stroke cutting off Nuada's hand. After a truce and further failed negotiations, Sreng challenges Nuada to single combat. Nuada asks that Sreng tie one of his hands behind his back to make it a fair fight, but the Fir Bolg champion refuses. The Tuatha choose to offer Sreng his choice of the provinces of Ireland for the Fir Bolg to inhabit while the Tuatha would take possession of the rest. Sreng chooses Connacht, and they make peace, the Tuatha still getting the better end of the bargain but not at the cost of their king's life. Nuada, now blemished, is exempt from ruling as king, and the Tuatha appoint Bres as the new king. This bad decision leads into the events of *The Second Battle of Moytura*.

Online Resource: CODECS's *Cath Muige Tuired Cunga* resource page, van hamel.nl/codecs/Cath_Muige_Tuired_Cunga

The Second Battle of Moytura

Other Names: Cath Maige Tuired, Cath Maighe Tuireadh Thúaidh, Cath Dédenach Maige Tuired

Like *The First Battle of Moytura*, *The Second Battle of Moytura* details the adventures of the Tuatha Dé Danann and their struggle with another set of enemies, the Fomorians. The Fomorians are described as a seafaring race of beings, although it is sometimes suggested they lived under the sea as well. The Fomorians were an ongoing threat who troubled some of the earlier inhabitants of Ireland. Since their former king Nuada lost his hand at the conclusion of *The First Battle of Moytura*, the Irish gods were forced to elect a new king. A king could not be blemished since his blemish or deformity would reflect on the health of the land. Bres, who is half Tuatha Dé Danann and half Fomorian, is given the kingship. Bres unfortunately shows favoritism to the Fomorian side of his heritage, and soon the Tuatha Dé Danann are tasked with doing heavy labor and paying excessive tribute to the Fomorians. Bres also proves to be a poor king in other areas as well. He makes poor judgments and his people soon go hungry. Bres is eventually dethroned, and the Tuatha reinstate Nuada, who had his severed hand magically restored. Interestingly, he does not grow another hand and is not given a magical one. The original hand has somehow been preserved and through magic reattached and made good as new.

Bres goes to his Fomorian brethren and asks for aid in retaking his throne. One of the Fomorian leaders, Balor of the Evil Eye, agrees to help him, and they are soon waging war against the Tuatha Dé Danann. Balor has an eye that when opened can destroy what it gazes upon. He is often depicted as a one-eyed giant, but there is no indication that he had a single eye, only that one eye has this destructive power while the other one functions normally.

Bres isn't the only half-Tuatha, half-Fomorian among the Tuatha Dé Danann. Lugh, who has both Tuatha and Fomorian heritage, arrives at court and impresses Nuada with his many talents. The Morrigan encourages Lugh to take up arms, and he is given command of the Tuatha's army. Lugh is the grandson of Balor, and there is a prophecy that Balor will be killed by his grandson, which does come to pass.

Before the two armies battle, the Irish gods boast about what powers and prowess they will display in battle. The Morrigan, as well as many of the other Irish gods, takes part in this boasting. The two groups battle one another and the Tuatha defeat their enemies. Nuada is killed alongside Macha. The two fighting and dying beside one another may indicate that Nuada was her husband. The Morrigan has very minor parts to play in this story but the small parts she does have are helpful in understanding her.

Online Resource: CELT's electronic edition of *Cath Maige Tuired: The Second Battle of Mag Tuired,* celt.ucc.ie//published/G300010/index.html

The Cattle Raid of Cooley

Other Names: Táin Bó Cúailnge

The Cattle Raid of Cooley, often simply referred to as the *Táin,* is part of the Ulster Cycle and revolves around the conflict between Ulster and Connacht over a magical bull. There are many versions of the Táin. Partial versions exist in the *Book of Dun Cow* and *The Yellow Book of Lecan,* while a third version, in the *Book of Leinster,* is probably an attempt to merge the other two versions into a cohesive whole. It can be difficult to understand everything happening in the *Táin* if you don't know many of the events that happen in other related stories. Thomas Kinsella's *The Táin* is a good place to start, since it starts off with relating the "pre-tales" that have a bearing on the events of the *Táin.* These include the boyhood adventures of Cuchulain and how Macha cursed the men of Ulster, a curse that plays a major role in crippling the men of Ulster during the *Táin.* Also included is the story of the feuding faery swine herders, which is often overlooked by modern readers but is pivotal to understanding the Morrigan's involvement in the *Táin.* The two bulls that are fought over in the Táin aren't really bulls at all: they are faeries who have transformed into bulls as a result of a quarrel many years before and continue to be reborn as various animals to continue their battle in the forms they take on. As they battle in various animal forms, there is no clear winner between the two, so they keep incarnating as different animals and the conflict between them continues. One could speculate that the Morrigan is only involved because at the center of the *Táin* there is an Otherworldly dispute that needs to be rectified. She doesn't really seem to be on the side of either Ulster or Connacht, helping both at various times, but her actions do ensure that there is finally a winner between the two quarreling bulls, the dispute can finally be called to an end, and they themselves can return to the Otherworlds.

The *Táin* revolves around Queen Maeve (also spelled Medb) of Connacht attempting to capture a magical bull in the possession of the king of Ulster. Her husband also possesses a magical bull, and to show she owns equal worth she must acquire its equal. At first, she tries to buy the bull, but when her offers of money and even sex are refused, she goes to war to obtain the bull. The men of Ulster are struck by Macha's curse, which was that they would be inflicted with the pain of childbirth in the hour of their greatest need. The young hero Cuchulain is the only one left unaffected and able to defend Ulster. This exemption from the curse is either because he is a demigod, being the son of Lugh and a mortal woman, or because he is beardless and thus not quite yet a man by the definitions of the curse. Cuchulain invokes the right to single combat at river fords, and Maeve is forced to halt her army's progress while each day she sends a champion to fight Cuchulain.

The Morrigan upholds a promise made earlier to Cuchulain to attack the hero while he is in battle in various animal forms. She attacks him in the form of an eel, a wolf, and a cow, and as she wounds the hero, he wounds her in turn. Perhaps because of his semidivine nature, any wound the hero dealt could not be healed without his blessing. After this encounter, the Morrigan appears to the hero as an old woman with a cow. He asks for a drink of her cow's milk and blesses her each time he drinks the milk. Each time he blesses her, one of her wounds heals. Eventually, the Ulster men recover from the curse and the two armies meet in battle. Maeve is forced to retreat, but the two bulls do meet with one another and begin to fight. The Ulster bull kills the other but is mortally wounded, spending several days wandering Ireland and shaking bits of the dead bull's flesh off his horns before he too dies. The faery squabble is resolved, since one bull has bested the other. Maeve's husband no longer has a magical bull, but neither does Ulster, so the war is over and everyone goes home, minus some magical cattle.

Online Resource: Vassar College's *Táin Bó Cúalnge* resource page, adminstaff .vassar.edu / sttaylor / Cooley /

The Cattle Raid of Regamna

Other Names: Táin Bó Regamna, The Cattle Raid of the Important Calf

This is one of the few that I rarely see mentioned by its English name, so looking for the Irish right off is best. *The Cattle Raid of Regamna* can be found in *The Yellow Book of Lecan*, a fourteenth-century manuscript.

This story serves as an alternative version of the Morrigan's encounter with Cuchulain found in *The Cattle Raid of Cooley*. In *The Cattle Raid of Cooley* she is disguised as a king's daughter who has fallen in love with the hero. When the hero turns down her offer of love and aid, she tells him she will hinder him instead, attacking him in various animal forms. An almost identical exchange of this is given in *The Cattle Raid of Regamna* but under different circumstances. This story occurs prior to the events of *The Cattle Raid of Cooley*. It begins when Cuchulain is woken up by a mysterious roar and sets out with his trusted charioteer, Lóeg, to investigate. Soon after, the two encounter a woman accompanied by a man driving a cow. The woman's chariot is rather odd. It is drawn by a single horse rather than the normal two. It also has one leg and the chariot's post running through the animal. Odd, right? Not to Cuchulain. He questions the woman, accusing her of stealing the cow and informs her that all the cattle of Ulster are under his protection. The woman claims to be a female poet, but Cuchulain doesn't really believe that. Eventually, Cuchulain jumps into her chariot and challenges her, only for her to turn into a black bird. Finally, he realizes he had been talking to the Morrigan. The Morrigan tells him that she has brought the cow from the faery mound of Cruachan to breed with a bull, basically telling him he has no business with this particular cow or what she does with it since it is not one of Ulster's cows. She then promises to attack when he is in battle as an eel, a wolf, and a cow. The same exchange between the Morrigan and Cuchulain found in *The Cattle Raid of Cooley* is repeated here. Each vows to attack the other, and the Morrigan describes the animals she will shape-shift into while coming against Cuchulain.

Online Resource: Internet Sacred Text Archive's transcription of A. H. Leahy's *Heroic Romances of Ireland*, volume 2 (London: David Nutt, 1901), sacred-texts.com/neu/hroi/hroiv2.htm

Dindshenchas

Other Names: The Bodleian Dinnshenchas, Dindsenchas, Dinnseanchas, Dinnsheanchas, Dinnśeanċas

The *Dindshenchas* is a collection of 176 poems and prose writings that tell the lore of place names around Ireland. It contains a wealth of lore, detailing the stories of many of the gods in relation to deeds connected to certain features of the land. One recension can be found in the twelfth-century *Book of Leinster*.

In this text we can find the story of Odras, a young woman whom the Morrigan transforms into a stream, as well as the Morrigan's son Meiche. These stories are short but appear nowhere else, making them valuable insights into the Morrigan.

In the story of Odras, the woman falls asleep while tending her cattle and the Morrigan appears and takes a bull. Instead of just letting the incident go, Odras pursues the Morrigan, almost reaching the Cave of Cruachan. But at the last minute she again decides she is tired and takes some time to sleep. The Morrigan appears again and sings spells of power over her, turning her into a small river. Remember, all the stories in the *Dindshenchas* revolve around place names, so the story is meant to explain the lore around this river.

The story of the Morrigan's son Meiche also revolves around the lore of a river. Meiche had three serpents in his three hearts, and it was determined that these snakes would one day grow so large that they would gobble up all of Ireland. Meiche is slain to save Ireland and his ashes are thrown into a river. The ashes apparently are also poisonous, and the river's waters boil and kill all the wildlife in the river.

Online Resource: CELT's electronic edition of *The Metrical Dindshenchas*, celt .ucc.ie//published/T106500B/

The Siege of Knocklong

Other Name: Forbhais Droma Dámhgháire

The Siege of Knocklong can be found in a fifteenth-century manuscript called the *Book of Lismore*. The manuscript was hidden, discovered only during renovations in 1814, in a recess of Lismore Castle in County Waterford. The book also contains other prose and stories about the lives of the saints. *The Siege of Knocklong* is invaluable for its descriptions of magical practices, in particular those used in warfare. While in other stories we are only told certain characters use magic to accomplish a task, the words and magical acts they use or say are not detailed.

The story is basically about ancient tax evasion. The siege begins with the steward of High King Cormac complaining that the royal coffers are empty. Cormac decides the solution to his problem is to force the men of Munster to pay additional taxes, so he gathers his army and his druids and marches on Munster to collect his tribute, despite being advised the additional tax is unjust. This culminates in a battle fought by both normal and magical means. High King Cormac marches on the men of Munster because they refuse to pay taxes. Cormac sets up his camp on the Hill of Knocklong while the king of Munster, Fiacha, makes camp at Glenbrohane. The struggle between the two lasts for over a year.

After several battles fail to bring the high king victory, he calls on his druids to use their magic to win. The druids use their magic to dry up all the water in the area. But Fiacha has his own druids, and he asks the druid Mug Ruith to restore the water and help them win the battle. With the druid Mug Ruith's help, the men of Munster are victorious and drive Cormac's army out of their lands.

Online Resource: CORPUS's *Forbuis Droma Damhghaire* resource page, van hamel.nl/codecs/Forbuis_Droma_Damhghaire

The Destruction of Da Derga's Hostel
Other Name: Togail Bruidne Dá Derga

The Destruction of Da Derga's Hostel can be found in the twelfth-century manuscript called the *Book of Dun Cow*. It tells the story of King Conaire's birth, mostly poor rulership as king, and his death as he subsequently goes about breaking every one of the *geasa,* or magical taboos, placed upon him.

When the high king of Ireland dies, a bull feast is performed to induce a vision of who the new king will be. The prophetic vision received in the bull feast is that a naked man will arrive at the hill of Tara, and that man would be the next king. Conaire does arrive at Tara naked and is made king. Conaire has several *geasa* and through various circumstances breaks all but one of them before his fatal encounter at the hostel. Early on he breaks a prohibition that will eventually lead to his downfall. This prohibition was that there would be no plundering or raiding during his reign. His foster brothers don't like this very much and secretly begin raiding the same farmer every year. The farmer complains to Conaire, but the matter is quickly dropped and ignored. Conaire's foster brothers begin to expand their plundering until eventually the problem is too big to ignore. Those caught raiding are sentenced to death, with the exception of his foster brothers, who are simply banished to Britain. This isn't a popular decision, and his banished foster brothers will later lead an invading force that kills Conaire.

When he stays at Da Derga's hostel, he encounters a woman, Badb, asking for entrance to the hostel. His final *géis* is that he cannot admit a single woman into his home after sunset. But if he refuses her, he is not upholding the rules of hospitality, which she mocks him for. He does admit her and breaks his final taboo. The hostel is attacked by Conaire's foster brothers, who have returned with a large armed force, a battle ensues, and the hostel is set on fire. Conaire is struck with a magical thirst that can't be sated, and he tasks his champion to get him water. His champion travels across Ireland with the king's cup, but either all the water has been used to quench the fire on the hostel, or he can't find water in any of the rivers. That the rivers will not fill the king's cup is another sign the land itself has turned against the king. Finally, he does find water and brings it back to the king, only to arrive as Conaire is being beheaded. The champion kills the men who have beheaded the king. Afterward, the apparently still animate and thirsty severed head drinks the water his champion had roamed all of Ireland to bring him and praises him in poetic verse.

Again, the Morrigan is not a main character, but her appearance as Badb in order to make an unworthy king break his final taboo makes this a worthwhile read for devotees of the Morrigan. The talking severed head is of course a bonus.

Online Resource: CELT's *The Destruction of Da Derga's Hostel,* celt.ucc.ie /published/T301017A.html

Bibliography

Ball, Martin J., and James Fife, eds. *The Celtic Languages*. London: Routledge, 1993.

Carmody, Isolde. "The Dindshenchas of the Barrow River—Berba." *Story Archeology* (blog), May 29, 2013. https://storyarchaeology.com/the-dindshenchas-of-the-barrow-river-berba/.

———. "The Mórrígan Speaks—Her Three Poems." *Story Archeology* (blog), June 23, 2016. https://storyarchaeology.com/the-morrigan-speaks-her-three-poems-2.

———. "Names of the Dagda." *Story Archeology* (blog), December 23, 2012. https://storyarchaeology.com/names-of-the-dagda/.

Clark, Rosalind. *The Great Queens: Irish Goddesses from the Morrígan to Cathleen ní Houlihan*. Gerrards Cross, UK: Colin Smythe, 1991.

Corlett, Christiaan. "Cursing Stones in Ireland." *Journal of the Galway Archaeological and Historical Society* 64 (2012): 1–20. https://www.jstor.org/stable/24612852?seq=1.

Daimler, Morgan. *The Dagda: Meeting the Good God of Ireland*. Pagan Portals. Alresford, Hants, UK: Moon Books, 2018.

———. *Irish Paganism: Reconstructing Irish Polytheism*. Pagan Portals. Alresford, Hants, UK: Moon Books, 2015.

———. "The Morrigan, The Dagda, and Unions." *Living Liminally* (blog), April 14, 2015. https://lairbhan.blogspot.com/2015/04/the-morrigan -dagda-and-unions.html.

———. *The Morrigan: Meeting the Great Queens.* Pagan Portals. Alresford, Hants, UK: Moon Books, 2014.

———. "The Morrigan's Peace Prophecy." Irish-American Witchcraft, *Patheos Pagan* (blog), November 17, 2015. https://www.patheos.com/blogs/agora /2015/11/irish-american-witchcraft-the-morrigans-peace-prophecy/.

———. "The Morrigan, Questions and Answers," Irish-American Witchcraft, *Patheos Pagan* (blog), November 17, 2017, https://www.patheos.com /blogs/agora/2017/11/irish-american-witchcraft-morrigan-questions -answers/.

———. "The Story of the Sword." *Living Liminally* (blog), July 16, 2014. https://lairbhan.blogspot.com/2014/07/the-story-of-sword.html.

———. *Where the Hawthorn Grows: An American Druid's Reflections.* Alresford, Hants, UK: Moon Books, 2013.

Epstein, Angelique Gulermovich. "War Goddess: The Morrigan and Her Ger-mano-Celtic Counterparts." PhD diss., UCLA, 1998.

Faraday, L. Winifred. *The Cattle-Raid of Cualnge.* London: David Nutt, 1904. https://books.google.vg/books?id=NofxTqgewBAC&source=gbs _navlinks_s.

Fraser, J., ed. and trans. "The First Battle of Moytura." *Ériu*, vol. 8. (1916): 1–63. https://www.jstor.org/stable/30005394?seq=1.

Gray, Elizabeth A., ed. and trans. *Cath Maige Tuired: The Second Battle of Mag Tuired.* Irish Texts Society, vol. 52. Dublin: Irish Texts Society, 1982.

Gwynn, Edward, trans. *The Metrical Dindshenchas.* 5 vols. Dublin: Royal Irish Academy, 1903–35.

Hennessy, W. M. "The Ancient Irish Goddess of War." *Revue Celtique* 1 (1870–72): 32–55.

Junger, Sebastian. *Tribe: On Homecoming and Belonging.* New York: Twelve, 2016.

Kinsella, Thomas, trans. *The Táin: Translated from the Irish Epic Táin Bó Cuailnge*. New York: Oxford University Press, 1969.

Leahy, A. H., trans. and ed. *Heroic Romances of Ireland*. Vol. 2. London: David Nutt, 1906. https://books.google.com/books?id=t31HAQAAIAAJ& source=gbs_navlinks_s.

MacAlister, R. A. Stewart, trans. *Lebor Gabála Érenn: The Book of the Taking of Ireland, Part IV*. Irish Texts Society, vol. 41. Dublin: Irish Texts Society, 1956. https://archive.org/details/leborgablare04macauoft/page/n5/mode/2up.

Matasovic, Ranko. *Etymological Dictionary of Proto-Celtic*. Boston: Brill, 2009.

Matthews, John. *Taliesin: The Last Celtic Shaman*. With Caitlin Matthews. Rochester, VT: Inner Traditions, 1991.

Mees, Bernard. *Celtic Curses*. Woodbridge, UK: Boydell Press, 2009.

Ó Dónaill, Niall. *Foclóir Gaeilge-Béarla*. London: Colton Book Imports, 1997.

O'Donovan, John, ed. and trans. *Annals of the Kingdom of Ireland by the Four Masters, from the Earliest Period to the Year 1616*. Vol. 1. Dublin: Hodges and Smith, 1848. https://books.google.com/books?id=Gb0_AAAAcAAJ& source=gbs_navlinks_s.

O'Donovan, John, trans. *Sanas Chormaic: Cormac's Glossary*. Edited by Whitley Stokes. Calcutta: O. T. Cutter, 1868. https://books.google.com /books?id=-ZANAAAAYAAJ&source=gbs_navlinks_s.

Ó Duinn, Seán, trans. *The Siege of Knocklong/Forbhais Droma Damhghaire*. Cork, Ireland: Mercier Press 1992. Electronic reproduction by Corpus of Electronic Texts. Transcribed and edited by Beatrix Färber and Ivonn Devine Nagai. Cork, Ireland: University College, 2014. https://celt.ucc.ie /published/T301044.html.

O'Grady, Standish Hayes. *Silva Gadelica (I–XXXI): A Collection of Tales in Irish*. Vol. 2, translation and notes. London: Williams & Norgate, 1892. https:// archive.org/details/silvagadelicaix00gragoog/page/n4/mode/2up.

O hOgain, Dáithi. *Myth, Legend, and Romance: An Encyclopaedia of Irish Folk Tradition*. New York: Prentice Hall, 1991.

Strachan, John, and J. G. O'Keefe. "Táin Bó Cuailnge," *Ériu* 2 supplement
(1905): 33–64.

Stokes, Whitley, trans. "The Destruction of Da Derga's Hostel." *Revue Celtique*
22 (1901): 9–61, 165–215, 282–329, 390–437. https://archive.org/details
/revueceltiqu22pari/page/8/mode/2up.

———. "The Prose Tales in the Rennes Dindshenchas," *Revue Celtique* 15
(1894): 272–336, 418–84. http://www.archive.org/stream/revue
celtiqu15pari#page/272/mode/2up.

———. "The Second Battle of Moytura." *Revue Celtique* 12 (1891): 52–130.
https://archive.org/details/revueceltiqu12pari/page/n5/mode/2up.

———. *Three Irish Glossaries: Cormac's Glossary Codex A, O'Davoren's Glossary,
and a Glossary to the Calendar of Oingus the Culdee.* London: Williams & Norgate, 1862. https://archive.org/details/cu31924026508238/page/n4
/mode/2up.

Stokes, Whitley, ed. and trans. *Acallamh na Senórach.* In *Irische Texte.* Edited
also by Ernst Windisch. 4th ser., vol. 1. Leipzig, Germany: Hirzel, 1900.
Electronic reproduction by Corpus of Electronic Texts. Transcribed and
edited by Donnchadh Ó Corráin. Cork, Ireland: University College, 1996.
https://celt.ucc.ie//published/G303000/index.html.

———. "The Bodleian Dinnshenchas." *Folk-Lore* 3 (1892): 467–516. https://
archive.org/details/folklore03folkuoft/page/466/mode/2up.

Smyth, Daragh. *A Guide to Irish Mythology.* Dublin: Irish Academic Press, 1988.

Westropp, Thomas Johnson. *Folklore of Clare: A Folklore Survey of County Clare
and County Clare Folktales and Myths.* Clare, Ireland: CLASP, 2000.

Williams, Mark. *Ireland's Immortals: A History of the Gods of Irish Myth.* Princeton, NJ: Princeton University Press, 2016.

Wimberly, Lowry C. *Folklore in the English and Scottish Ballads.* New York: Frederick Ungar, 1928.

Index

U

Ulster, 13, 22, 44, 71, 79, 168, 170, 171, 205, 206, 228, 241–243
Undry, 142
Unshin, 26
UPG, 2, 12, 19, 103, 109, 111–114, 116–121

V

venomous, 104, 107, 174
victory, 31–34, 37–39, 61, 199–202, 204, 205, 211, 214, 217, 221, 229, 235, 245
vulture, 114, 115, 175

W

Washer at the Ford, 12, 23, 37, 38, 76, 103, 105, 106, 197–199, 201, 205
wolves (mac tíre), 34, 44, 92–94, 97, 98, 232, 235, 242, 243

To Write to the Author

If you wish to contact the author or would like more information about this book, please write to the author in care of Llewellyn Worldwide Ltd. and we will forward your request. Both the author and the publisher appreciate hearing from you and learning of your enjoyment of this book and how it has helped you. Llewellyn Worldwide Ltd. cannot guarantee that every letter written to the author can be answered, but all will be forwarded. Please write to:

Stephanie Woodfield
⅟ Llewellyn Worldwide
2143 Wooddale Drive
Woodbury, MN 55125-2989

Please enclose a self-addressed stamped envelope for reply,
or $1.00 to cover costs. If outside the U.S.A., enclose
an international postal reply coupon.

Many of Llewellyn's authors have websites with additional information and resources. For more information, please visit our website at http://www.llewellyn.com